IMAGES
*of America*

# SAN FRANCISCO'S WEST OF TWIN PEAKS

**ON THE COVER:** Snow falling in San Francisco always makes for a historic day. This is a snow-covered Mount Davidson on December 11, 1932. Dairy cows still graze across from the new Miraloma Park neighborhood under construction on the eastern slope of the city's highest hill before its summit is made into a city park and crowned with the world's largest cross. (Courtesy Miraloma Park Improvement Club.)

IMAGES
*of America*

# SAN FRANCISCO'S WEST OF TWIN PEAKS

Jacqueline Proctor

ARCADIA
PUBLISHING

ISBN 978-0-7385-4660-5

Published by Arcadia Publishing
Charleston, South Carolina

Printed in the United States of America

Library of Congress Catalog Card Number: 2006924383

For all general information contact Arcadia Publishing at:
Telephone 843-853-2070
Fax 843-853-0044
E-mail sales@arcadiapublishing.com
For customer service and orders:
Toll-Free 1-888-313-2665

Visit us on the Internet at www.arcadiapublishing.com

*As a plaque on a special Mount Davidson rock once stated, this book is now "dedicated to Madie D. Brown, who found beauty in flower and tree on this lofty hill. Through her untiring pleas, these acres have been set aside as a city park that all may enjoy their beauty and find refreshment of the soul."*

# Contents

# Acknowledgments

One of the reasons I love my tiny San Francisco home is its view of the city's highest point. I am also proud to have a relic of San Francisco's colorful history, a giant concrete cross lit by Pres. Franklin D. Roosevelt, in my very own neighborhood. So I was very alarmed when a judge decided that the park should either be sold or the landmark at its summit be destroyed. With other neighborhood leaders, we created the Friends of Mount Davidson Conservancy in 1986 to protect our special part of the city. Our research to support historical landmark designation sparked my interest in finding out more about the rich, but yet to be fully published, history about the area known as West of Twin Peaks. Why did the president light the cross? Why did the committee of arrangements include the builders of the surrounding neighborhoods and the first woman elected to the board of supervisors? These were the questions that inspired me to dig deeper.

My heartfelt thanks to Dave Bisho, Mary Shea, Margie Whitnah, Gary Holloway, Elaine Blair, Richard Brandi, and Woody LaBounty, cofounder of the Western Neighborhoods Project, for their warm encouragement and wonderful help with this project. I wish to thank my son Aaron Proctor for designing my business cards and web site, www.mtdavidson.org, along with my husband, Ron Proctor, for his untiring technical assistance. I also wish to express my deep appreciation and respect to those who contributed the information and images that made this book possible:

Ron and Joann Davis; Denis Pinto; Bob, Paula, and Michael DeLiso; Glenn Gullmes; Elizabeth Mettling; Ken and Kathy Hoegger; Kathy Rawlins and the Miraloma Park Improvement Club; John Pommon; Bertha Jones; Jeannie Davis MacKenzie; Greg Gaar; Tasia Melvin; Greg Clinton, Nanette Asimov, and Kathleen Beitiks of the Westwood Park Association; Bill and Peg Kaplan; Joann Wentker; Jim Ferry; John Pflueger; Miraloma Community Church; Carolyn Wade; Tom O'Neil; Beverly Coughlin; the California Association of Realtors; Virginia Larribeau; John Pinkerton; David Atkins; Jack Tillmany; Bill Moore; Corinne Bryan; Inge Horton; Jane Radcliffe, Daphne Powell, Jennifer Heggie, and the Sunnyside Neighborhood Association; Nelson Foss; Sean Elsbernd; Mike Jones; Susan Yip; Robert Karis; Paul Ishkanian; Josephine Salbolboro; Sally Tobin; Roxanne Makasdjian; Beryl Banks; Glenn Koch; and Sue Kirkham.

# Introduction

> As the group found themselves deeper in the wood . . . peace and quiet were so profound that it seemed almost unbelievable that the noise and roar of a great city was only a few minutes behind them. . . . The solitude of the forest . . . conveyed a sense of vastness quite as real as one would experience among the age-old monarchs of the High Sierras. . . . The undergrowth and flowers looked as if they might have been there for centuries . . . (At the summit was) a clear vision of the great panorama that spread before the eye . . . on the far eastern horizon stood the bold figure of Mt. Diablo, to the west could be seen the boundless Pacific, with the headlands of Point Reyes and Point San Pedro forming widespread arms of welcome to those who enter the Golden Gate. (Below were) tall monuments of steel and concrete wherein were housed thousands of busy minds . . . Myriads of moving objects were, without doubt, hurrying hither and thither, all within vision of Mt. Davidson, yet the noise and tumult of it all was absent.

This experience of hiking Mount Davidson, written by George Decatur in 1923, is available for the public to enjoy today. Pres. Franklin D. Roosevelt lit the historic monument that crowns it in 1934 at the invitation of Madie Brown, the woman who led the campaign to make it a city park. She wrote to him, "I have dared to dream that you would press a button in Washington, D.C., which in turn would light for the first time this giant cross in San Francisco. . . . It seems most appropriate that you, who have brought light to many a darkened American home and who through your New Deal has instilled the principles of the Golden Rule into American business, should take part in this cross-lighting ceremony."

At 938 feet above sea level, Mount Davidson is not only the highest geographic point of the world-famous San Francisco skyline, but it offers an insider's view of the development of the city from its heart, west of the Twin Peaks. Originally named Blue Mountain by noted scientist and surveyor George Davidson, Mount Davidson Park provides a peaceful oasis of public open space in the middle of one of the densest cities in the United States. At its summit is a time capsule with a transcript of the title signed by the first Mexican governor of California, Pio Pico, granting ownership of the mountain to Don Jose de Jesus Noe, the last Mexican *alcalde* (mayor) of Yerba Buena. Noe was only the first of many San Francisco mayors who have been drawn to the area. The city's fourth mayor, Cornelius Garrison, bought Noe's rancho from John Horner in 1855. Adolph Sutro, the 21st mayor, purchased 1,200 acres from the estate of Francois Pioche. Mayor George Christopher later had a dairy business nearby, Mayor John Shelley built a home in Sherwood Forest, Mayor George Moscone lived in the same neighborhood, and Mayor Art Agnos lived down the hill in West Portal.

Adolph Sutro left his tree-covered Rancho San Miguel property to a charitable trust. After developer A. S. Baldwin determined its potential value, Sutro's heirs had the trust invalidated by the California Supreme Court. Buying the land to develop into housing, Baldwin followed the lead of Behrend Joost's Sunnyside District, using "sunny" advertising to attract potential residents to the "foggy outside lands" west of Twin Peaks. Joseph Leonard built the world's largest sundial. Miraloma Park had a home called Sunshine Gables. To further entice potential buyers, these new City Beautiful–inspired residence parks, including Balboa Terrace, Ingleside Terraces, Westwood Park, Mount Davidson Manor, Westwood Highlands, Monterey Heights, and

Sherwood Forest had homes designed by leading architects along landscaped and view-enhancing curvilinear boulevards. But it would take the help of Mayor "Sunny Jim" Rolph to expand the public transportation available to these new "suburbs in the city" before the children of the gold rush and the 1906 earthquake, along with others from around the world, came in search of the American dream.

After A. S. Baldwin built trails up to the top of the city's highest hill, hiker and YMCA director George Decatur was inspired to organize the first of what would become an annual Easter sunrise event there in 1923. With Baldwin's wife, Emma, donating the six-acre summit, they raised funds during the Great Depression to build the world's largest cross. Designed by the creators of San Francisco's tallest buildings, George Kelham and Henry Brunnier, Governor Rolph laid the first cornerstone.

Decades after World War II, gourmet Tower Market and the gigantic Sutro Tower became the most well-known entrance gates to the West of Twin Peaks District, which was home to many San Francisco notables, including architect Milton Pflueger; engineer Henry Brunnier; television personalities Art Linkletter and George Fenneman; Gov. Edmund G. "Pat" Brown and his son Jerry Brown, governor and mayor of Oakland; Dr. Carlton Goodlett, publisher of the *Sun Reporter*; Calvin Simmons, conductor of the Oakland Symphony; police chiefs Al Nelder and Fred Lau; Evelyn Cisneros and Stephen Legate of the San Francisco Ballet; Jazz saxophonist Joe Henderson; San Francisco 49er Abe Woodson; city attorney Louise Renne; celebrity Carol Channing; San Francisco Giant Willie Mays; opera singer Helen Dilworth; and others whose creativity, spirit, and imagination make San Francisco what it is today.

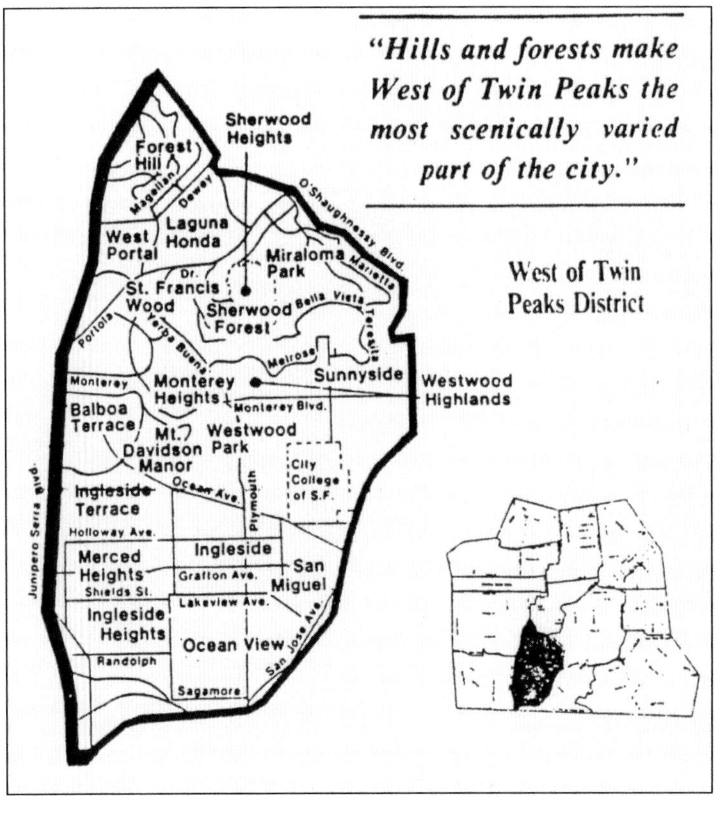


The area of San Francisco known as West of Twin Peaks is large, and its boundaries vary. This book focuses on neighborhoods in the vicinity of Mount Davidson developed by Behrend Joost and the Residential Development Company that include Balboa Terrace, Ingleside Terraces, Mount Davidson Manor, Monterey Heights, Westwood Park, Westwood Highlands, Sherwood Forest, Miraloma Park, and Sunnyside.

# *One*

# BIRTH OF A BENEVOLENT CITY

## THE CALIFORNIA DREAM

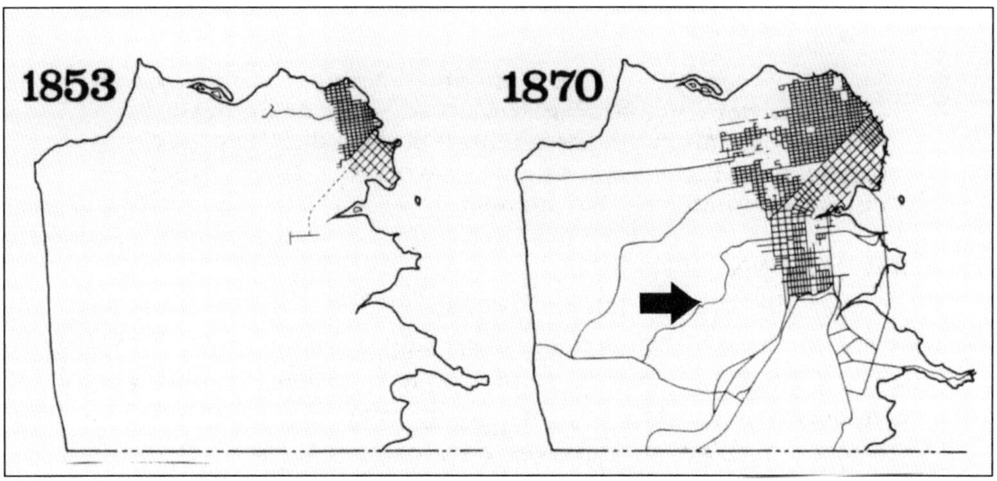


San Francisco was first developed on what is now its most eastern boundary alongside San Francisco Bay. The first owner of the area now known as West of Twin Peaks was Don Jose de Jesus Noe. The 4,443 acres of land were granted to him in 1846. By 1852 and California statehood, Noe sold most of his Rancho San Miguel to John Horner. This 1870 map marks Mount Davidson and the road that became present-day Portola Drive, built across the middle of the rancho by its fourth owner, Francois Pioche. (Courtesy San Francisco Planning Department.)

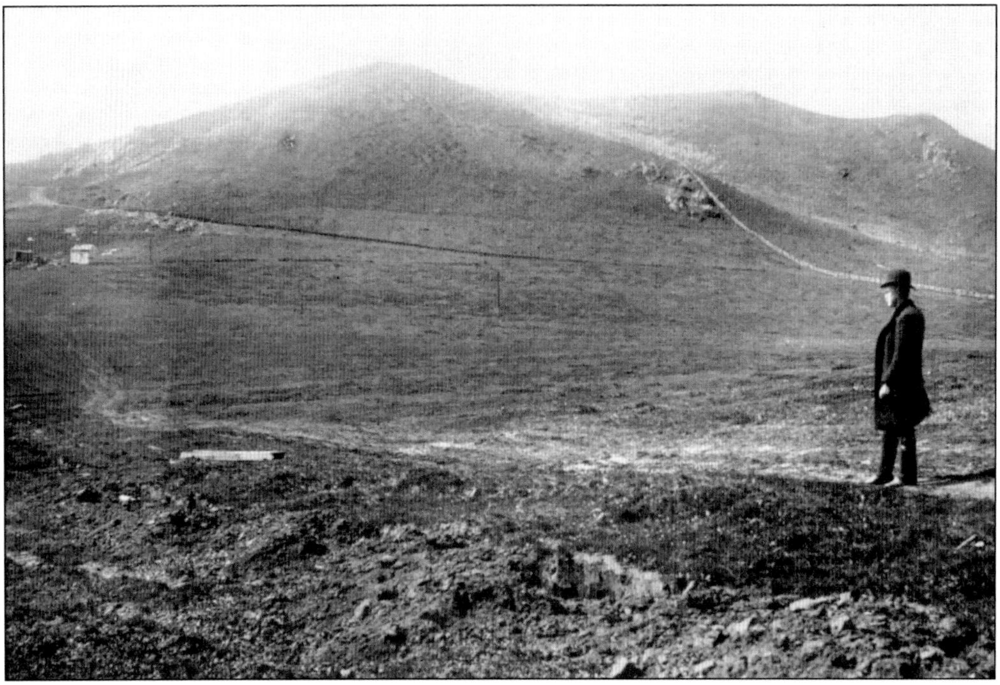

In 1852, scientist George Davidson mapped the mountain now named for him. The color of its wildflowers inspired him to name it Blue Mountain. In 1879, he built the West Coast's first astronomical observatory in San Francisco. Davidson persuaded James Lick to fund building the world's largest observatory of its time on the Bay Area's highest peak, Mount Hamilton. (Courtesy private collection.)

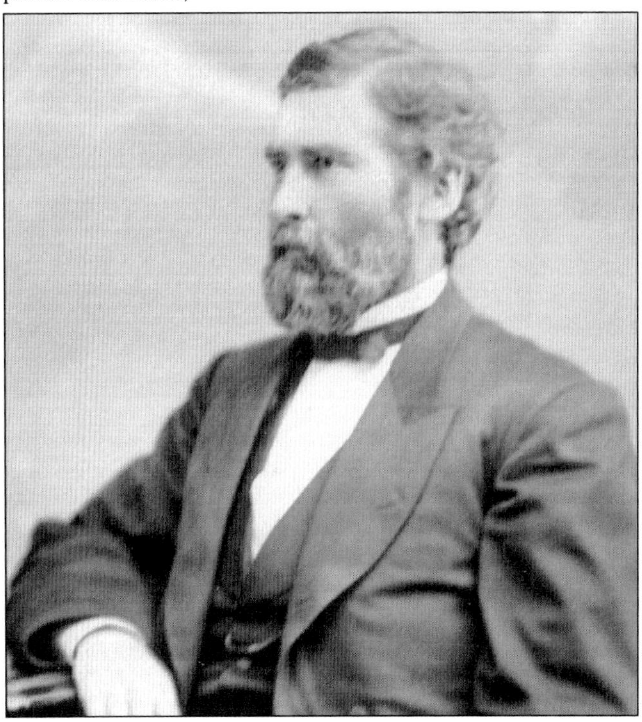

Born in England, Davidson was one of the greatest men ever to serve with the U.S. Geodetic Coast Survey. Before arriving here in 1850, he helped survey the coastline of New England, the California/Nevada border, the Alaskan coastline, and Panama (looking for a possible canal route). In 1900, Davidson wrote that he had traveled 401,888 miles—roughly 16 times the circumference of the world. (Courtesy Ron Proctor.)

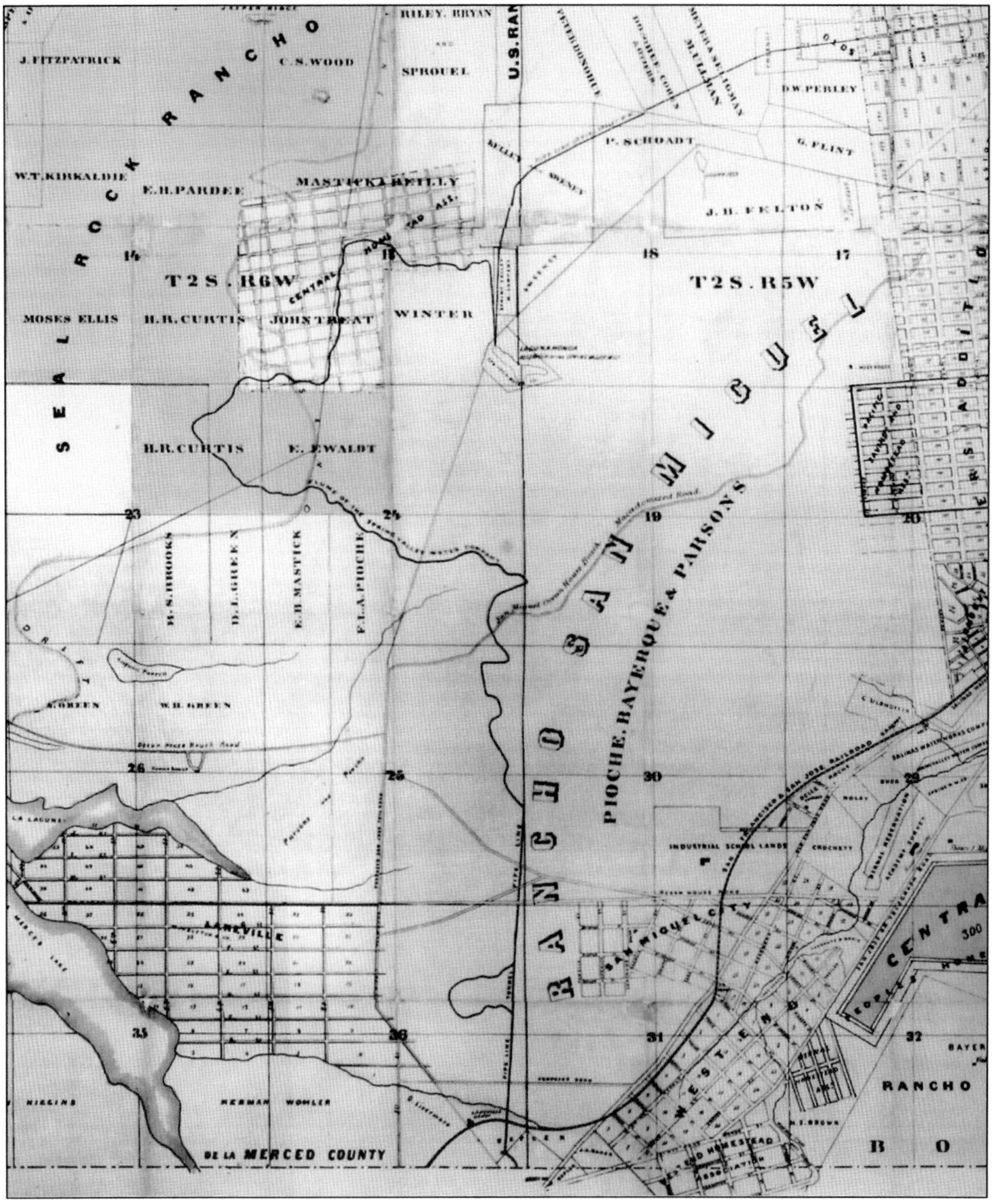


This map of Rancho San Miguel shows Pioche, Bayerque, and Parsons owning it in 1864. Francois Pioche was in Chile when he decided to join the gold rush to San Francisco in 1848 with Julius Bayerque. By the mid-1850s, they had established a mercantile and banking house. Pioche went back to his native Paris to boost the future of San Francisco. With 6 million francs to invest, he proceeded to become one of its primary builders. A noted *bon vivant*, Pioche gave lavish parties for the men and women of importance. He is credited with getting the city off to its start as an epicurean delight by bringing 40 Parisian chefs and a boatload of French wines so San Franciscans unable to afford the grand tour could find out for themselves what they were missing. (Author's collection.)

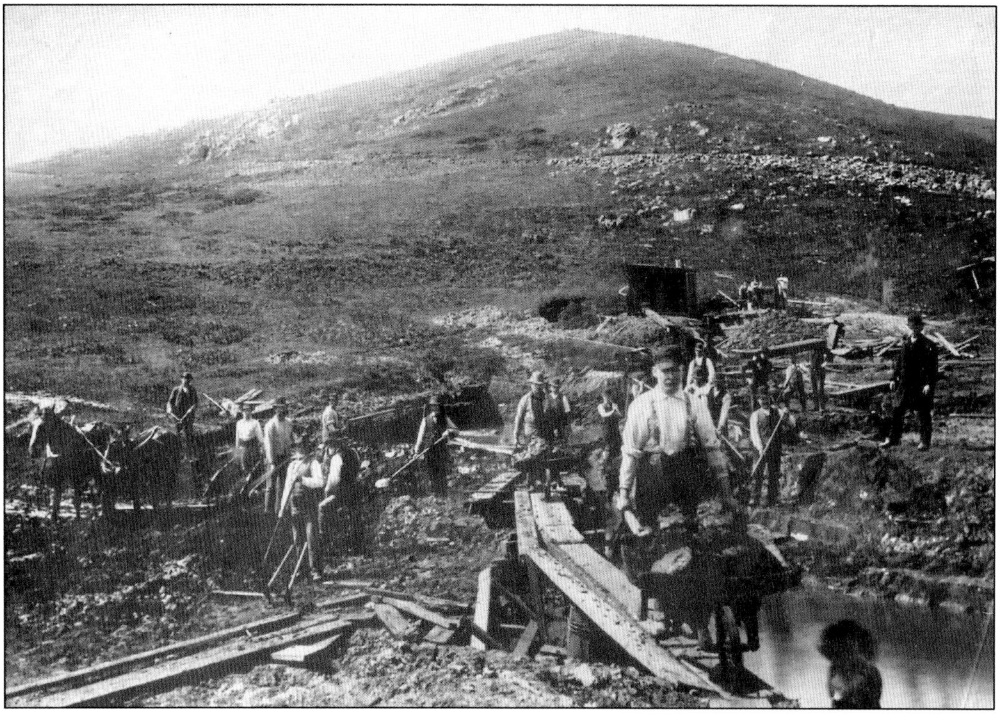

Men are at work here on the Bethlehem Spring in 1891. The Islais and Salinas Water Company developed Islais Creek below Blue Mountain into one of the city's first water supplies. With financing from Pioche, it became part of the Spring Valley Water Company, producing 200,000 gallons per day. Since water to area homes came from wells, the earliest recorded hookup was not until 1909 at 663 Mangels Avenue. (Courtesy Ken Hoegger.)

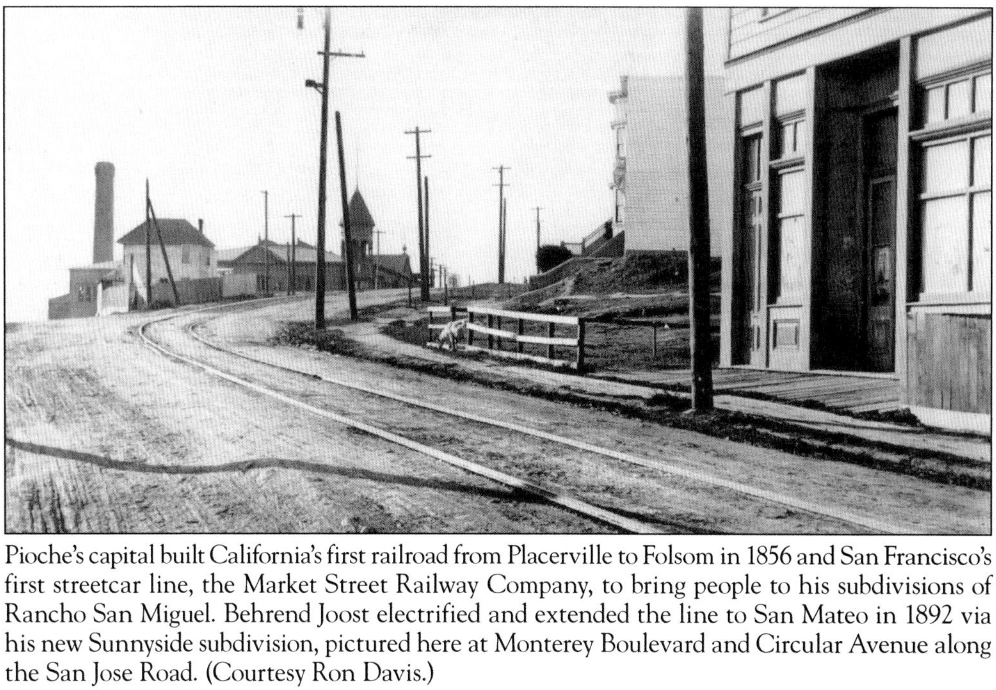

Pioche's capital built California's first railroad from Placerville to Folsom in 1856 and San Francisco's first streetcar line, the Market Street Railway Company, to bring people to his subdivisions of Rancho San Miguel. Behrend Joost electrified and extended the line to San Mateo in 1892 via his new Sunnyside subdivision, pictured here at Monterey Boulevard and Circular Avenue along the San Jose Road. (Courtesy Ron Davis.)

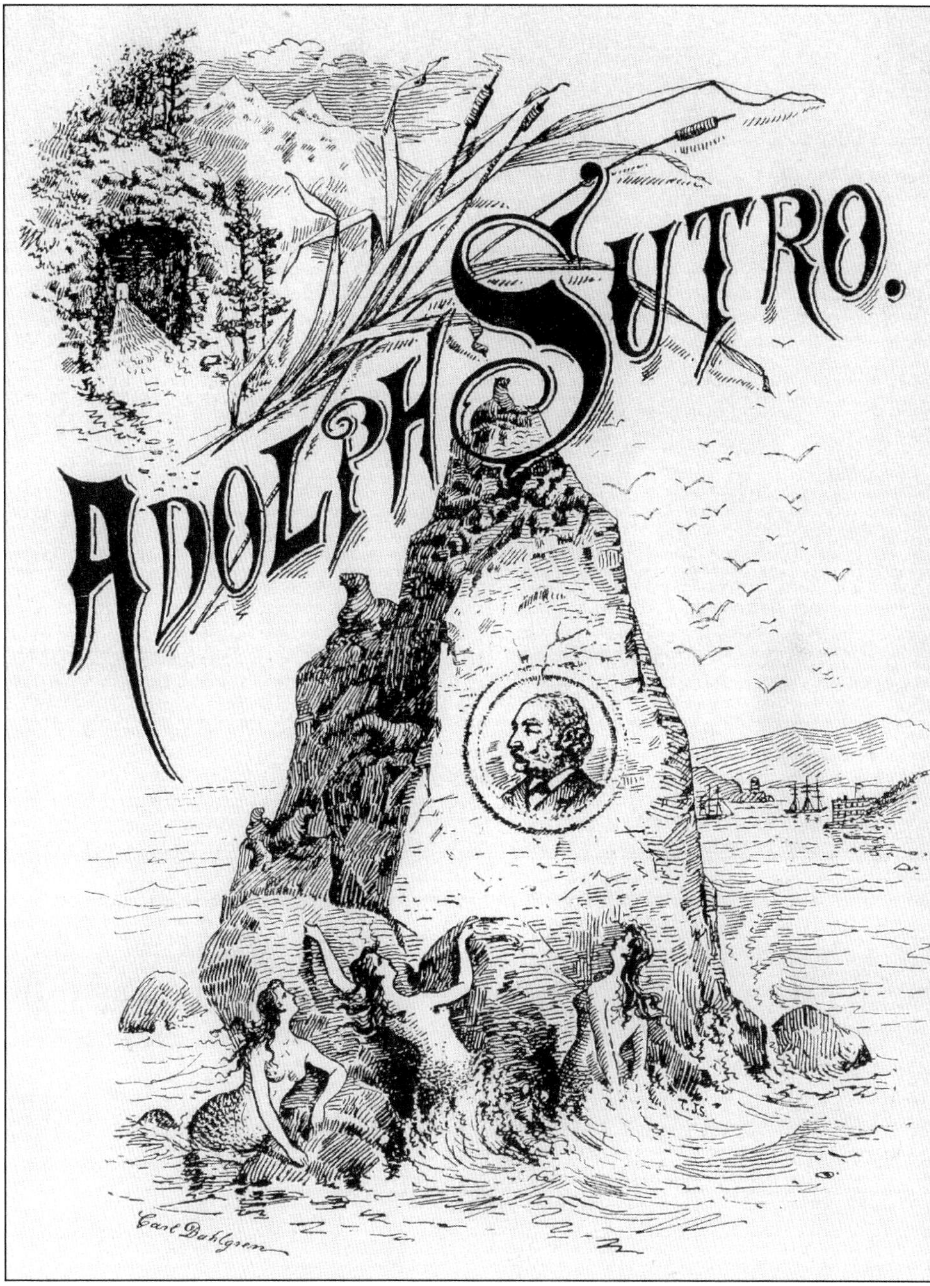


When Edgar Allen and Hosea Grosch died shortly after their discovery of silver at Mount Davidson, located above Virginia City, Nevada, people believed the place was cursed. But in 1865, engineer Adolph Sutro developed a plan of how to mine the silver safely. Mark Twain wrote, "The Sutro Tunnel is to plow through the Comstock Lode from end to end, at a depth of two thousand feet, and then mining will be easy and comparatively inexpensive; and the momentous matters of drainage, and hoisting and hauling of ore will cease to be burdensome." Completion of the seven-mile-long tunnel in 1879 was celebrated with a victory parade through it led by former president Ulysses S. Grant. With his fortune, Sutro bought 1,200 acres of Rancho San Miguel encompassing most of present-day West of Twin Peaks in 1880. (Courtesy Glenn Koch.)

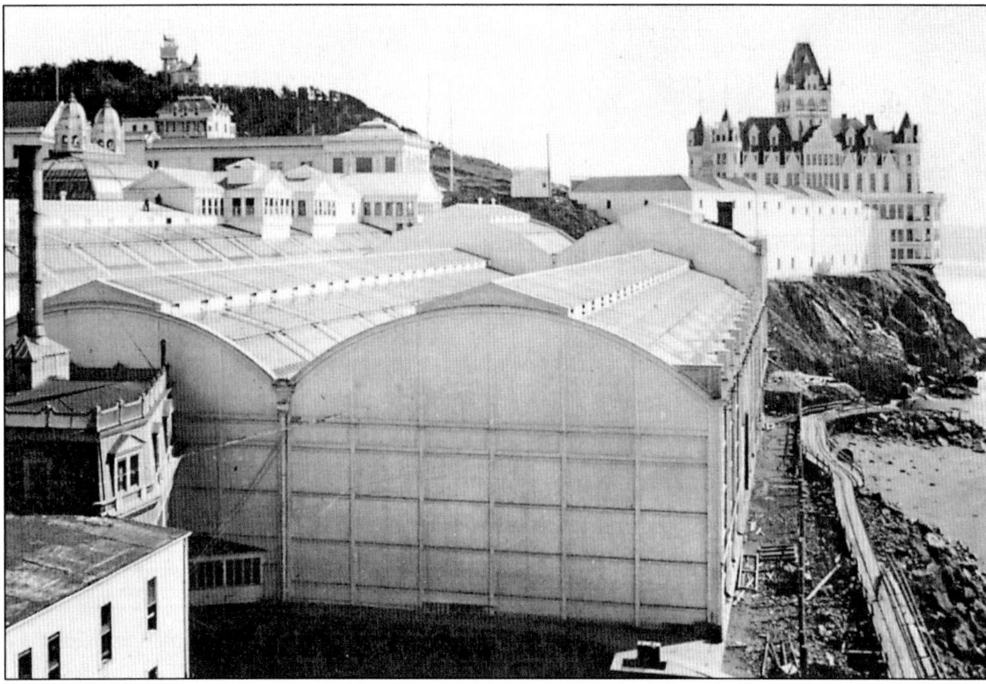

Mayor of San Francisco from 1895 to 1897, Adolph Sutro built a home overlooking his Cliff House Restaurant and Sutro Baths (the world's largest swimming pool) at Seal Rock. The public was welcome to stroll around on his estate, although smoking was not permitted. Here he hosted everyone from Oscar Wilde to President Harrison. (Courtesy Margie Whitnah.)

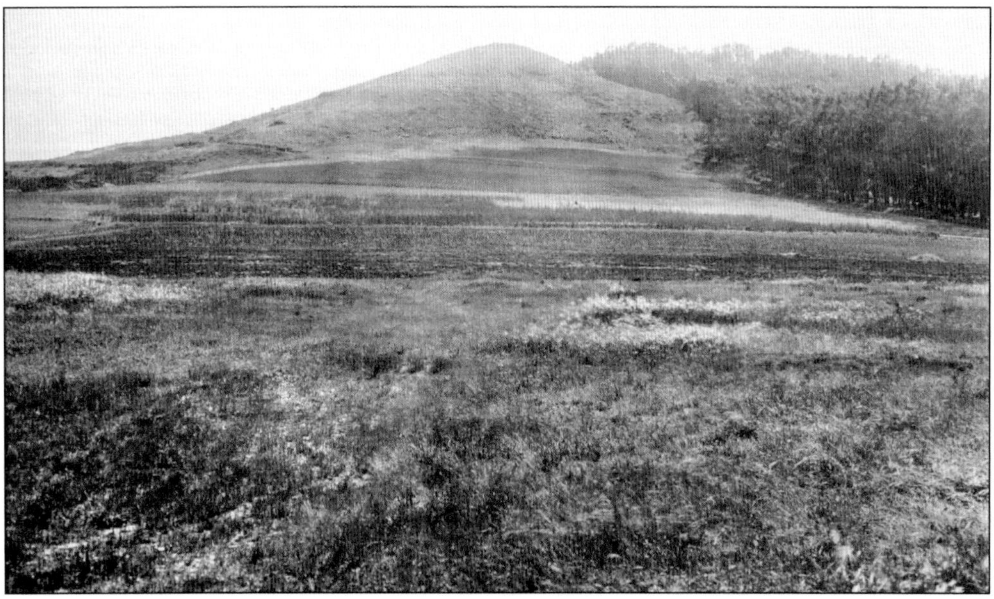

The *San Francisco Chronicle* reported in 1929 that when Joaquin Miller was planting trees in the East Bay, he "envisioned the beauty to Adolph Sutro that might be created by trees on the San Miguel Hills." Sutro's "gift to the beauty of San Francisco" started with enlisting children to plant trees on the first Arbor Day in 1886. By 1910, the stately trees of Sutro Forest had caused all traces of Blue Mountain's former bleakness to disappear. (Private collection.)

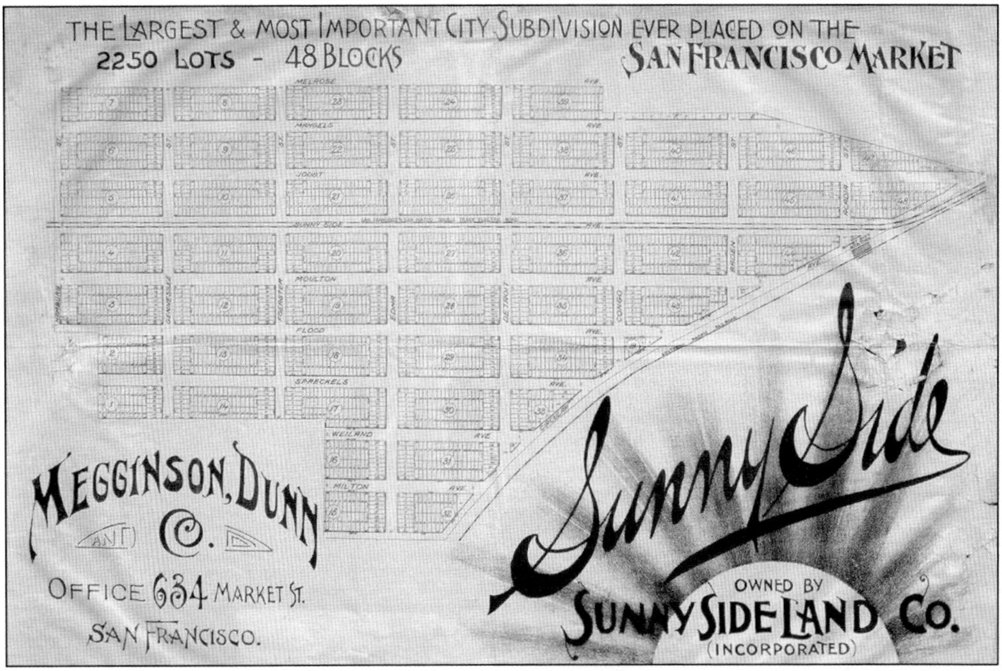


Behrend Joost, the "grand old man of Twin Peaks," bought a portion of Rancho San Miguel from Leland Stanford in 1891 with a fortune he made from a contract to dredge the Panama Canal. After getting out of the canal venture before it failed, Joost's investment in Sunnyside, "the magnificent" subdivision, was the largest to date in San Francisco with 2,250 lots for sale. (Courtesy California State Library, Sutro Branch.)

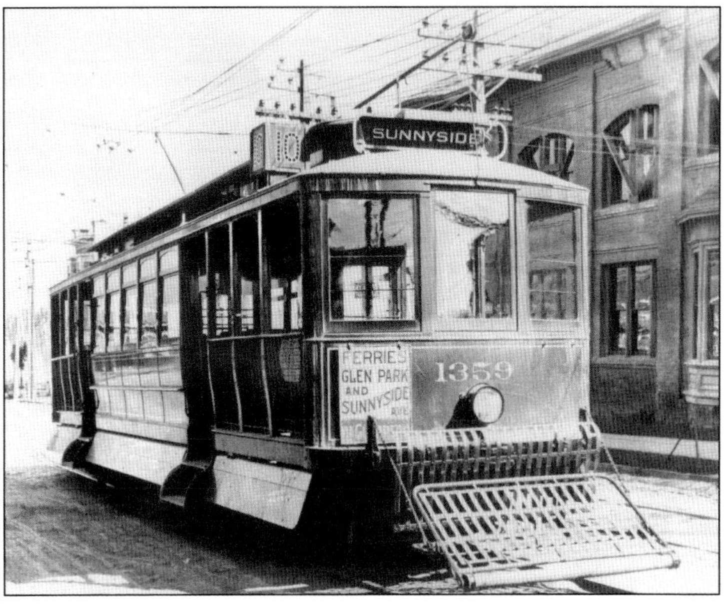


Joost opened the city's first interurban electric streetcar line in 1892. Running all the way to San Mateo, it conveniently passed through Sunnyside. Both ventures became investment failures, however, and Joost sold out his interests with less than 5 percent of Sunnyside built upon by 1900. The Market Street Railway later purchased the streetcar line for an extension of the No. 10 line to Gennessee Street. (Courtesy Ron Davis.)

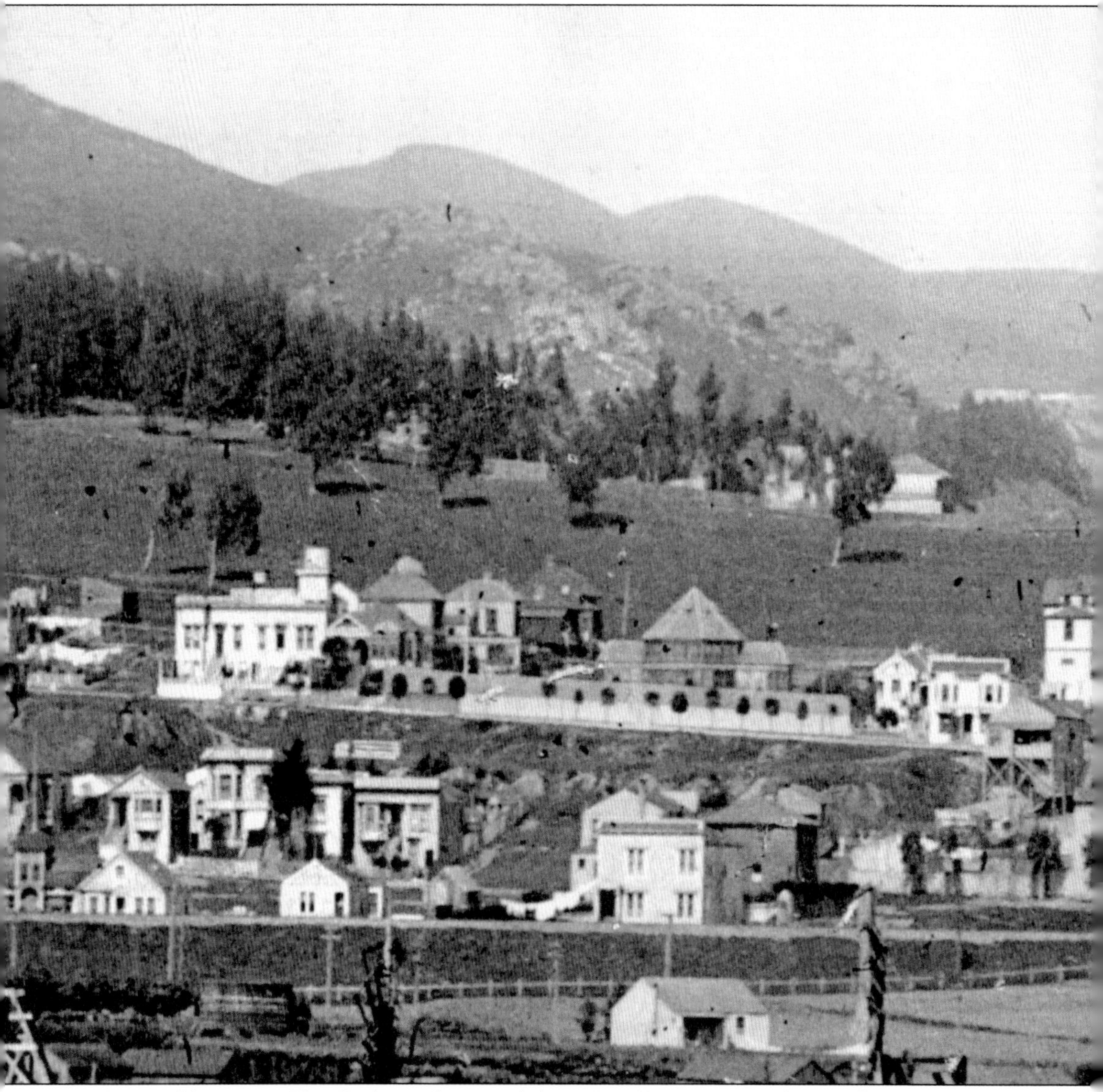

Situated between Glen Park on the east (where San Francisco used to end), Sutro's forest on the west, and the Industrial School on the south, Sunnyside was one of the first neighborhoods built west of the Twin Peaks. H. Taylor, a grip man on Joost's railway, built a home in 1893 near where the Sunnyside Conservatory (above) would later be constructed. Taylor owned seven lots, with a total frontage of 175 feet, building his own Victorian house at 230 Sunnyside Avenue. In

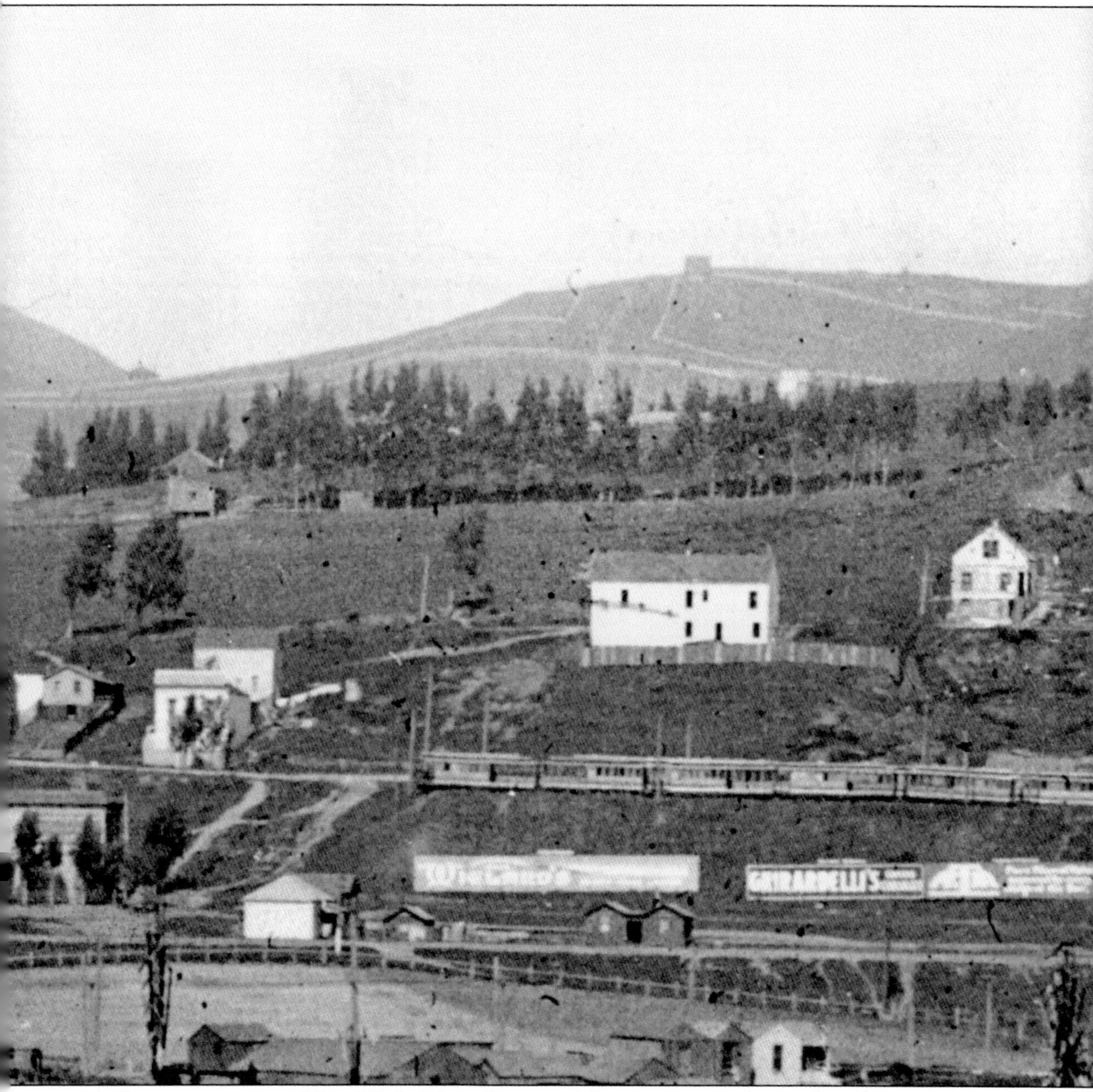


1898, the property was sold to W. A. Merralls, one of the greatest mechanical minds of all time, with money he earned from inventing a ventilation system for the New York City subway system. By 1914, he had added both a conservatory and an observatory to the property. (Courtesy of private collection.)

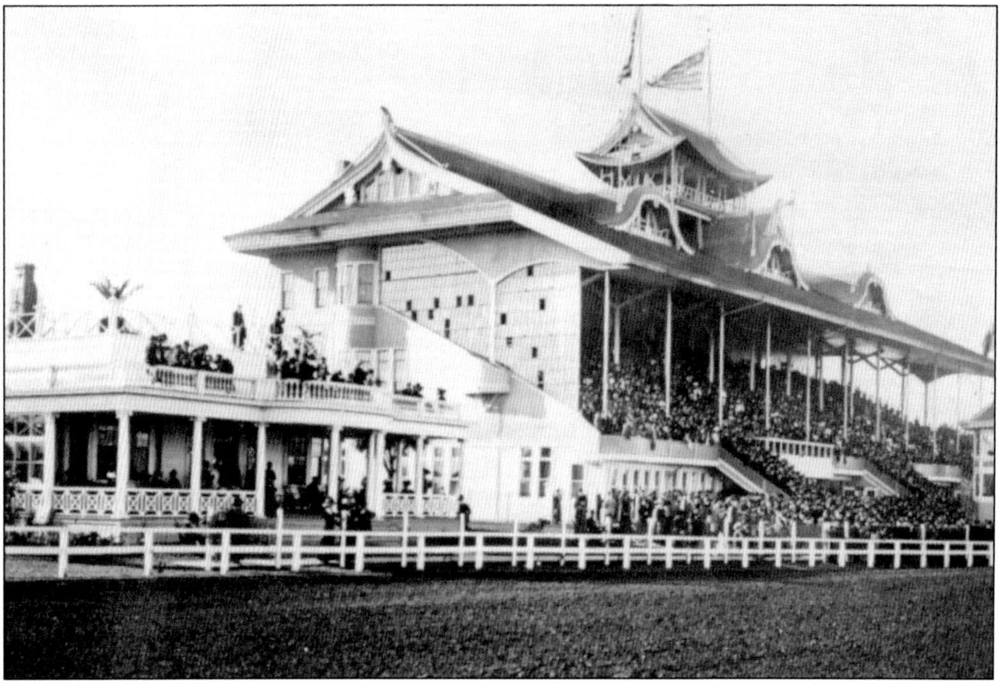

Gambler Edward Corrigan bought 148 acres of Rancho San Miguel to build the Ingleside Race Track. Not satisfied with the way things were run at the Bay District Track, he formed the Pacific Coast Jockey Club with A. A. Spreckels and Henry J. Crocker to build "the most sumptuous racing course in the west." It opened in 1885 before a crowd of 8,000 and operated regularly through 1905. (Courtesy Margie Whitnah.)

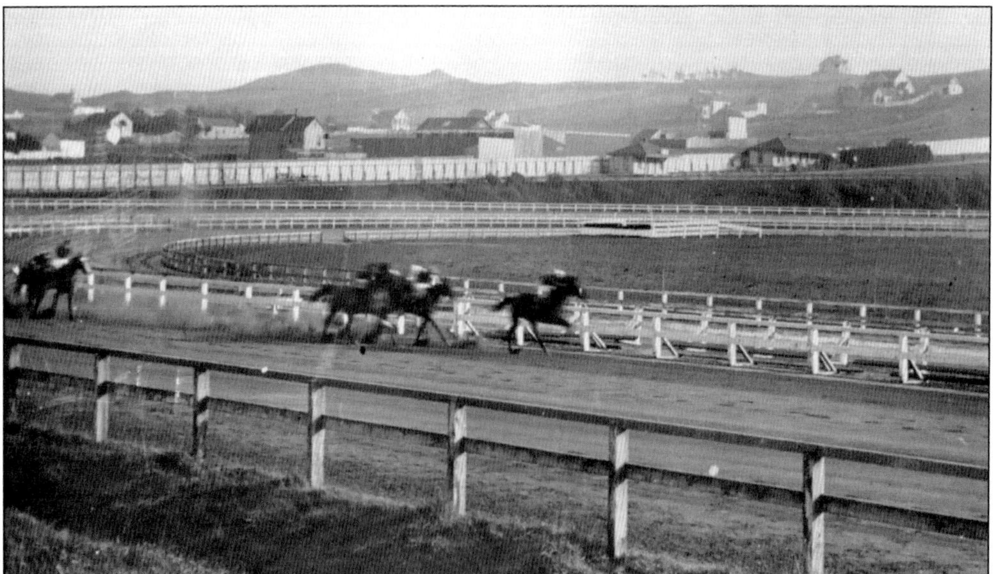

The Ingleside Horse Racing Track was also the site of California's first automobile race in 1900. The winner, and the only car of eight to finish, was White Steam engineer Walter Grothe, who drove the oval in one minute, 22 seconds. (Courtesy Margie Whitnah.)

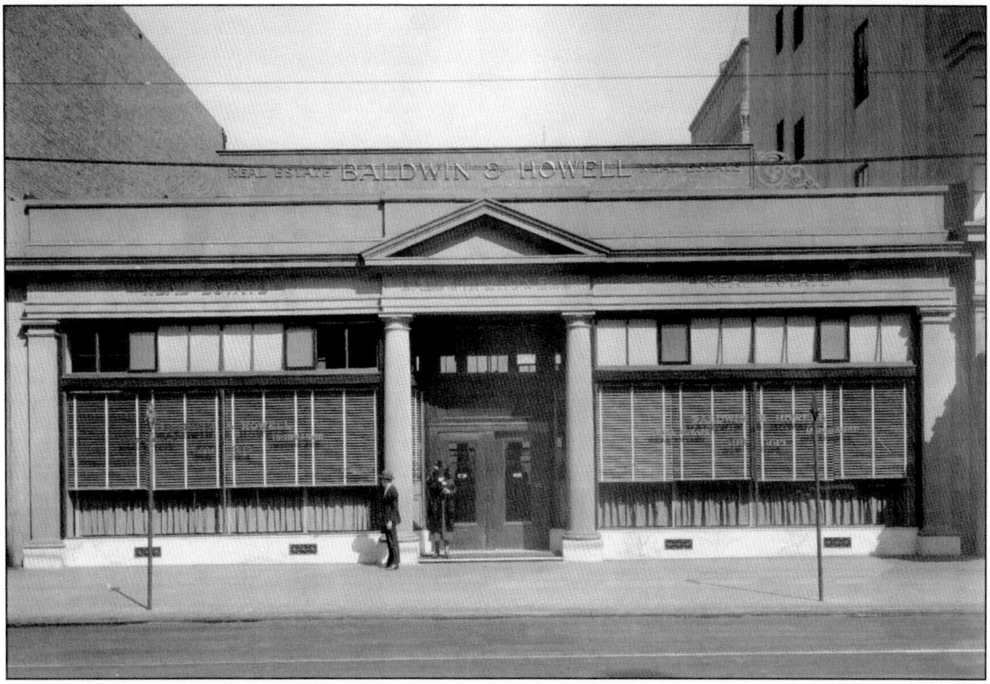


The Baldwin and Howell Real Estate Company was established in 1885. Josiah Howell was the first president of the real estate board in 1905. A. S. Baldwin, appraiser of Adolph Sutro's estate, bought it for development after the California Supreme Court overturned the gift of that land to an educational trust. From their office at 318–324 Kearny Street, Baldwin and Howell began developing Rancho San Miguel for housing in 1912. (Courtesy Westwood Park Association.)

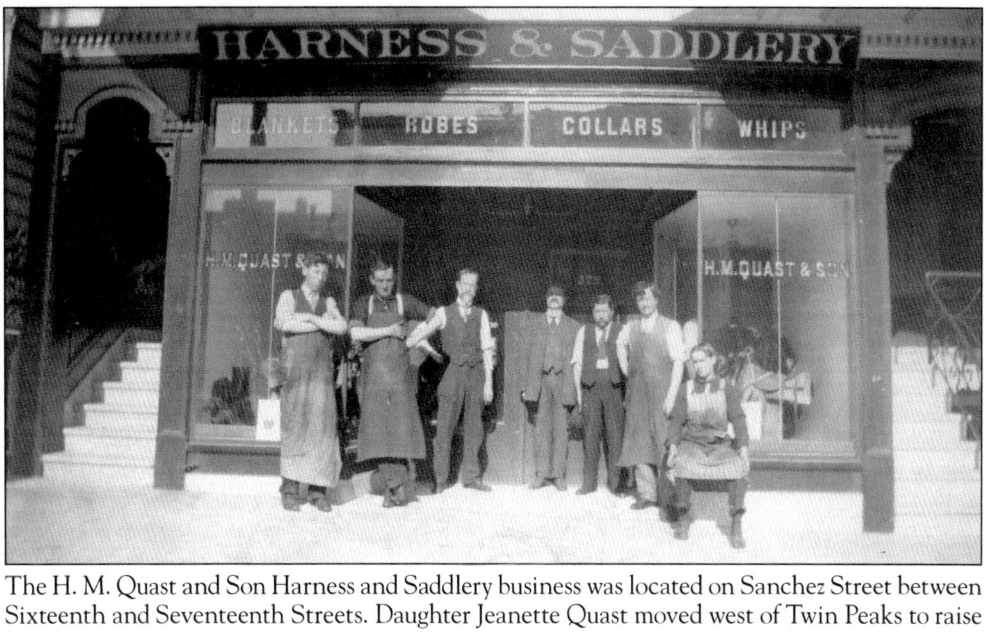


The H. M. Quast and Son Harness and Saddlery business was located on Sanchez Street between Sixteenth and Seventeenth Streets. Daughter Jeanette Quast moved west of Twin Peaks to raise her family on Mount Davidson. Herman M. Quast came to San Francisco from his native Germany around 1870, when San Francisco had the highest percentage of foreign-born inhabitants of any major city in America. (Courtesy Jeanne Davis MacKenzie.)

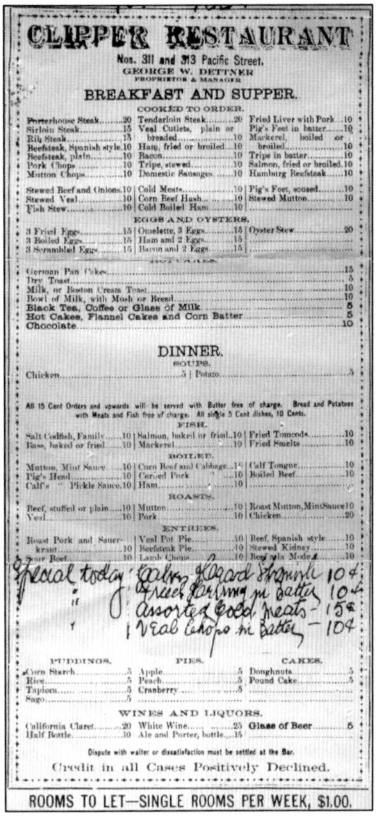

# CLIPPER RESTAURANT

Nos. 311 and 313 Pacific Street.
GEORGE W. DETTNER
PROPRIETOR & MANAGER

## BREAKFAST AND SUPPER.

COOKED TO ORDER.

| | | | | | |
|---|---|---|---|---|---|
| Porterhouse Steak | 20 | Tenderloin Steak | 20 | Fried Liver with Pork | 10 |
| Sirloin Steak | 15 | Veal Cutlets, plain or breaded | 10 | Pig's Feet in batter | 10 |
| Rib Steak | 15 | Ham, fried or broiled | 10 | Mackerel, boiled or broiled | 10 |
| Beefsteak, Spanish style | 10 | Bacon | 10 | Tripe in batter | 10 |
| Beefsteak, plain | 10 | Tripe, stewed | 10 | Salmon, fried or broiled | 10 |
| Pork Chops | 10 | Domestic Sausages | 10 | Hamburg Beefsteak | 10 |
| Mutton Chops | 10 | | | | |
| Stewed Beef and Onions | 10 | Cold Meats | 10 | Pig's Feet, soused | 10 |
| Stewed Veal | 10 | Corn Beef Hash | 10 | Stewed Mutton | 10 |
| Fish Stew | 10 | Cold Boiled Ham | 10 | | |

EGGS AND OYSTERS.

| | | | | | |
|---|---|---|---|---|---|
| 3 Fried Eggs | 15 | Omelette, 3 Eggs | 15 | Oyster Stew | 20 |
| 3 Boiled Eggs | 15 | Ham and 2 Eggs | 15 | | |
| 3 Scrambled Eggs | 15 | Bacon and 2 Eggs | 15 | | |

HOT CAKES.

| | |
|---|---|
| German Pan Cakes | 15 |
| Dry Toast | 5 |
| Milk, or Boston Cream Toast | 10 |
| Bowl of Milk, with Mush or Bread | 10 |
| **Black Tea, Coffee or Glass of Milk** | 5 |
| **Hot Cakes, Flannel Cakes and Corn Batter** | 5 |
| **Chocolate** | 10 |

## DINNER.

SOUPS.

Chicken ... 5 | Potato ... 5

All 15 Cent Orders and upwards will be served with Butter free of charge. Bread and Potatoes with Meats and Fish free of charge. All single 5 Cent dishes, 10 Cents.

FISH.

| | | | | | |
|---|---|---|---|---|---|
| Salt Codfish, Family | 10 | Salmon, baked or fried | 10 | Fried Tomcods | 10 |
| Bass, baked or fried | 10 | Mackerel | 10 | Fried Smelts | 10 |

BOILED.

| | | | | | |
|---|---|---|---|---|---|
| Mutton, Mint Sauce | 10 | Corn Beef and Cabbage | 15 | Calf Tongue | 10 |
| Pig's Head | 10 | Corned Pork | 10 | Boiled Beef | 10 |
| Calf's " Pickle Sauce | 10 | Ham | 10 | | |

ROASTS.

| | | | | | |
|---|---|---|---|---|---|
| Beef, stuffed or plain | 10 | Mutton | 10 | Roast Mutton, Mint Sauce | 10 |
| Veal | 10 | Pork | 10 | Chicken | 20 |

ENTREES.

| | | | | | |
|---|---|---|---|---|---|
| Roast Pork and Sauerkraut | 10 | Veal Pot Pie | 10 | Beef, Spanish style | 10 |
| Sour Beef | 10 | Beefsteak Pie | 10 | Stewed Kidney | 10 |
| | | Lamb Chops | 10 | Beef a la Mode | 10 |

Special today: [illegible] 10¢
" [illegible] in Batter 10¢
" Assorted Cold Meats – 15¢
" Veal Chops in Batter – 10¢

| PUDDINGS. | | PIES. | | CAKES. | |
|---|---|---|---|---|---|
| Corn Starch | 5 | Apple | 5 | Doughnuts | 5 |
| Rice | 5 | Peach | 5 | Pound Cake | 5 |
| Tapioca | 5 | Cranberry | 5 | | |
| Sago | 5 | | | | |

WINES AND LIQUORS.

| | | | | | |
|---|---|---|---|---|---|
| California Claret | 20 | White Wine | 25 | **Glass of Beer** | 5 |
| Half Bottle | 10 | Ale and Porter, bottle | 15 | | |

Dispute with waiter or dissatisfaction must be settled at the Bar.

Credit in all Cases Positively Declined.

ROOMS TO LET—SINGLE ROOMS PER WEEK, $1.00.

This menu is from the Clipper Restaurant, which was started in 1871 by George Dettner, whose parents arrived from Alsace before the gold rush. After 1883, he started the Dettner Printing House on Howard Street. Son Ernest built the German-style home at 75 Upper Terrace from earthquake bricks in 1915. Granddaughter Elvira married Jack Granfield and lived in Ingleside Terraces, which was built on the old Ingleside Racetrack. (Courtesy Dave Bisho.)

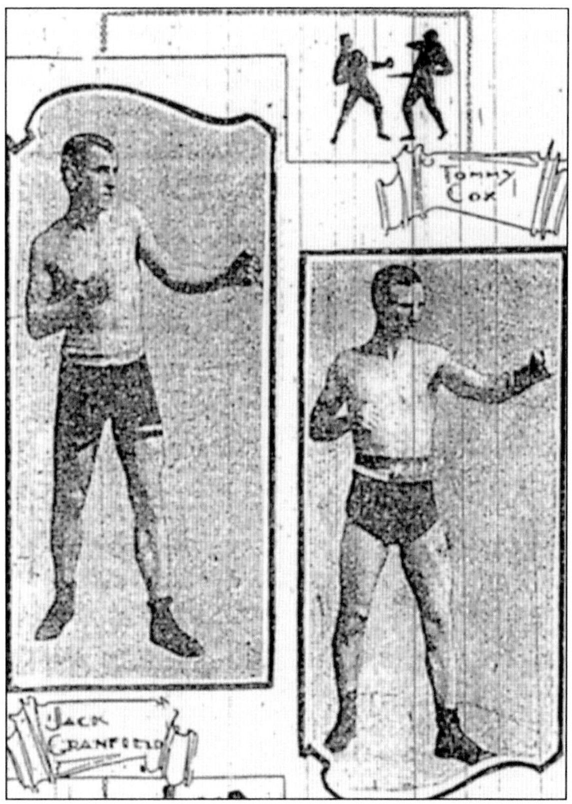


Jack Granfield boxed semiprofessionally as one of the early members of the Olympic Club. Born on Jesse Street in San Francisco and the son of a potato-famine Irish immigrant from County Kerry, Ireland, it was anticipated that Jack would put up a stirring preliminary battle with Tommy Cox before the main event between the "Fighting Dutchman" Charles Thurston and Otto Crib of Australia at the Mechanics' Pavilion in 1901. (Courtesy Dave Bisho.)

# *Two*

# LIVABLE NEIGHBORHOODS

## UTOPIAN DREAM IN THE OUTSIDE LANDS

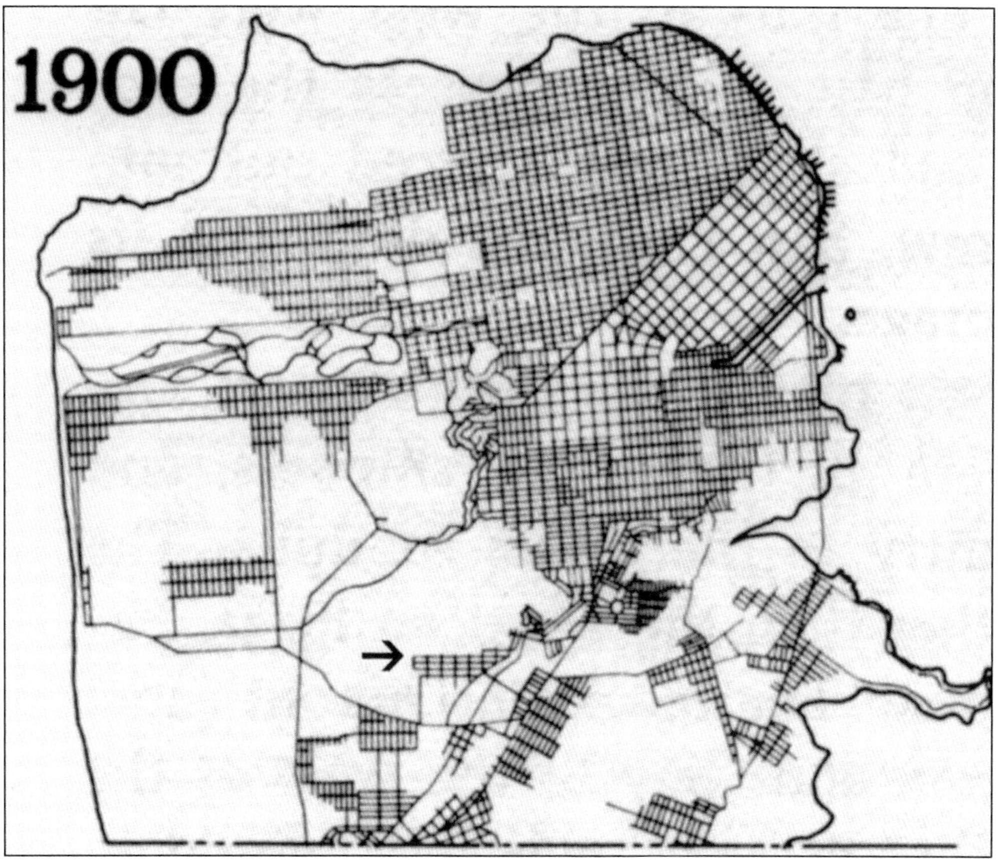


By 1900, the Sunnyside District was constructed as far west as Hamburg Street, and A. S. Baldwin was in court to develop the area west and north of it after the death of Adolph Sutro. San Francisco, the state's most populous city, had reached 350,000 as Los Angeles surpassed 100,000. (Courtesy San Francisco Planning Department.)

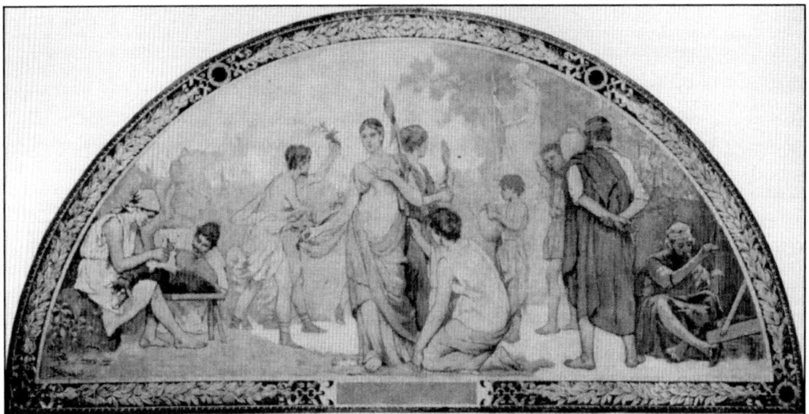

LIFE.

By Walter MacEwen.

*From the Decorative Painting in the Manufactures and Liberal Arts Building.*

## INTRODUCTION

THE Columbian Exposition of 1893 is not yet seen in the perspective of history, but it is possible already to summarize certain impressions and to suggest a consensus of opinion which will affect the historical verdict. So far as the plans are concerned which transformed a strip of outlying lake shore into a beautiful system of sites, roadways, water ways, and landscape art, there is no place for criticism. The general design of the buildings, and the results attained by that ungrudging co-operation of architects, artists, and builders, suggested in Mr. Burnham's article, have given to the world a universal exposition which is confessedly more beautiful in general design than its predecessors at Paris, Vienna, Philadelphia, or elsewhere. If it is true, as some foreign critics have urged, that the architecture does not represent creation, it is none the less true that it stands for a command of selection, assimilation, and harmonious combination, a largeness of purpose, discretion, and perception of æsthetic fitness, which have drawn from a less captious foreign visitor—Mr. Walter Besant—the verdict that "nowhere, at any time, has there been presented to the world any group of buildings so entirely beautiful in themselves, and in their arrangement, as this group at Chicago, which they call the World's Fair."

Daniel Burnham's architectural design for Chicago's Columbian Exposition of 1893 started a revolution in city planning across the country—the City Beautiful movement. Cameron Binkley describes this movement in San Francisco as being driven by the ethos of middle-class environmentalism and a desire for beauty, order, system, and harmony. He stated, "City Beautiful enthusiasts promoted the creation of monumental public structures, park-like boulevards and the use of urban planning and sanitary engineering." Binkley went on to say that women were especially involved in this movement "planting trees and flowers, promoting parks and playgrounds, cleaning up garbage, regulating utility poles, billboards, and nuisance industries, and promoting zoning restrictions. This work combined women's interests in nature, art, health, and society." Burnham developed a City Beautiful plan for San Francisco in 1905, recommending hilltops remain free of development, underground transit go through the Twin Peaks, and that new streets follow the natural contours of the city's hills. (Author's collection.)

On April 18, the Wednesday after Easter Sunday in 1906, an estimated 8.3 magnitude earthquake shook San Francisco, causing this damage to a "corruptly" constructed city hall before it and much of the rest of the city was destroyed by fire. Future West of Twin Peaks resident Jack Granfield resourcefully used bricks from city hall to start a business repairing streets. (Courtesy Jeanne Davis.)

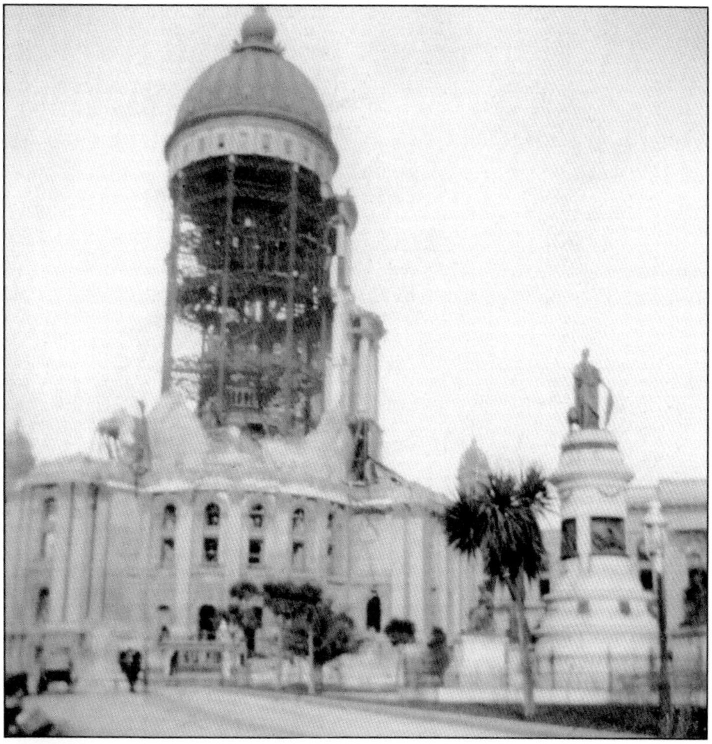

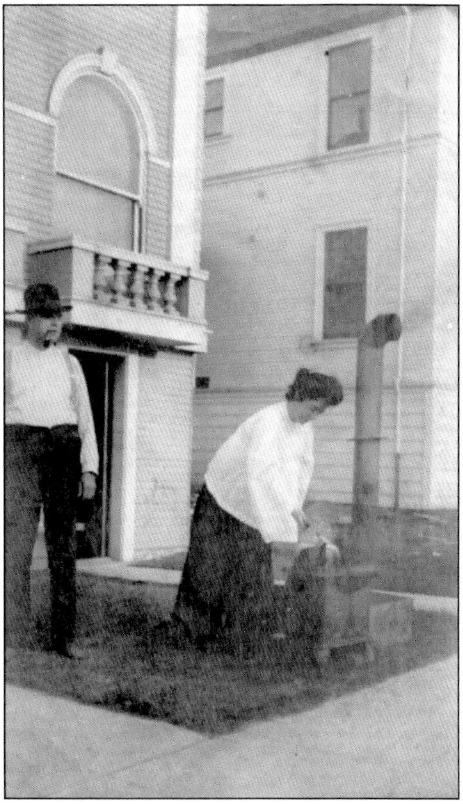

The day after the earthquake, the Weir and Shank families were happy to be safe, taking photographs outside their undamaged home at 61 Fifth Avenue near Lake Street to show they were okay. For six weeks, no indoor fires were allowed anywhere in the city. Charlotte Weir, here with her brother-in-law John Shank, cooked meals for her family and refugees camping at the nearby Presidio. (Courtesy Elizabeth Mettling.)

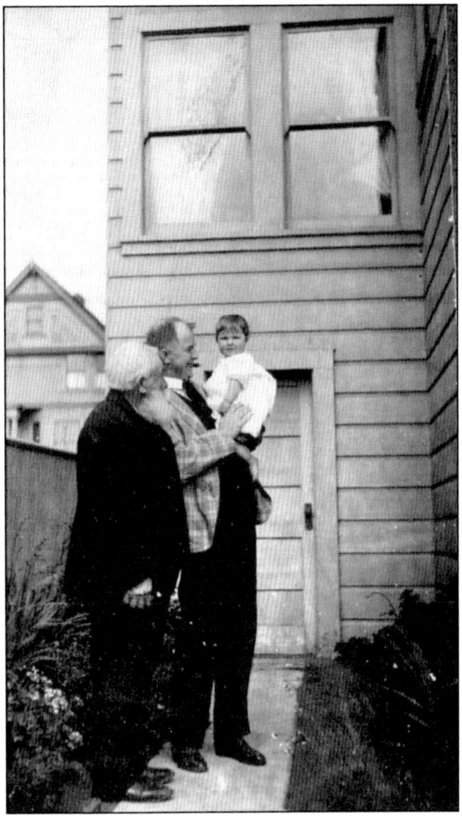

Future West of Twin Peaks resident Sally Shank, being held by her dad John, was glad to find her baptism record at her family's church after her birth certificate was destroyed in the earthquake. Grandfather James Weir came to San Francisco from Australia in 1852 on the same boat as Leland Stanford. He made a living in construction while he searched for silver in his Nevada mine. (Courtesy Elizabeth Mettling.)

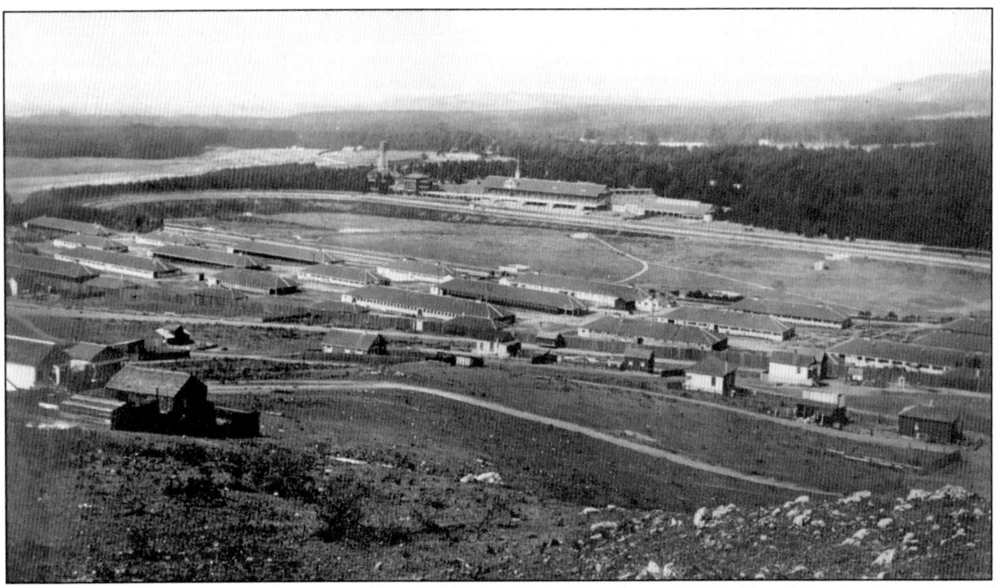

Thomas Williams, the new owner of the Ingleside Race Track in 1905, offered his facilities free of charge for the City of San Francisco to provide more permanent housing to earthquake refugees living in tent cities. Windows were installed in the horse barns, which were also cleaned and painted. The Ingleside Model Camp opened for 484 men and women in October 1906. The track never reopened for business after the earthquake. (Courtesy Margie Whitnah.)

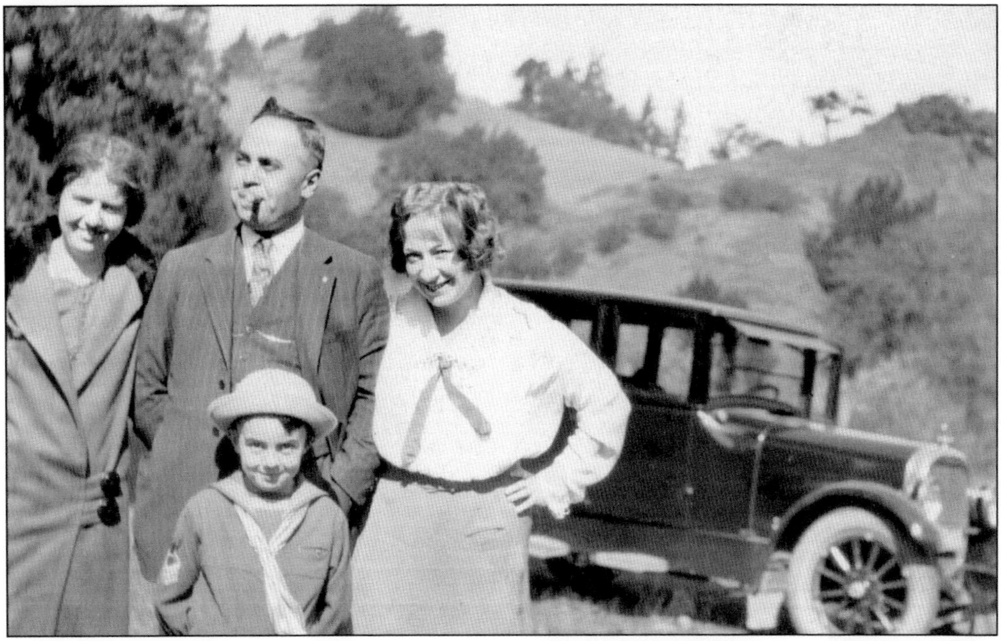

In 1905, 15-year-old Mark Pommon left his native Zakynthos, Greece, to visit San Francisco. Engulfed by the 1906 earthquake, he found work clearing rubble for $5 a day. He then headed to the logging camps in Mendocino and saved his earnings for a job where he could wear a white collar. Pommon is pictured here with his wife, Violet (left), son Dan, and a friend in the 1920s. (Courtesy John Pommon.)

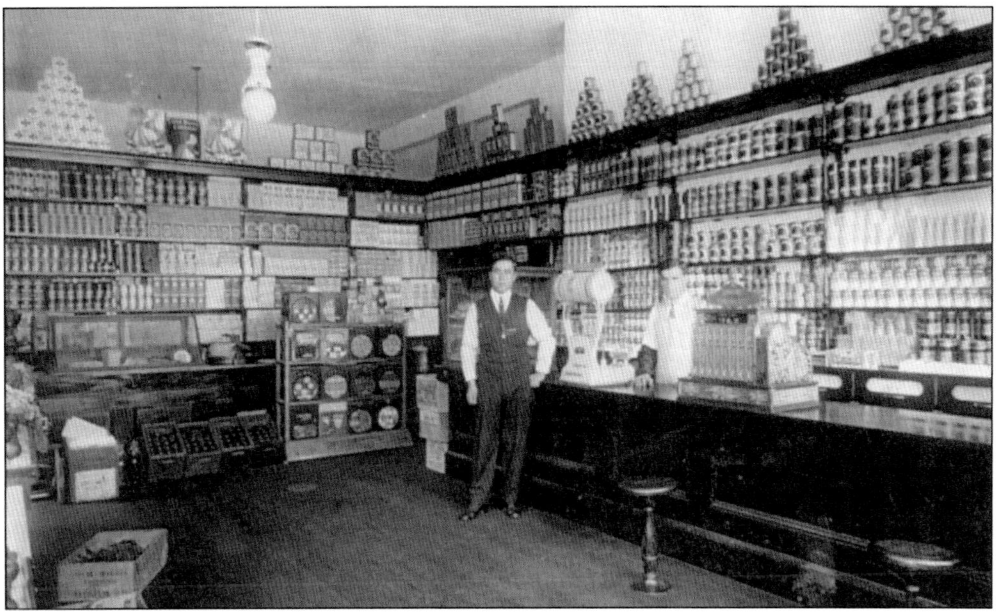

In 1916, Pommon bought Dudley's Market in downtown San Francisco that he ran for 23 years, wearing a suit to work each day. But Mark had a dream to open a place for one-stop shopping—a novel idea in those days of storefront butchers, green grocers, and fishmongers. This creator of Tower Market said he "looked at what was then a no-man's-land west of Twin Peaks and just bet the city would grow in that direction." (Courtesy John Pommon.)

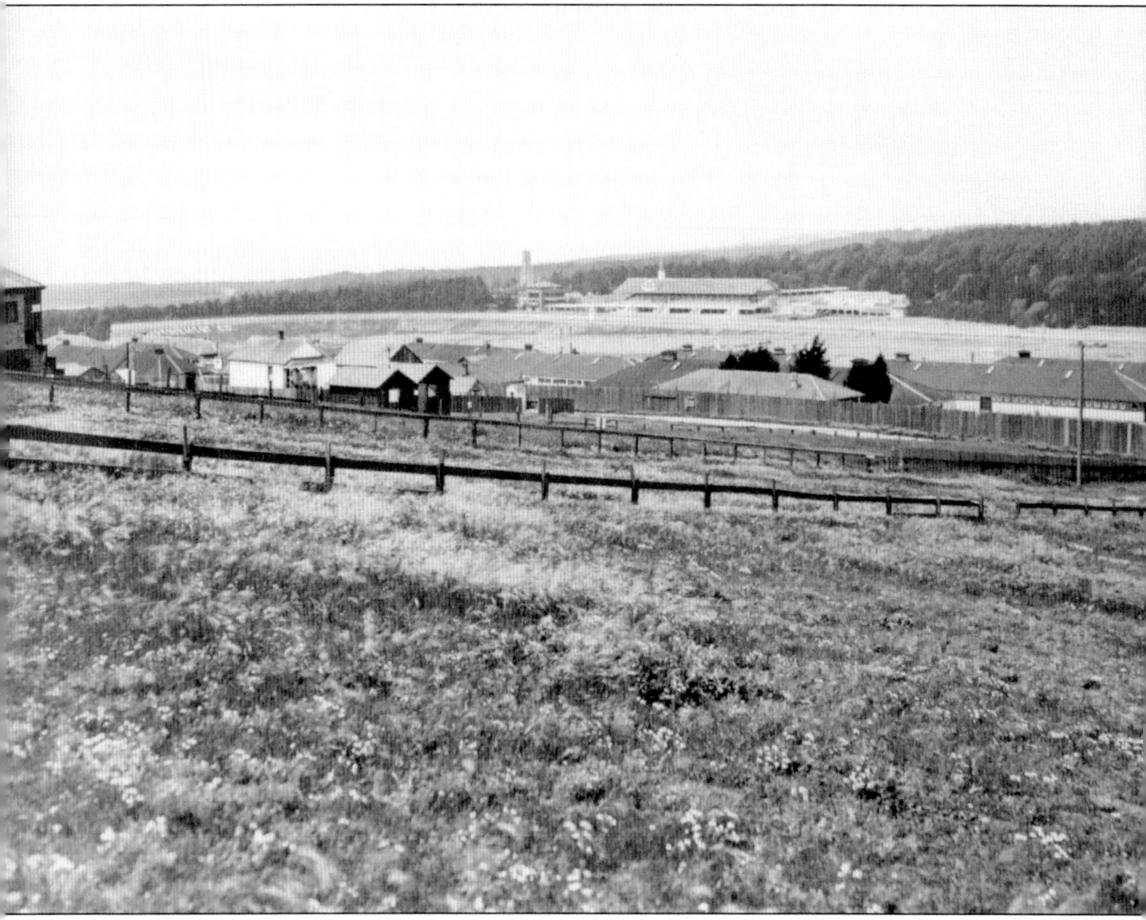

A. S. Baldwin's appraisal included this photograph of the 724 acres west of Twin Peaks and south of Mount Davidson that his Residential Development Corporation bought from Sutro's Estate for $1,417,877 in 1911. Here he would build the Westwood Park, Balboa Terrace, Ingleside Terraces, Mount Davidson Manor, Monterey Heights, and Westwood Highlands neighborhoods, utilizing Daniel Burnham's City Beautiful ideas to keep earthquake survivors from moving out of San

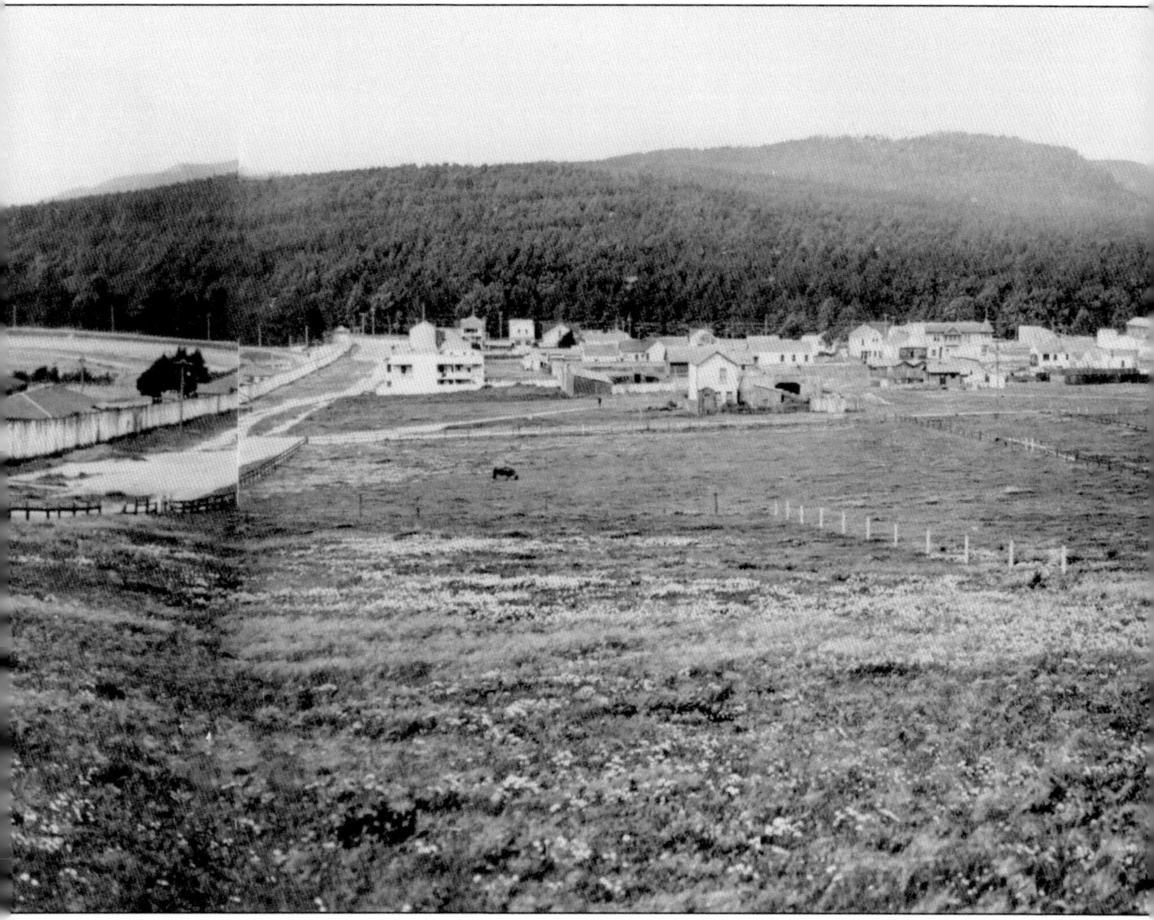

Francisco. Noting these are now some of the city's most attractive neighborhoods, even though they were built without any government intervention or direct support, Patrick McGrew states, "These homes will never be found in the tourist brochures that describe the sites of San Francisco, for none are located in the tourist zone. . . . These are the homes where San Franciscans live—a 'home city. A good place in which to live.' " (Courtesy Miraloma Park Improvement Club (MPIC).)

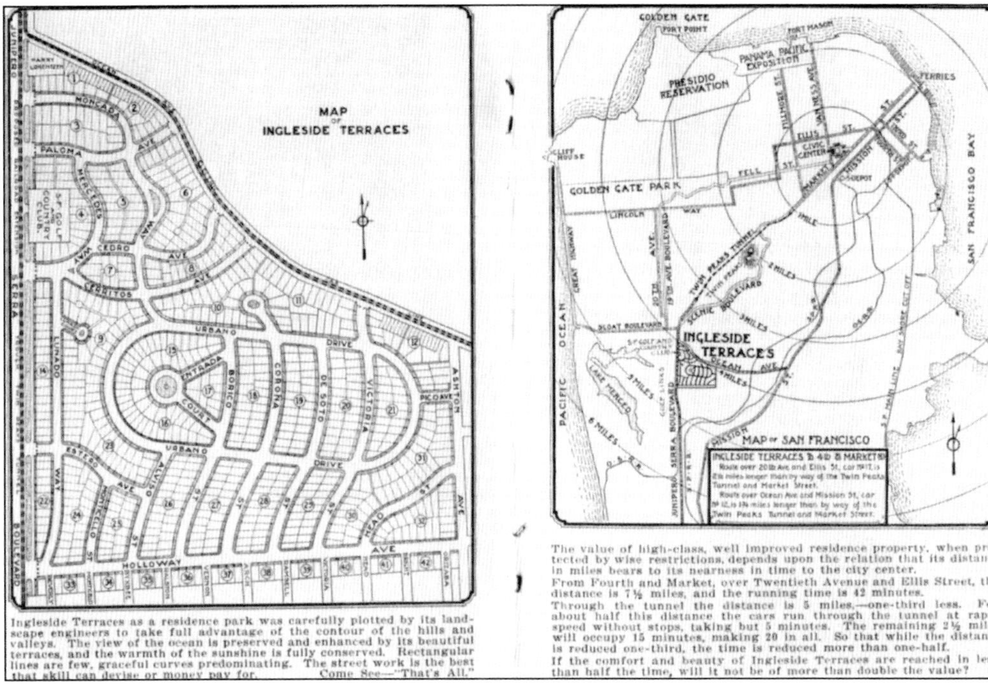


Ingleside Terraces, pictured on these maps, was built on the site of the old racetrack and opened in 1913. The 613 parcels, spread over 148 acres, were purchased for $2,500 per acre. The tract was designed and developed by Joseph Leonard, who made the neighborhood among the first in San Francisco to feature wide, smooth streets to accommodate the automobile. (Courtesy Margie Whitnah.)

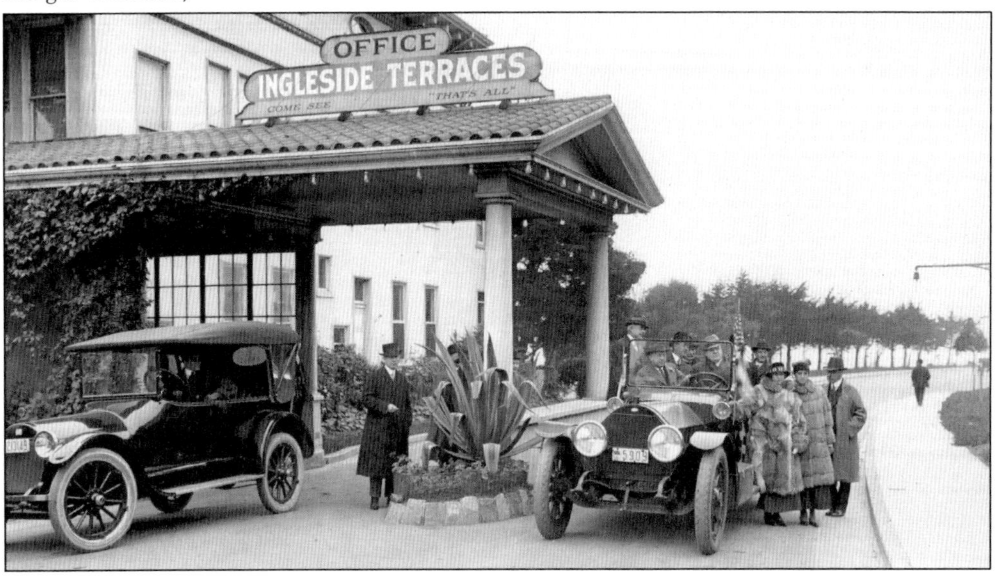


The racetrack clubhouse was used for the Ingleside Terraces sales office at the southeast corner of Cerritos Avenue and Moncada Way. The carriage entrance was on Cerritos, and the south side of the clubhouse faced what is now Urbano Drive, which follows the old racetrack. The homeowners association met there until 1930, when it was removed for more housing. (Courtesy Westwood Park Association.)

Ingleside Terraces brochures touted oversized lots ranging from 50 to 80 feet in width and 120 to 200 feet in depth, making "crowded conditions impossible." Homes were "honestly built, not to sell, but for someone to live in," with plenty of elbow room and fresh air. In addition, they had "clean and healthful surroundings—physically and morally; with kindly neighbors who are neither very rich, nor very poor." (Courtesy California Historical Society.)

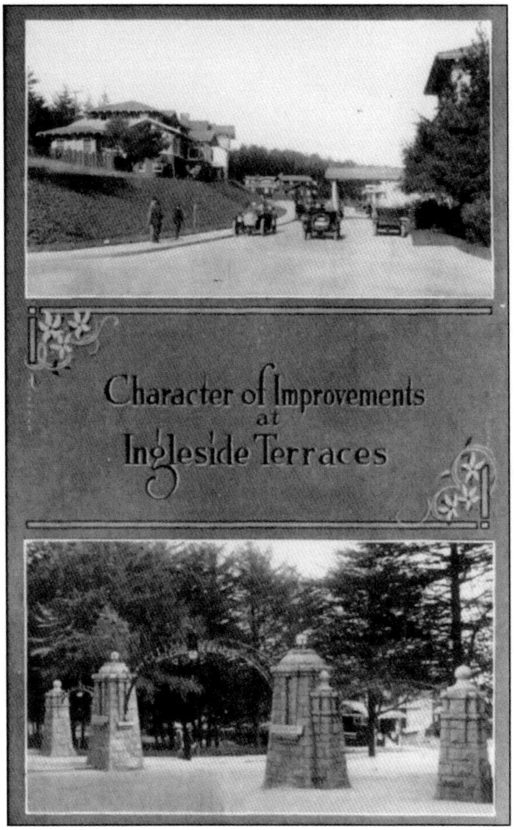


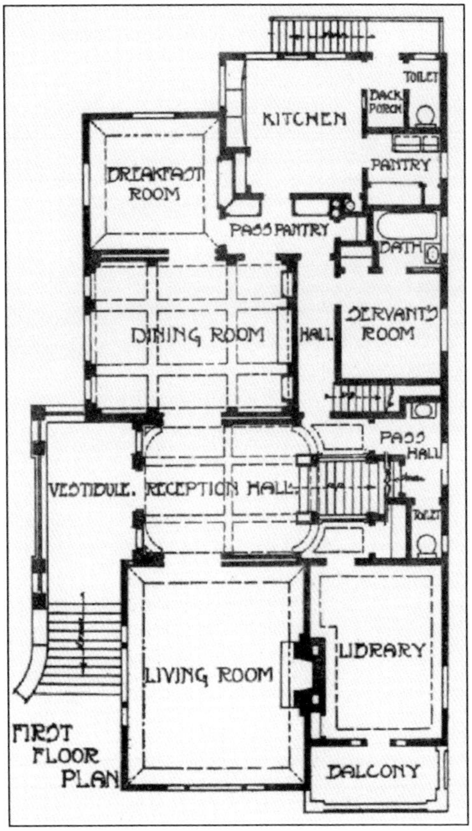


In 1914, the subdivision featured four plans ranging from $20,000 for a large home with servants quarters, to the smallest with two bedrooms for $6,000. Ingleside Terraces was advertised to be large enough to have room for "people of varied means and tastes," who could equally share in the view, climate, and street improvements. (Courtesy Margie Whitnah.)

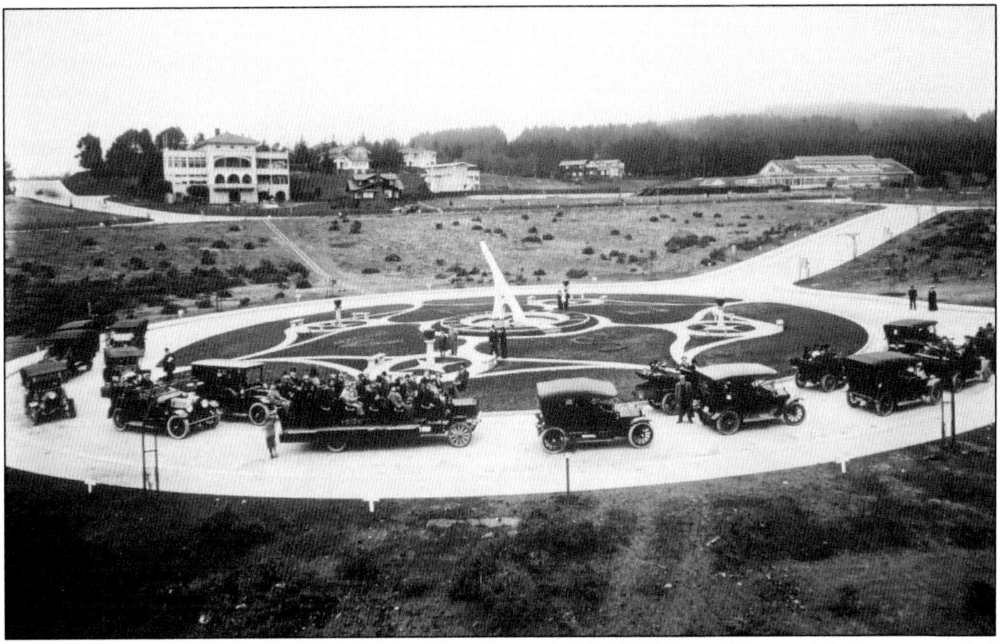

The sales brochures distributed at this 1913 ceremony for the building of the world's largest sundial to commemorate the opening of the Panama Canal noted (after the 1906 earthquake) that a child's future largely depended on his environment and that San Francisco had suffered from not encouraging the construction of attractive homes. "Homes need protection and she has not afforded it. Houses on twenty-five foot lots have driven thousands across the bay or peninsula." (Courtesy Margie Whitnah.)

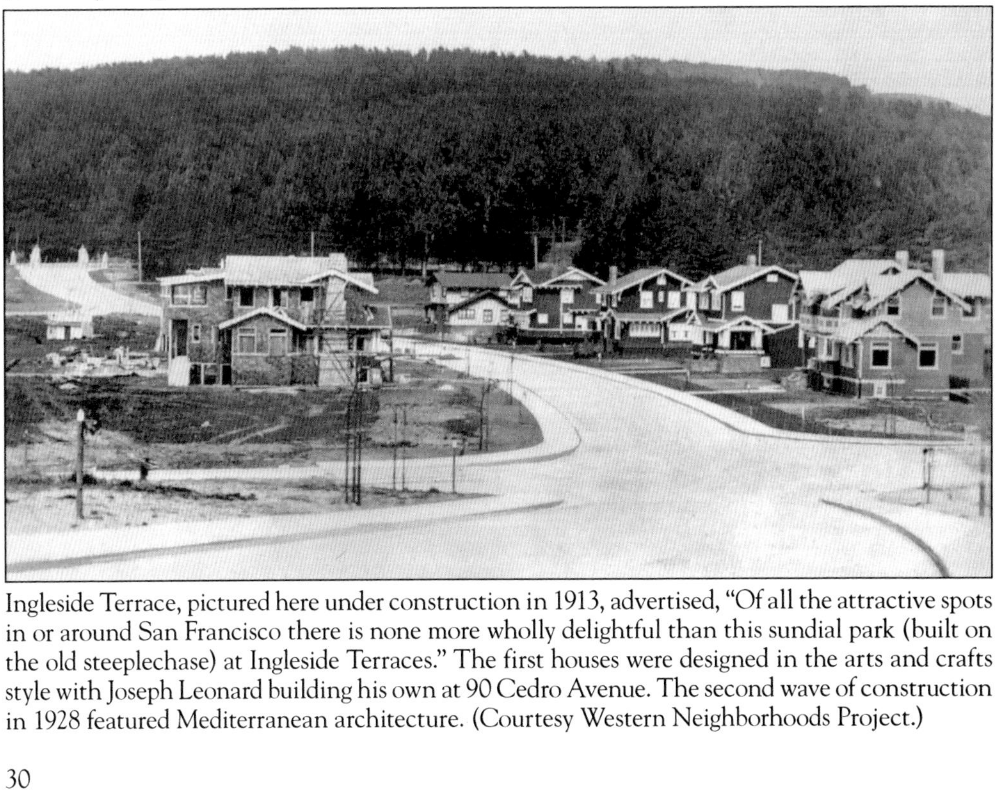

Ingleside Terrace, pictured here under construction in 1913, advertised, "Of all the attractive spots in or around San Francisco there is none more wholly delightful than this sundial park (built on the old steeplechase) at Ingleside Terraces." The first houses were designed in the arts and crafts style with Joseph Leonard building his own at 90 Cedro Avenue. The second wave of construction in 1928 featured Mediterranean architecture. (Courtesy Western Neighborhoods Project.)

This Ingleside Terraces brochure boasted that the historic coincidence of "the final blast at Panama, that permitted the waters of the Atlantic and the Pacific to intermingle, should occur on the same day that the Sundial at Ingleside was dedicated may not be at first apparent," but the "kiss of the oceans" would be making an earthquake-recovering San Francisco a great city once again. (Courtesy Margie Whitnah.)

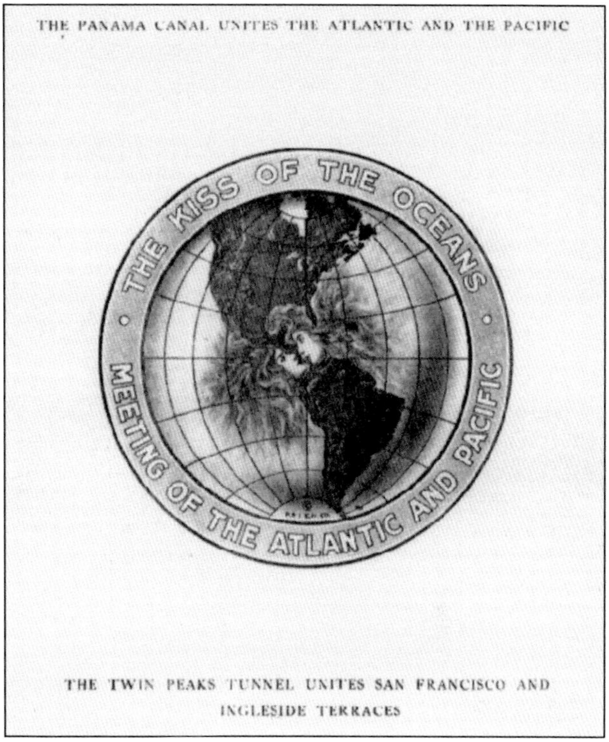


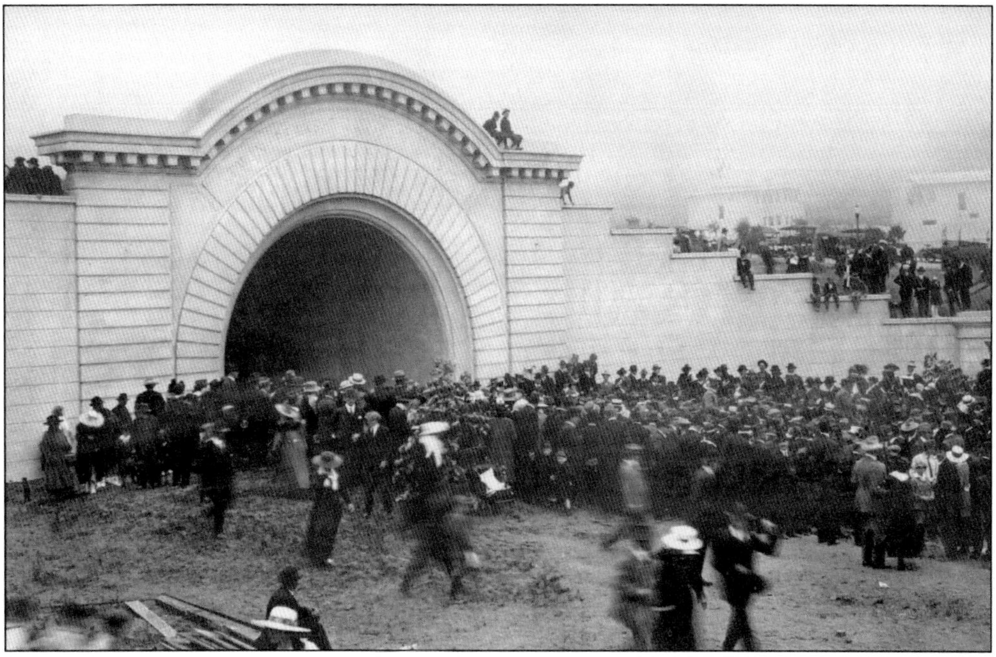

Like Adolph Sutro, Joseph Leonard and A. S. Baldwin struck it rich with an amazing tunnel. The extension of the streetcar line from downtown 12,000 feet below Twin Peaks to West Portal, the longest municipally owned tunnel (two and a quarter miles) devoted to rapid transit, would dramatically improve sales of their new "suburbs in the city" around Mount Davidson. (Courtesy Ken and Kathy Hoegger.)

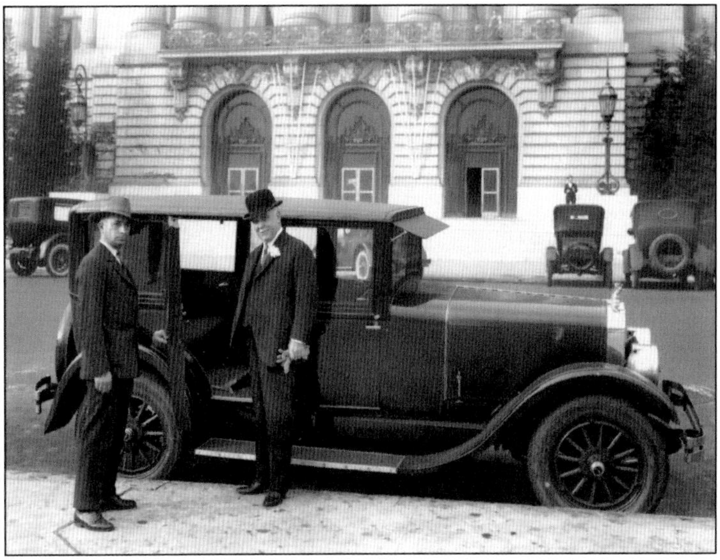

Mayor "Sunny Jim" Rolph remarked at the dedication ceremonies for the Twin Peaks Tunnel on July 14, 1917, that "westward the course of Empire takes its way." He aggressively pursued growth of a government-controlled transit system in San Francisco as a way to encourage development of new neighborhoods. (Courtesy Ron Davis.)

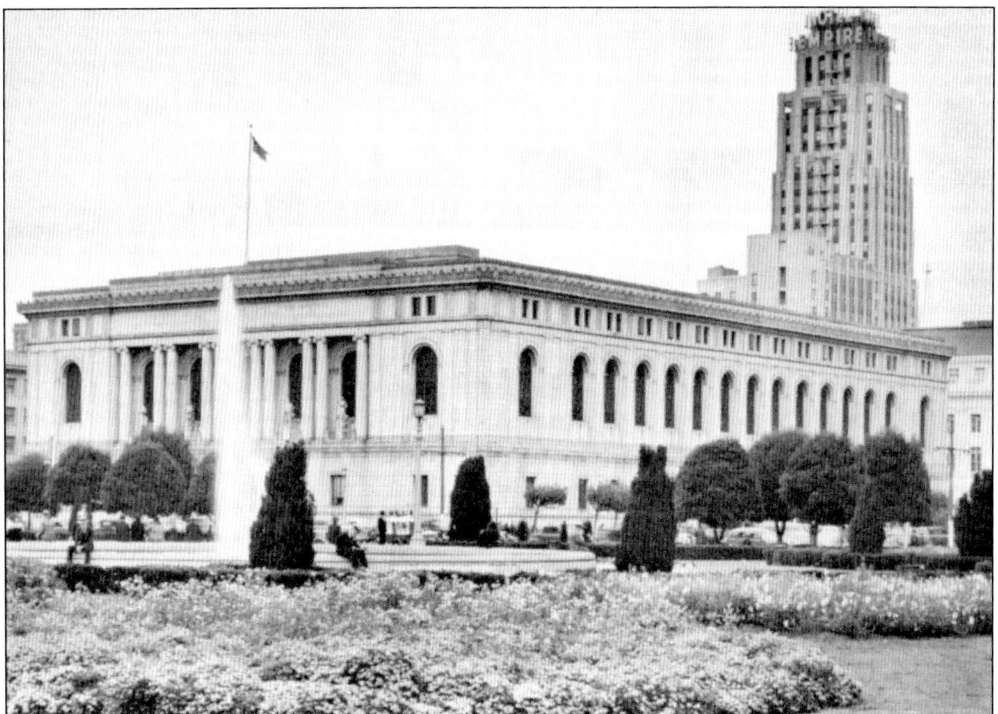

Educated at Harvard and L'Ecole des Beaux Arts in Paris, architect George Kelham came to San Francisco to oversee the construction of a new Palace Hotel to replace the one destroyed in 1906. He stayed to design the landmark Sharon Building on New Montgomery Street. In 1916, he won the competition to build the new city's main library, pictured here, on the former site of city hall. (Author's collection.)

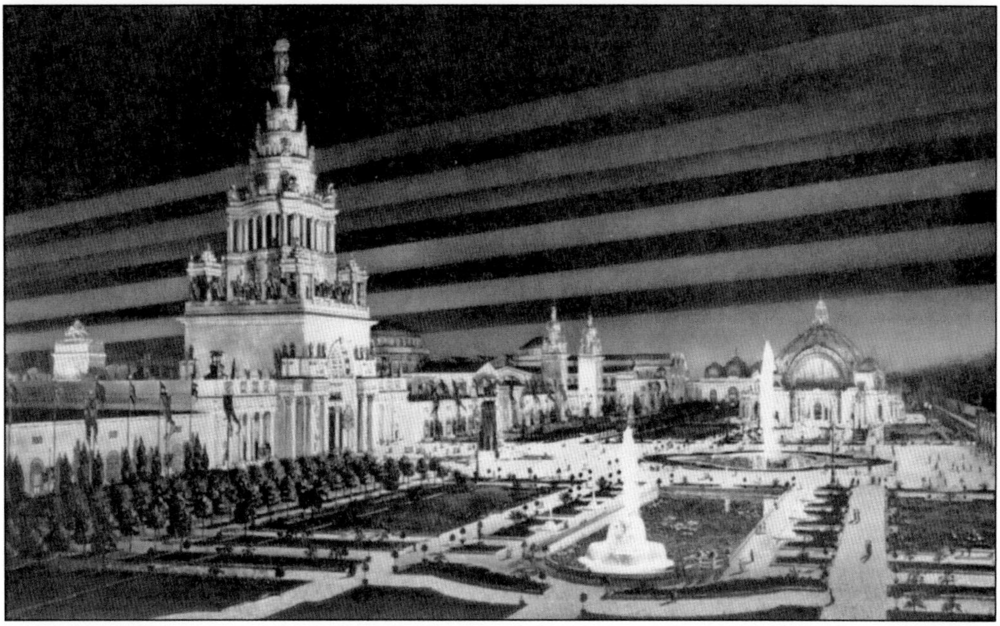

All of San Francisco celebrated the opening of the Panama Canal with its Panama-Pacific International Exposition in 1915 to show the world it had recovered from the earthquake devastation. George Kelham was appointed chief of architecture. The illuminating system adopted at the exposition was described in its program as the culminating example of "recent attainment in lighting great areas which has been accomplished in the electrical world." (Courtesy Ron Davis.)

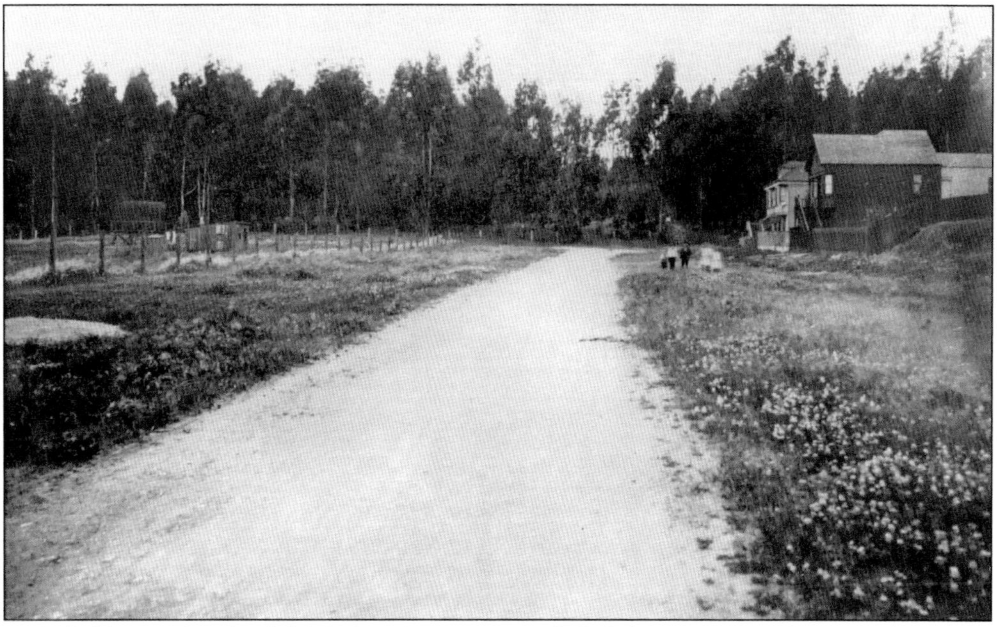

A. S. Baldwin's plan for Adolph Sutro's property included the extension of Sunnyside Avenue past Hamburg Street through the "Great Sutro Forest" all the way to the old Ingleside Racetrack. By the mid-1920s, Sunnyside Avenue was extended and renamed Monterey Boulevard to provide access to Westwood Park and other new neighborhoods built west of Twin Peaks. (Courtesy Ken and Kathy Hoegger.)

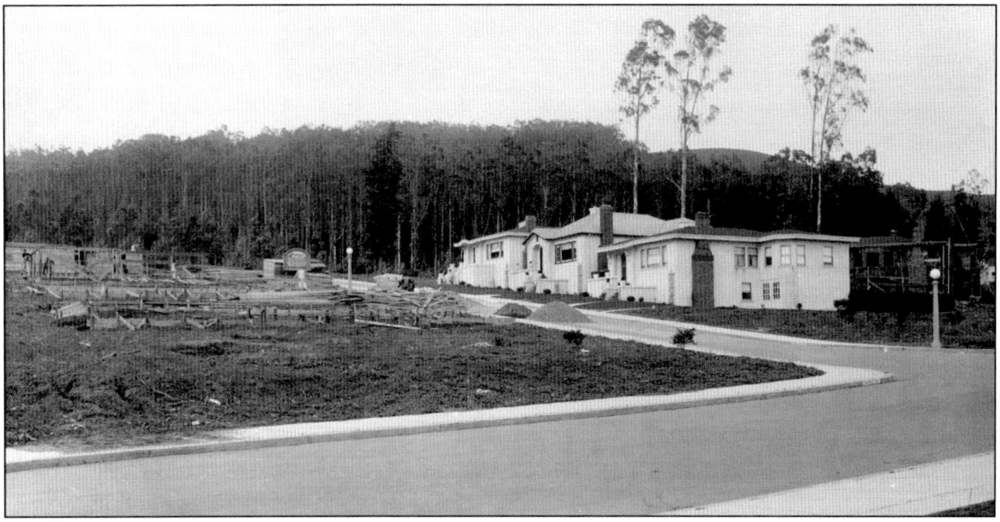

This is a 1917 photograph of construction starting on Westwood Park, which was advertised as "being for families of average means." It featured bungalow arts and crafts architecture with elaborate entrance gates designed by Louis Christian Mullgardt, an architect for the 1915 Panama-Pacific International Exposition. The same year, San Francisco appointed its first planning commission to implement land-use controls and establish separate zones for residential, commercial, and industrial uses. (Courtesy Westwood Park Association.)

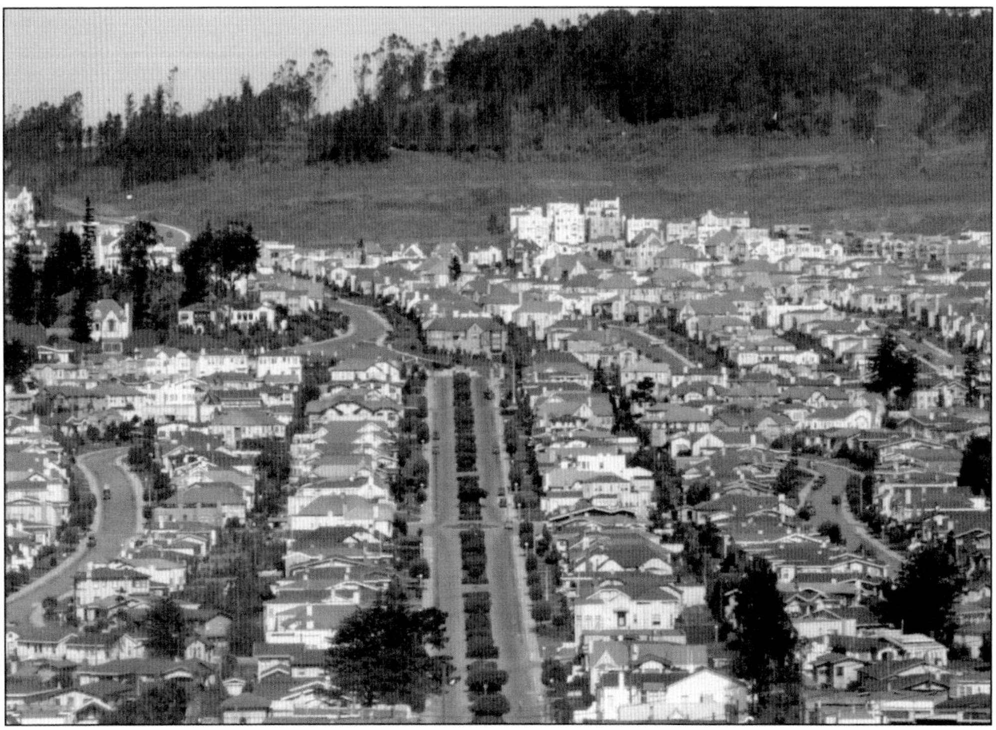

John M. Punnett designed these neighborhood streets to take advantage of the beautiful panorama of the location. Except for the esplanade or "parked boulevard" of Miramar Avenue and the short intersecting streets near the center, there is not a single straight street in Westwood Park pictured here in 1920s. (Courtesy private collection.)

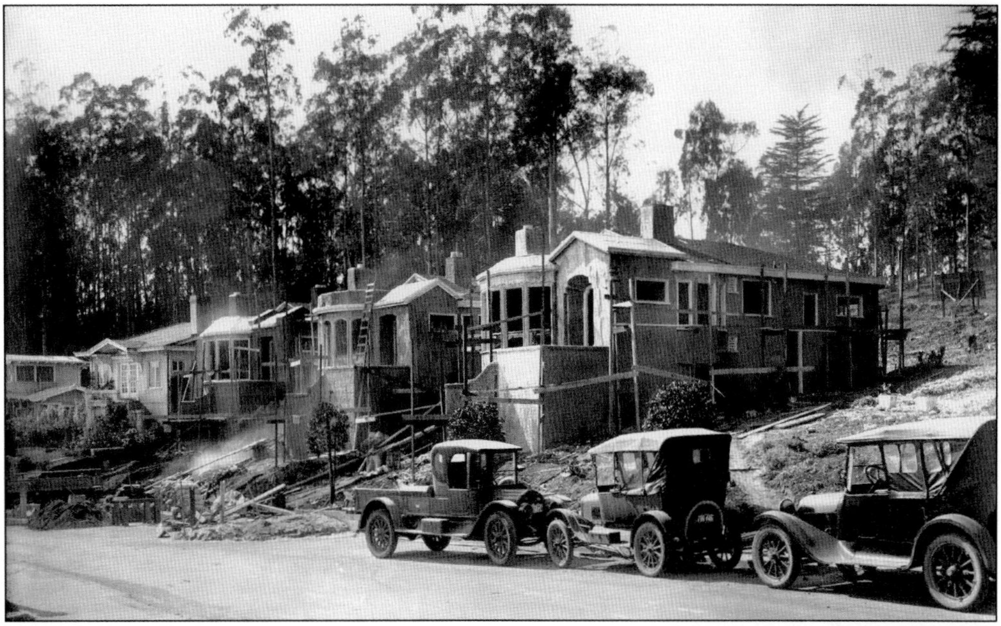

Advertisements hint of the original ownership of Jose Noe, stating, "The Charm of Westwood Park Bungalow Homes is largely due to the painstaking care and skill with which 'Westwood' builders have planned each individual home. Whether the motif be taken from the romantic days of California's Spanish pioneers, the substantial lines of Merrie England or the stately mansion of ye Colonial days, it always harmonizes with the general grouping." (Courtesy Westwood Park Association.)

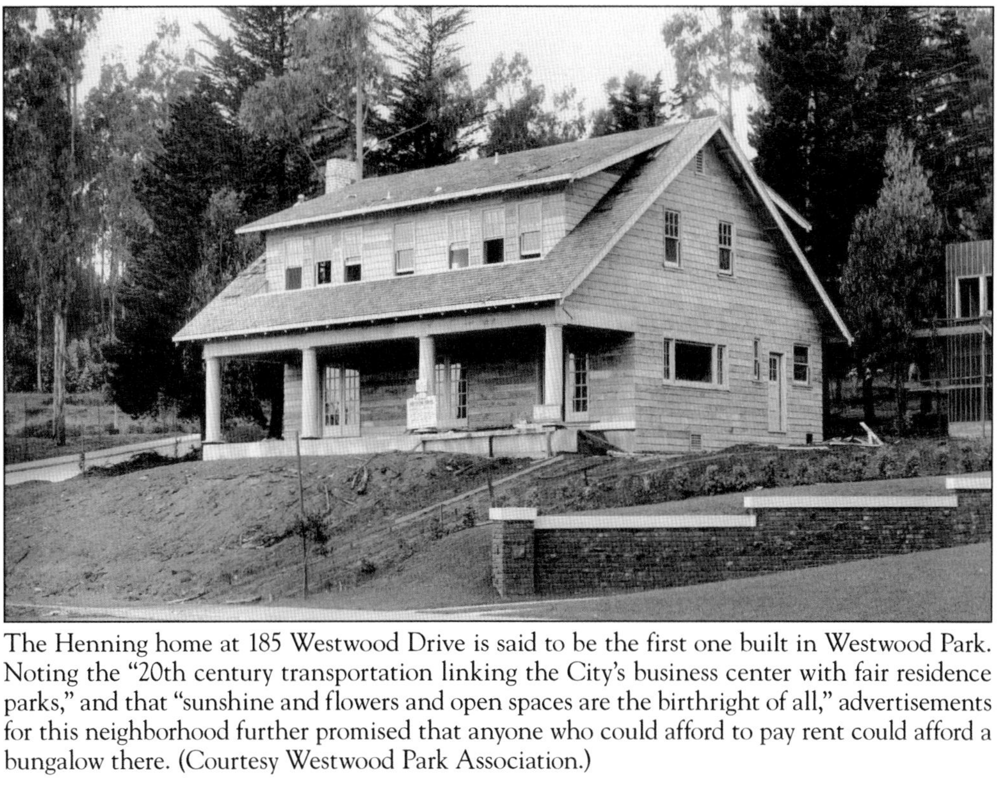

The Henning home at 185 Westwood Drive is said to be the first one built in Westwood Park. Noting the "20th century transportation linking the City's business center with fair residence parks," and that "sunshine and flowers and open spaces are the birthright of all," advertisements for this neighborhood further promised that anyone who could afford to pay rent could afford a bungalow there. (Courtesy Westwood Park Association.)

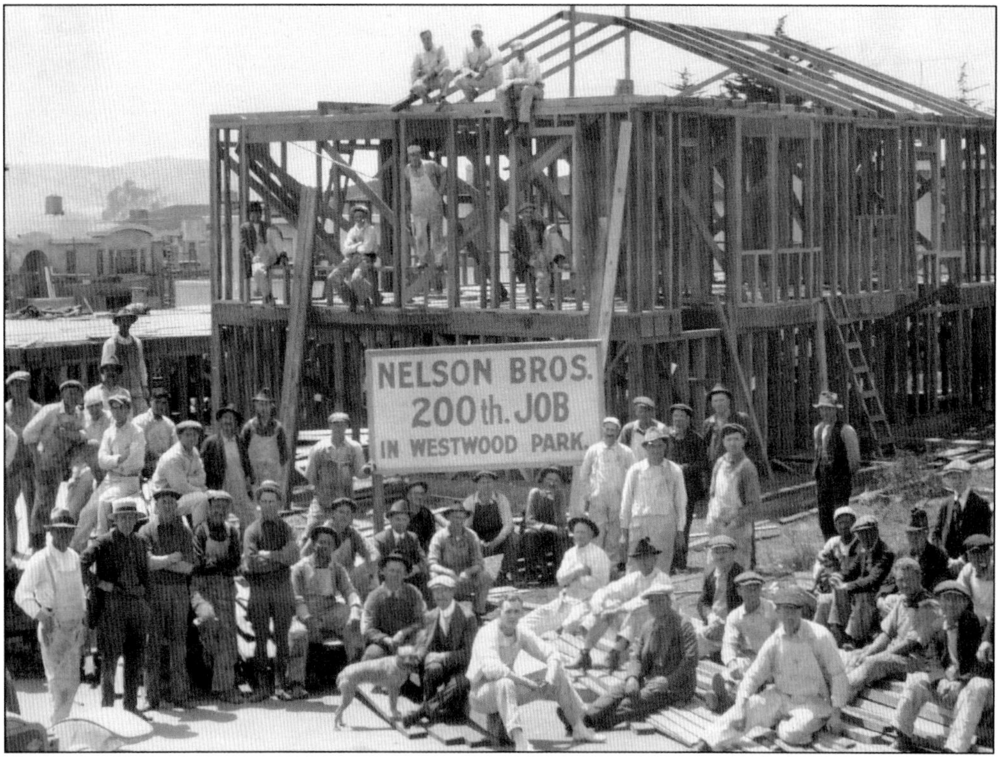


Workmen gather to celebrate the completion of Nelson Brothers' 200th house of the nearly 350 they built in Westwood Park through 1923. Hans Nelson came from Sweden to join his brother Martin. Nelson Foss recalls, "My grandfather decided that pounding nails wasn't what he was cut out for. So they built a house, sold it, and made some money. He said, 'We can keep the money, or use it to build two houses.'" (Courtesy Westwood Park Association.)

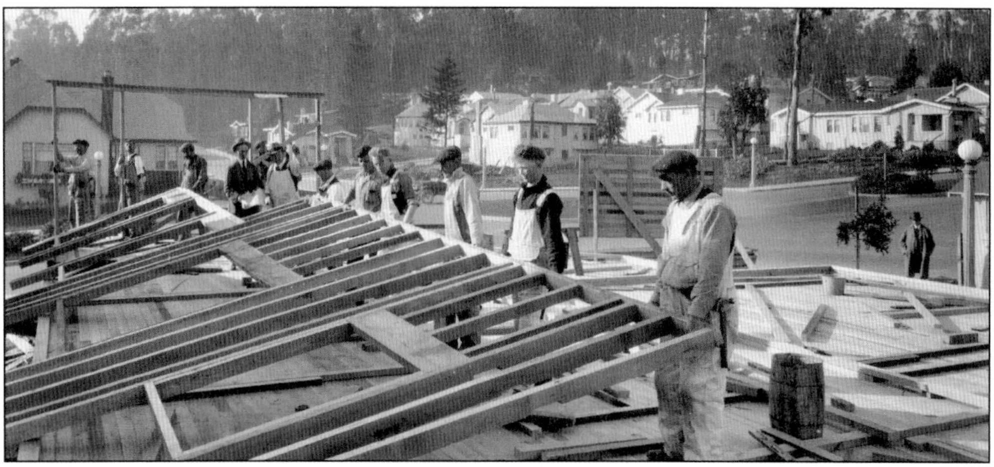

Hans Nelson, in suit and tie, is pictured here supervising the construction of this Westwood Park home. The Craftsman-style architecture focused on the quality of workmanship. The *San Francisco Chronicle* reported, "Every carpenter, every plasterer, every laborer, seems to take an unusual pride in his particular contribution of handiwork that is forming this home." The opportunity to live in a suburban-style home near the conveniences of downtown advertised Westwood Park as "San Francisco's Ideal Home Tract." (Courtesy Westwood Park Association.)

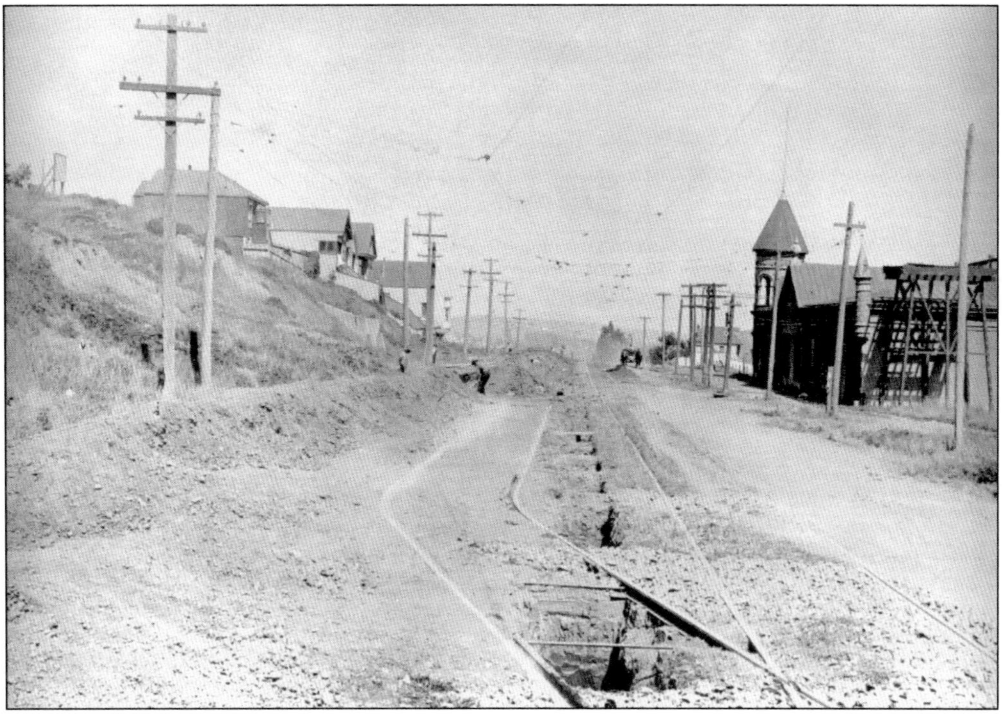

By 1909, Rogers and Stone Company was advertising lots for sale in Sunnyside, "a sheltered location near the great Sutro Forest in the center of San Francisco," from $400 to $600. In 1914, improvement of Sunnyside Avenue east of Baden Street was underway in the still-undeveloped neighborhood. The electric powerhouse for the railway built by Behrend Joost is at right. (Courtesy Ken and Kathy Hoegger.)

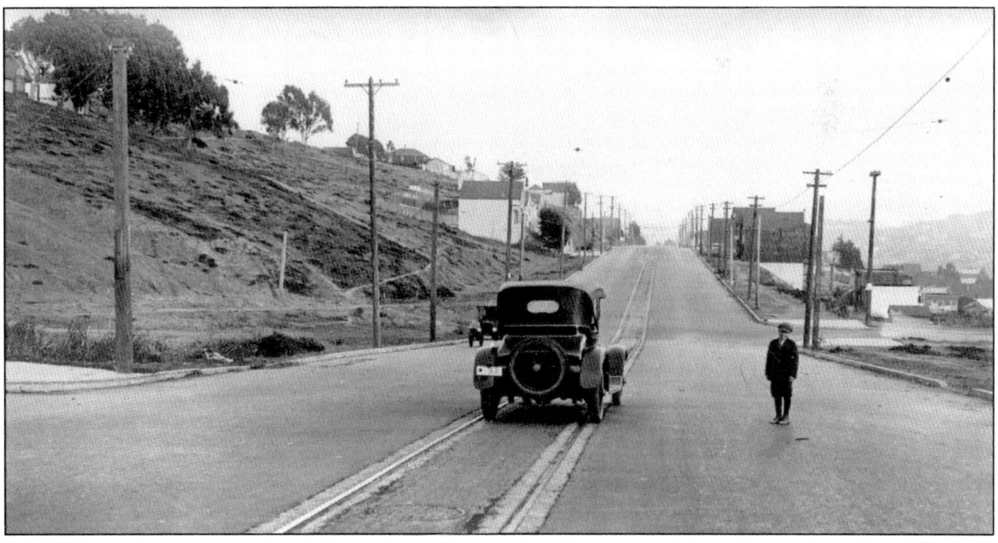

By 1915, work was completed here along Sunnyside Avenue at Edna Street. Resident Thomas Malim wrote, "From Baden to Gennessee Street, the line was a single track, with two bypass tracks a block apart. Occasionally the schedules for the cars would overlap, and the outbound passengers would have to disembark several blocks from the end of the line." (Courtesy Ken and Kathy Hoegger.)

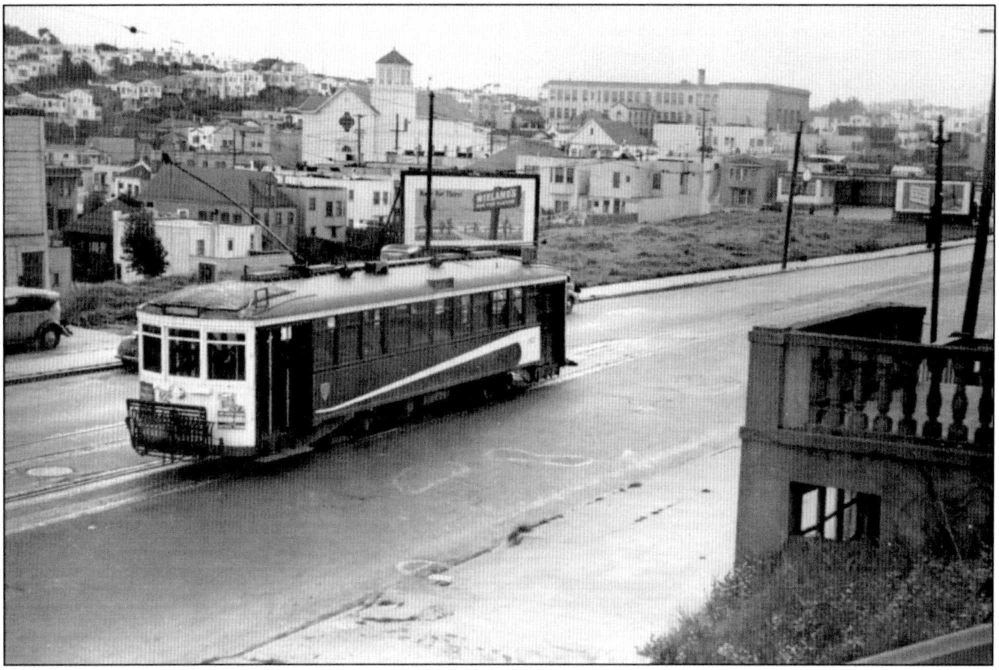

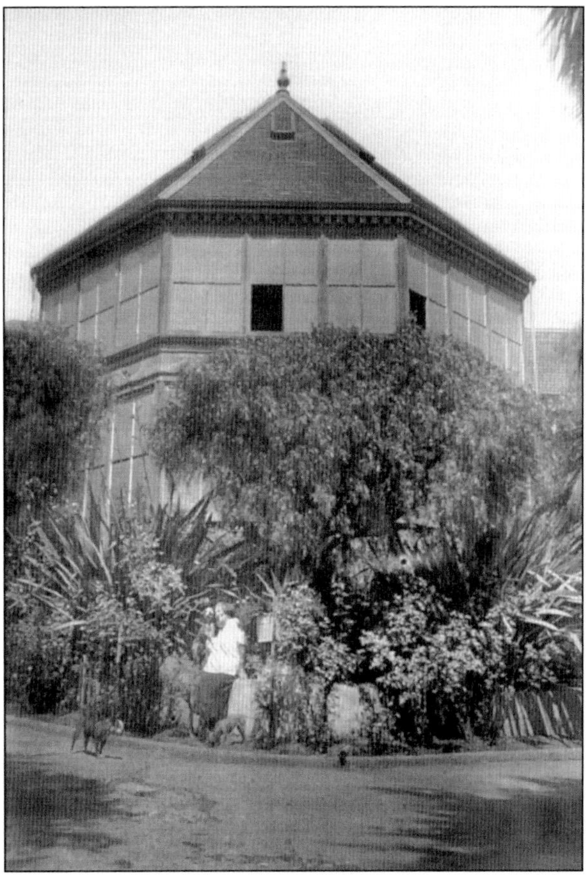

This is the No. 10 Sunnyside streetcar near Detroit Street in 1939, with Sunnyside School in the background. It ran from the ferries from Mission, Fourteenth, Guerrero, San Jose Avenue, Thirtieth, Chenery, Diamond, and Monterey Boulevard to Gennessee Street and Westwood Park. In 1942, poor tracks were one of the reasons the office of defense transportation decided to abandon the route during wartime. Muni's J extension follows part of the route today. (Courtesy Ken Hoegger.)

Mr. Merrall's widow and son stayed on the Sunnyside Conservatory property until 1916. It then lay vacant until Mr. and Mrs. Ernest Van Beck purchased it in 1919. As pictured here, they enlisted craftsmen to return the conservatory and grounds to their previous appearance. In 1952, Mrs. Van Beck sold the eastern-most lot to the Andersons, where they built their home at what is now 234 Monterey Boulevard. (Courtesy Friends of Sunnyside Conservatory.)

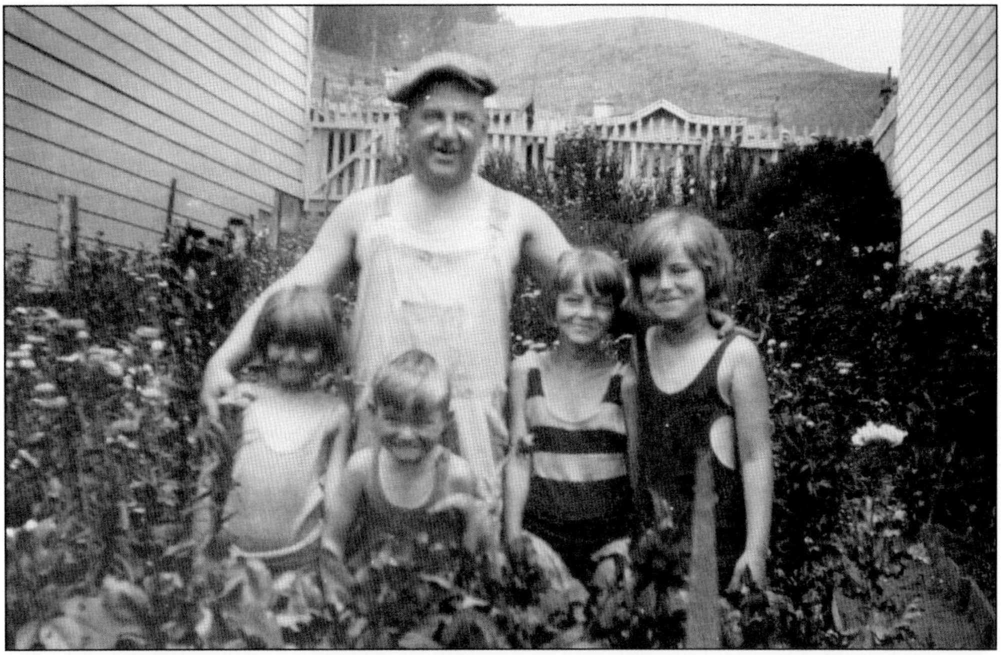

This view of a Sunnyside Avenue backyard near Gennessee Street was captured in 1915 when vegetable and dairy farmers still sparsely settled the neighborhood. Resident Harry Mazza, who lived next door to the house his parents bought in 1910, recalled, "When his mother baked bread in her backyard oven, she made extra for the neighbors. The neighborhood women delivered babies. . . . He and his friends swam in a pond on Detroit Street." (Courtesy private collection.)

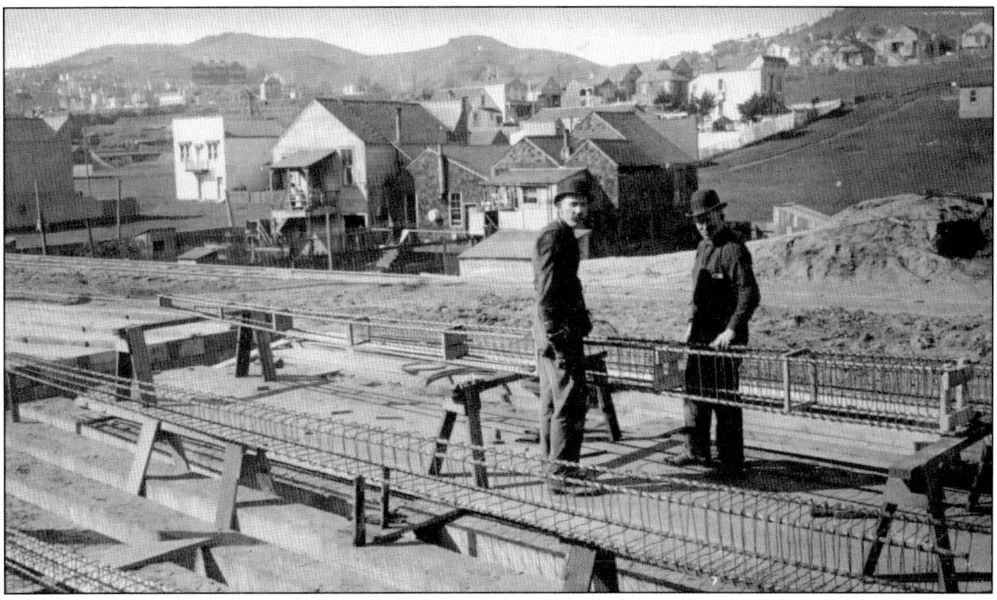

Freshwater Islais Creek began on the southern slope of Twin Peaks, just north of Portola Drive. The creek coursed through Glen Canyon, at what is now Bosworth Street, until it reached the bottom over which the Mission Viaduct was built in 1911. (Sunnyside and Mount Davidson are in the background.) Islais Creek then widened between Niagara and Geneva Avenues to form Lake Geneva. (Courtesy Ken and Kathy Hoegger.)

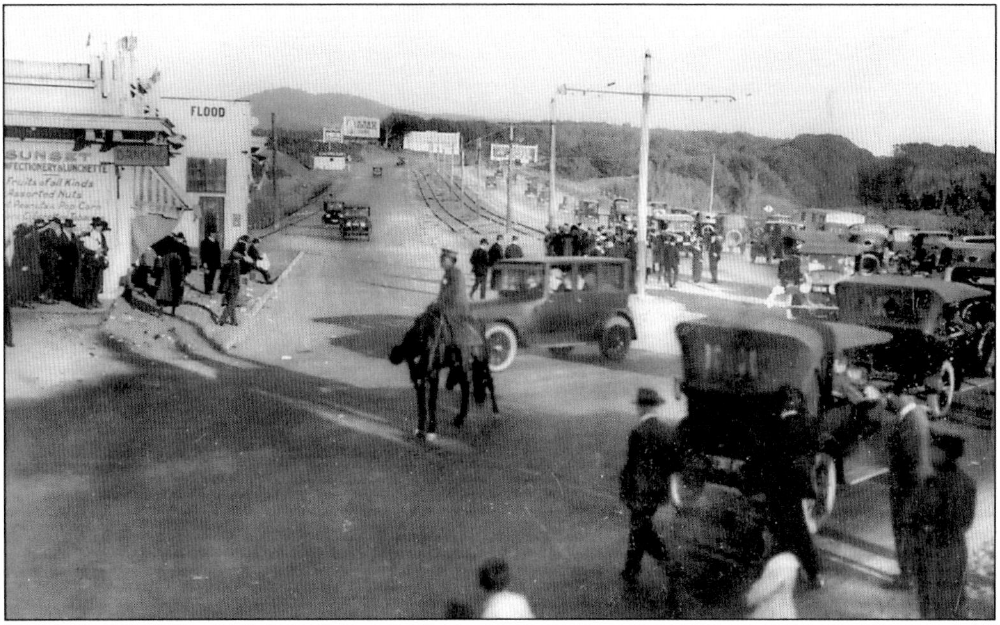


While James Rolph was mayor from 1911 to 1930, city engineer Michael O'Shaughnessy designed and constructed a network of boulevards in the undeveloped western half of the city. The opening of Sloat Boulevard in 1919 further improved the accessibility to West of Twin Peaks District subdivisions. (Courtesy Ken and Kathy Hoegger.)

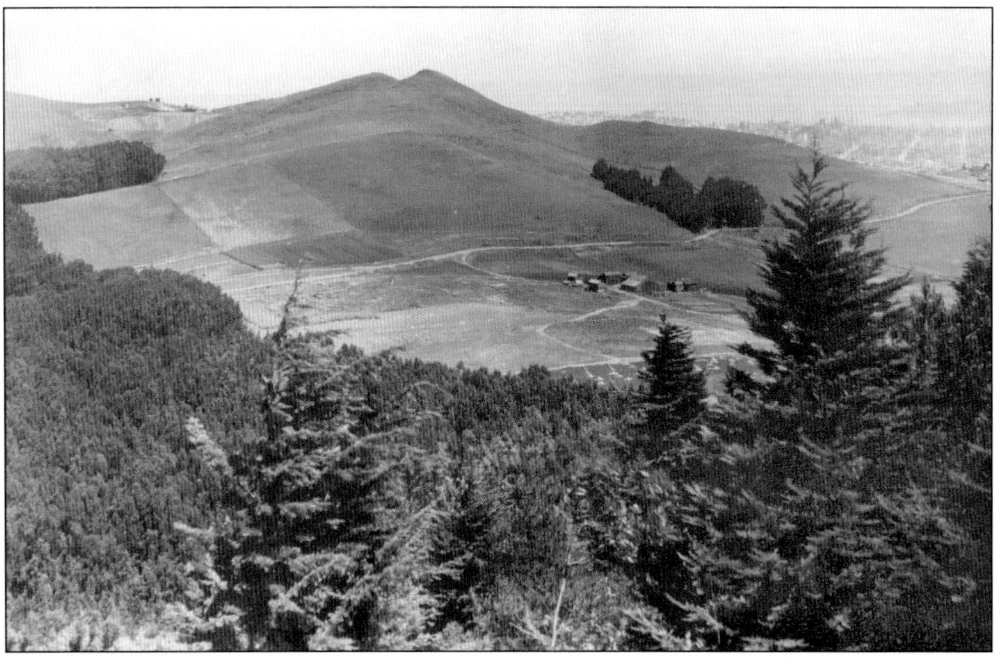

This was the view of the Twin Peaks and downtown from Blue Mountain when the Sierra Club asked that it be renamed for their charter member, George Davidson. After the ceremony was delayed because of a storm, weather bureau chief Alexander McAdie declared, "Postpone it if you wish, but I will be there." Standing alone, he delivered his address to the wind and rain and proclaimed the new name Mount Davidson in 1911. (Courtesy private collection.)

# *Three*

# Women's Suffrage and Prohibition

## Daring to Dream

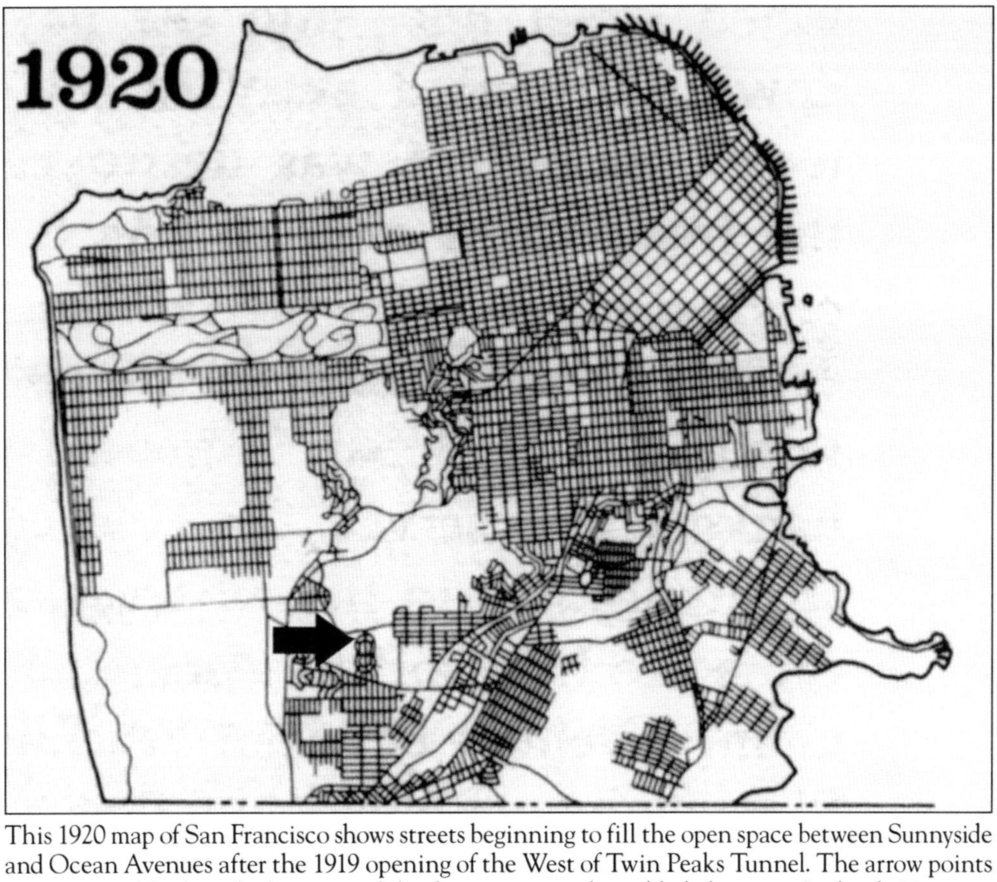


This 1920 map of San Francisco shows streets beginning to fill the open space between Sunnyside and Ocean Avenues after the 1919 opening of the West of Twin Peaks Tunnel. The arrow points to Westwood Park with the route of the former racetrack visible below it in Ingleside Terraces. (Courtesy San Francisco Planning Department.)

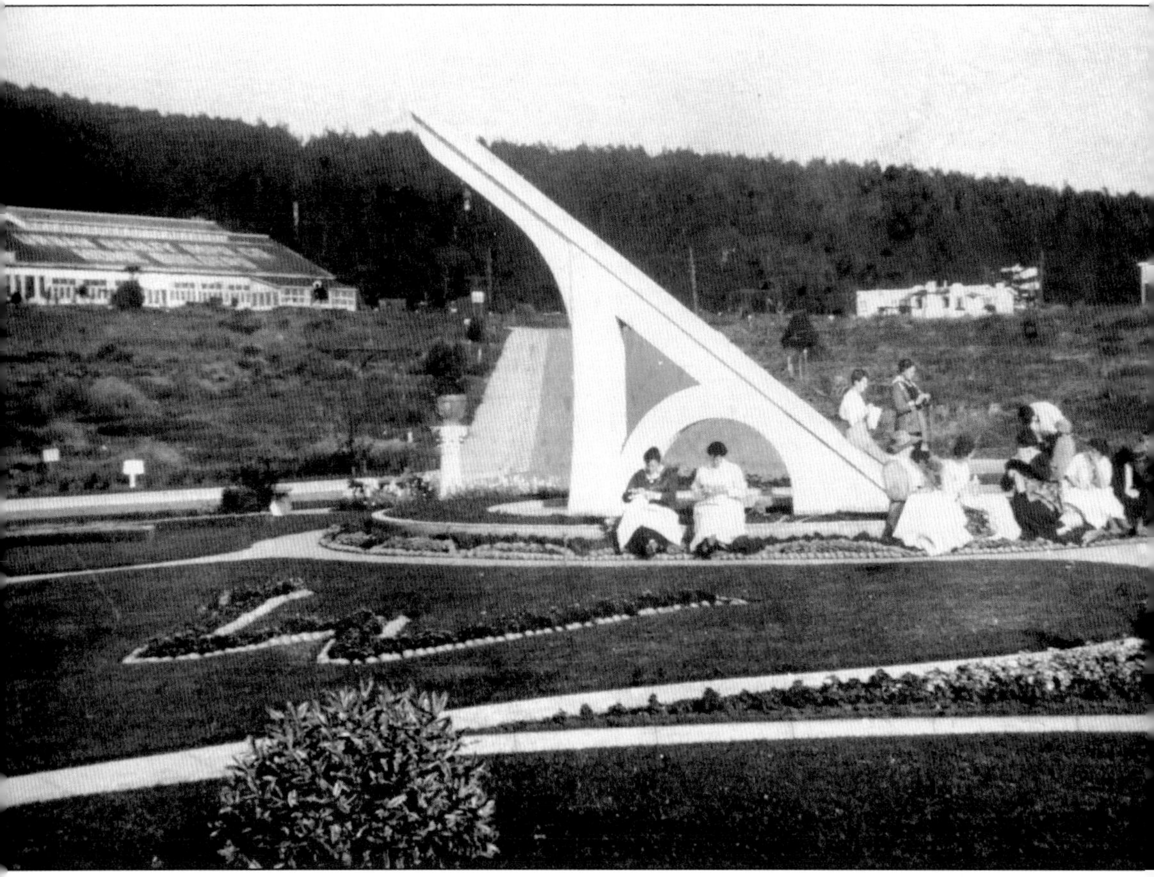

The rising role of women in decision-making during the time that women's suffrage was being voted upon may be one reason for this photograph of a sewing circle around the Ingleside Terraces sundial. Cameron Binkley has documented how women were also often responsible for the type of civic action that brought real change to public policy by leading and organizing campaigns to create or preserve special places. This was especially the case in California, where they often "worked both in support of and in deference to men's efforts" as a group rather than individually. Binkley highlights how the California Federation of Women's Clubs greatly enhanced women's social and political influence "with the conviction that nature and beauty, intelligently designed urban space, and outdoor activity could help inoculate against the ills of urban growth in a too rapidly industrializing America." (Courtesy Western Neighborhoods Project.)

In 1918, Elvira Dettner had been promised the prestigious first violin spot in the Lowell High School Orchestra. After the teacher chose a boy instead because "he was a boy," Elvira transferred to Polytechnic High School, where they were happy to give her the first violin position. She continued to bring music to her family and community after she married John Granfield and moved to Ingleside Terraces. (Courtesy Dave Bisho.)

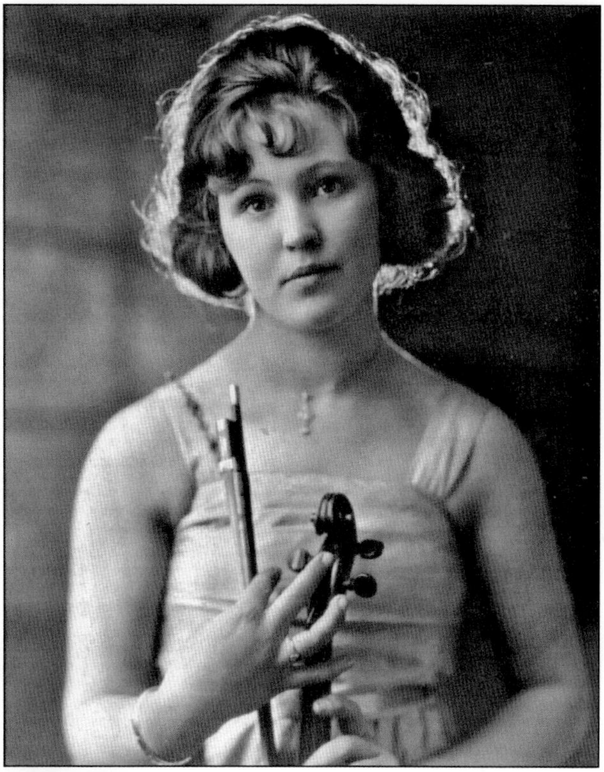

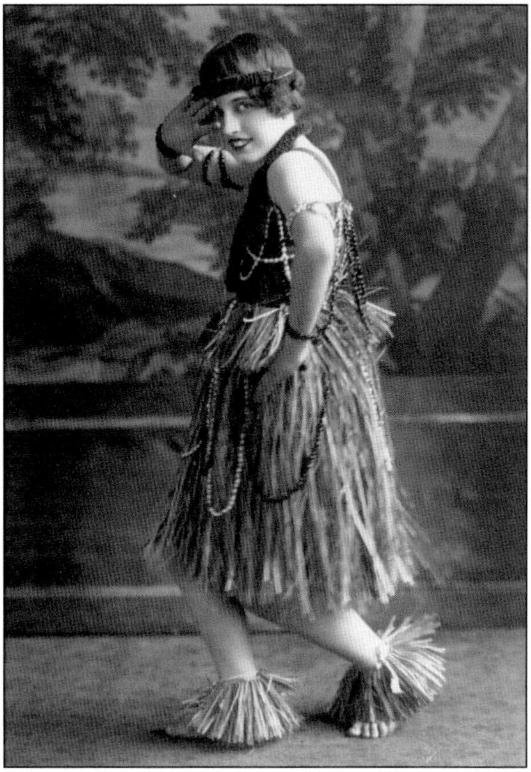

San Francisco native Jeanette Quast loved to dance in the 1920s. Growing up around her father's saddlery business, she moved to Hawaii to teach after earning her degree at the University of California. There she met her husband-to-be, Stanley Davis. They married in San Francisco and bought a new home on the east slope of Mount Davidson in Miraloma Park. (Courtesy Jeanne Davis MacKenzie.)

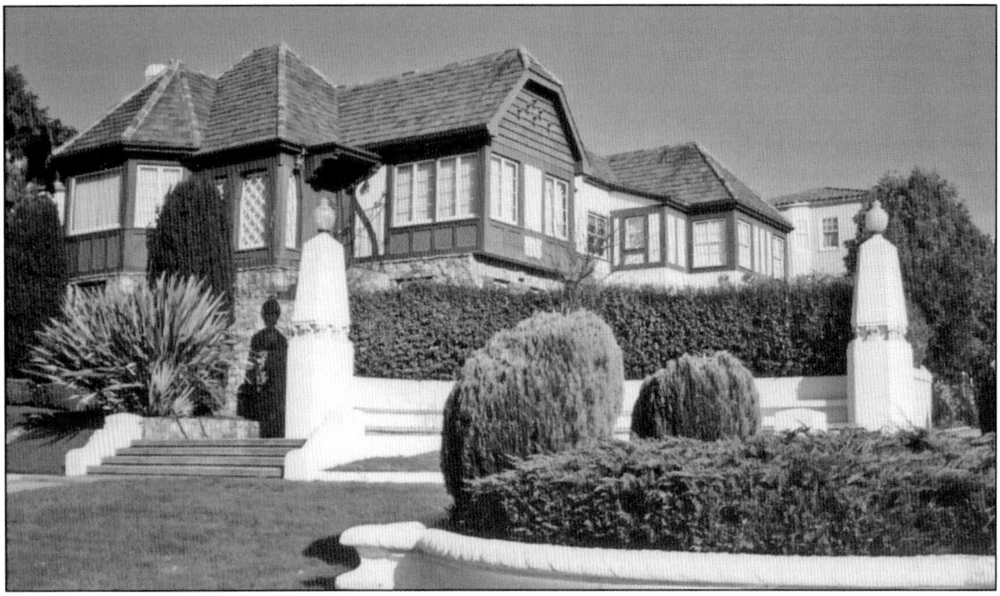

This is the grand City Beautiful entrance to Balboa Terrace, a neighborhood developed by Baldwin and Howell in 1912 but not built until after completion of the Twin Peaks Tunnel. Years later, it was described in an article about the West of Twin Peaks District as a "pleasant place to go home to" with "the respectability of St. Francis Wood at a lesser scale and one might hope, price." (Author's collection.)

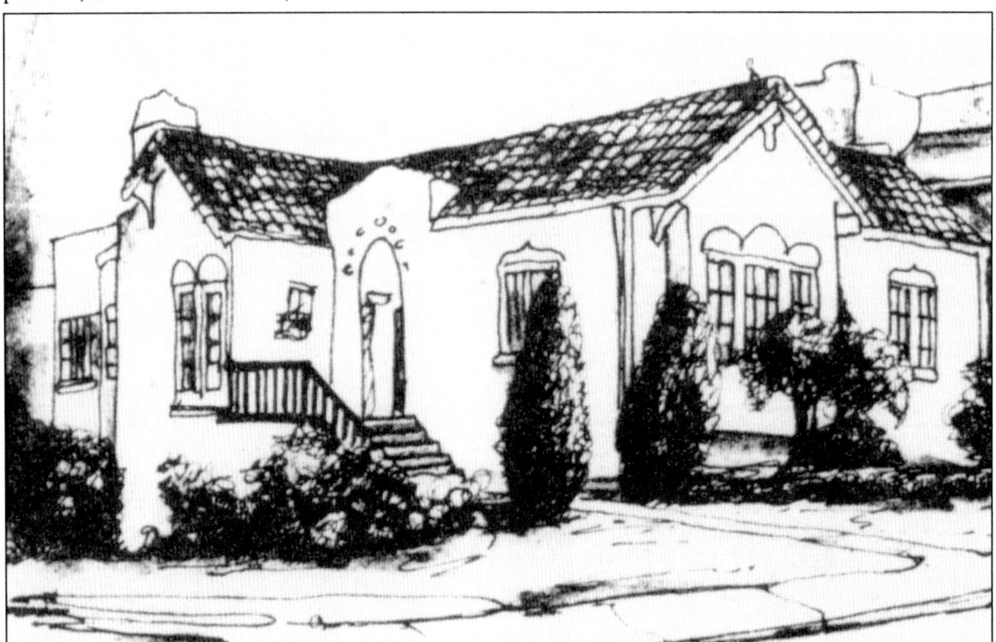

The neighborhood's construction was progressive so as to eliminate scattered buildings. Street pavement, sidewalks, and the ornamental lighting would be installed in each block before the next one was started. Home designs varied from "the villa of the Italian Renaissance to English Cottage." The majority "by popular demand, are Italian or Spanish design," as pictured in this sketch of 346 Benito Way. (Courtesy Bill Kaplan.)

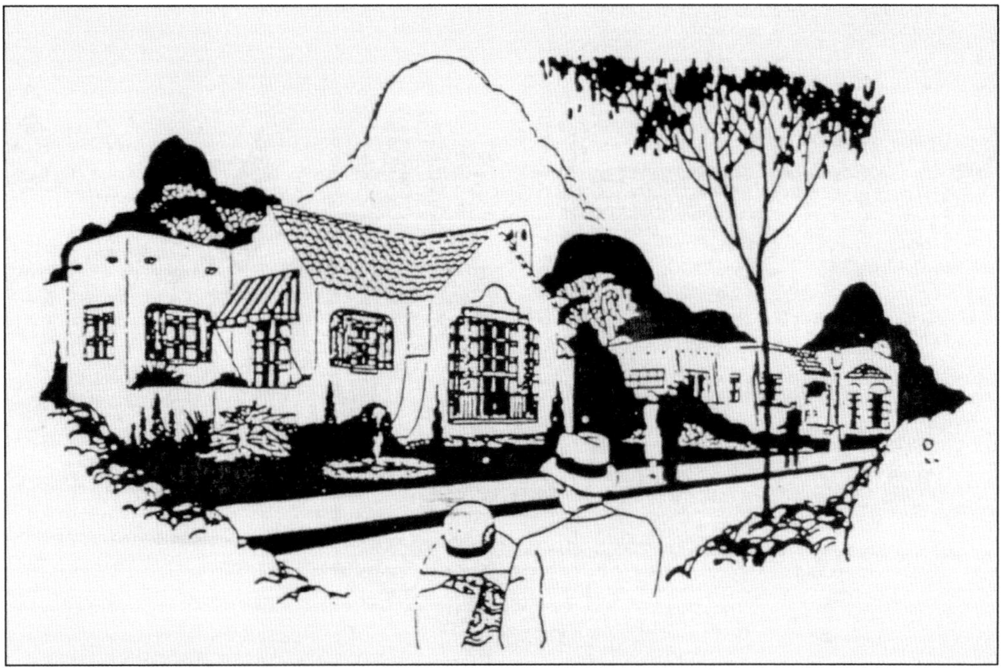

A 1926 article by K. K. Barton in *The Home Designer* described the development of "this exceptional piece of property" by experts under the personal supervision of owners Ernest and Oscar Heuter made Balboa Terrace "one of the showplaces of the Bay Region." Lang Realty was in charge of sales. (Courtesy Bill Kaplan.)

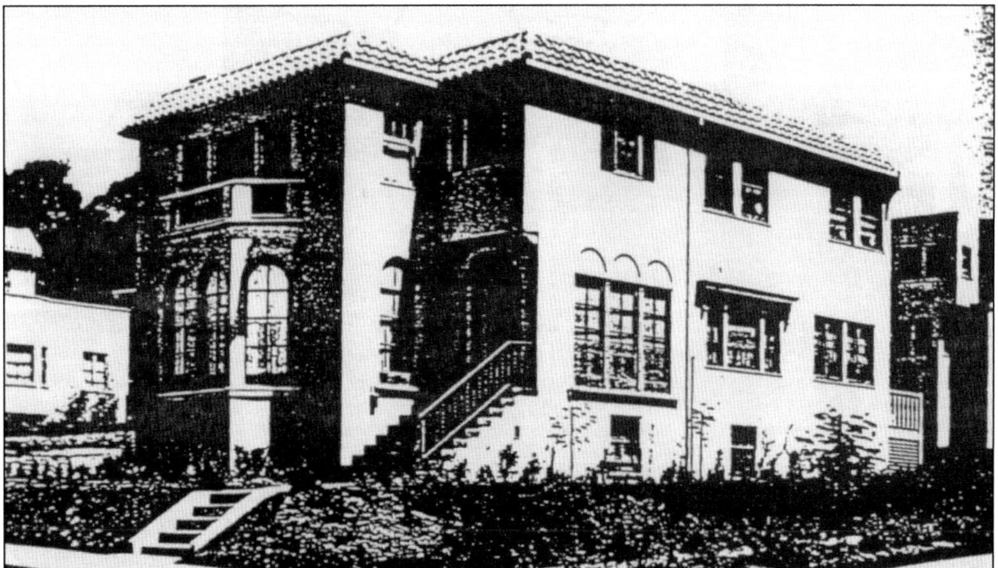

With homes selling for $10,000 to $20,000, K. K. Barton noted that individual home design was an important consideration, "so that the house of one influence does bear to foreign a relationship to its neighbor." The firm belonging to Harold Stoner completed the majority of the design work, resulting in "a harmony of design and finish." (Courtesy Bill Kaplan.)

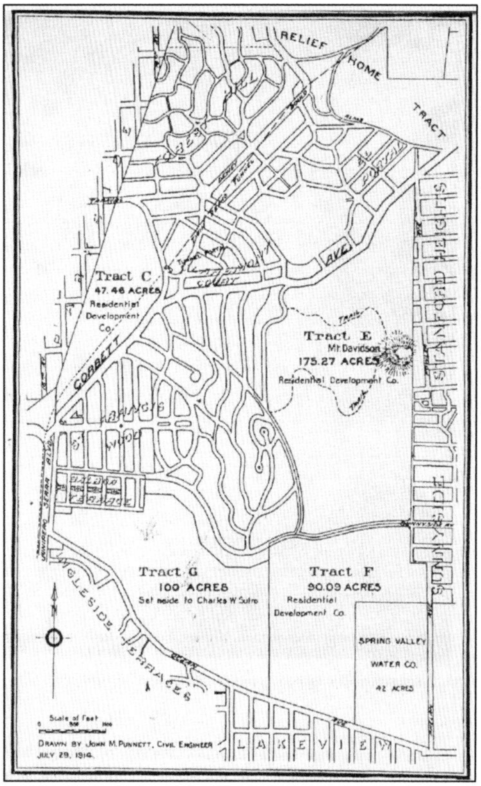


John Punnett's 1914 map shows streets never built in Leland Stanford's Heights on the east side of Mount Davidson. Punnett designed curvilinear streets instead for the Miraloma Park subdivision of former Stanford and Sutro land. The Meyer Brothers purchased 208 acres, stating 350 home sites were from the Sutro estate and "1,650 sites were from Wells Fargo and Company and others as far away as France." (Courtesy Western Neighborhoods Project.)

Stanford Heights Reservoir was constructed in 1923. At 618 feet in elevation, the city's second-highest reservoir holds 12.9 million gallons. San Francisco's water supply was developed as a series of different pressure districts, incorporating the Spring Valley and San Francisco City Water Works reservoirs and pipelines into the system. The city's highest tank was added to Mount Davidson in 1953, holding 75,000 gallons. (Courtesy private collection.)

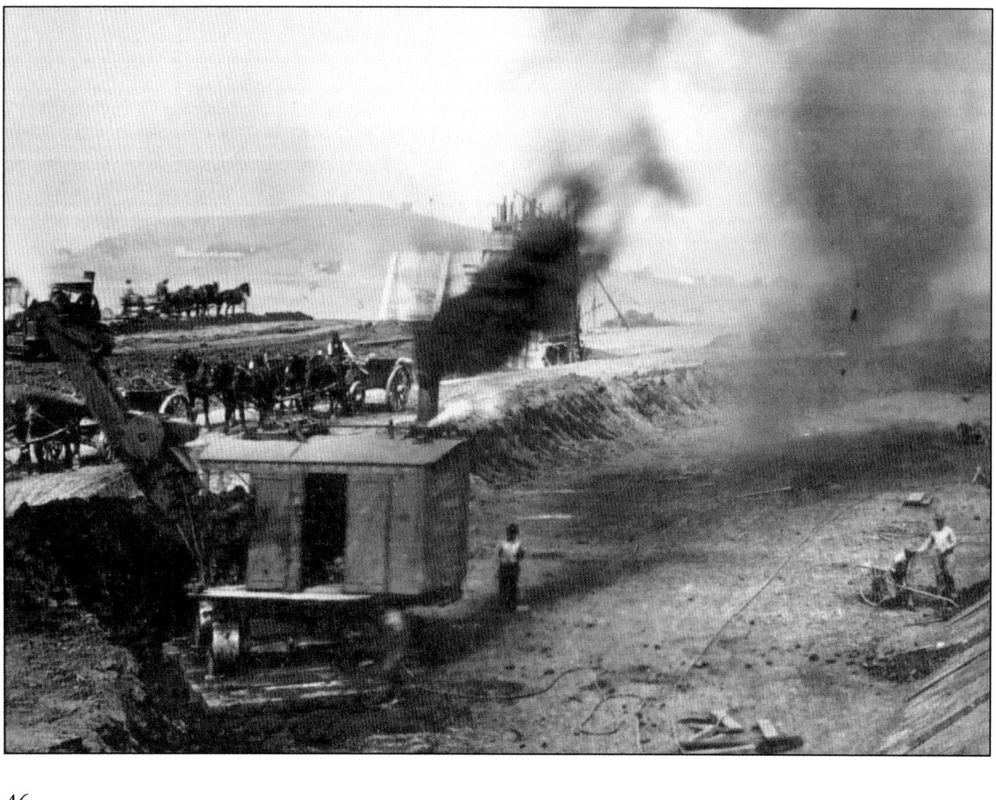

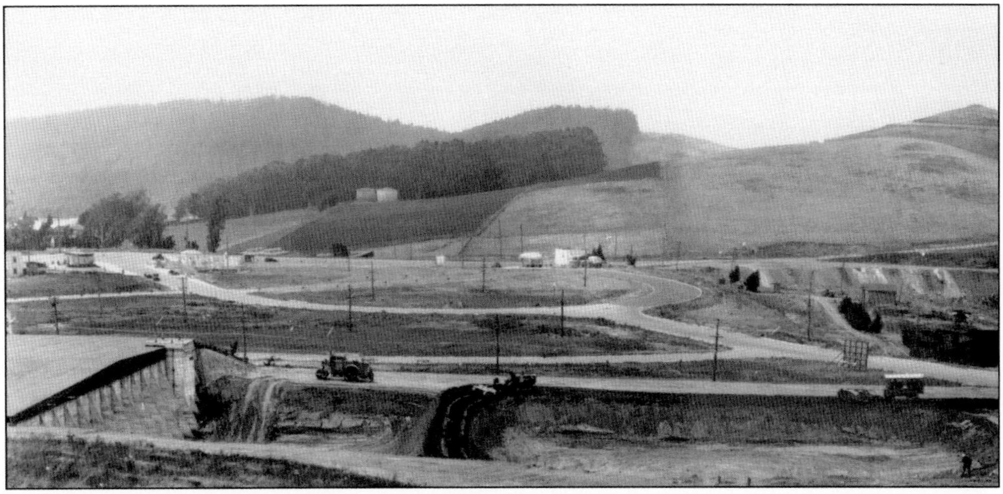

Looking north from the reservoir, the old Stanford Heights water tanks are visible across the Portola Drive entrance to Miraloma Park. Meyer Brothers called it a city in itself and a suburban home center where mass production provided home-ownership opportunities for those of average means. The subdivision of one-story, over-garage homes with individualized designs was the largest of the City Beautiful neighborhoods to be built. (Courtesy private collection.)

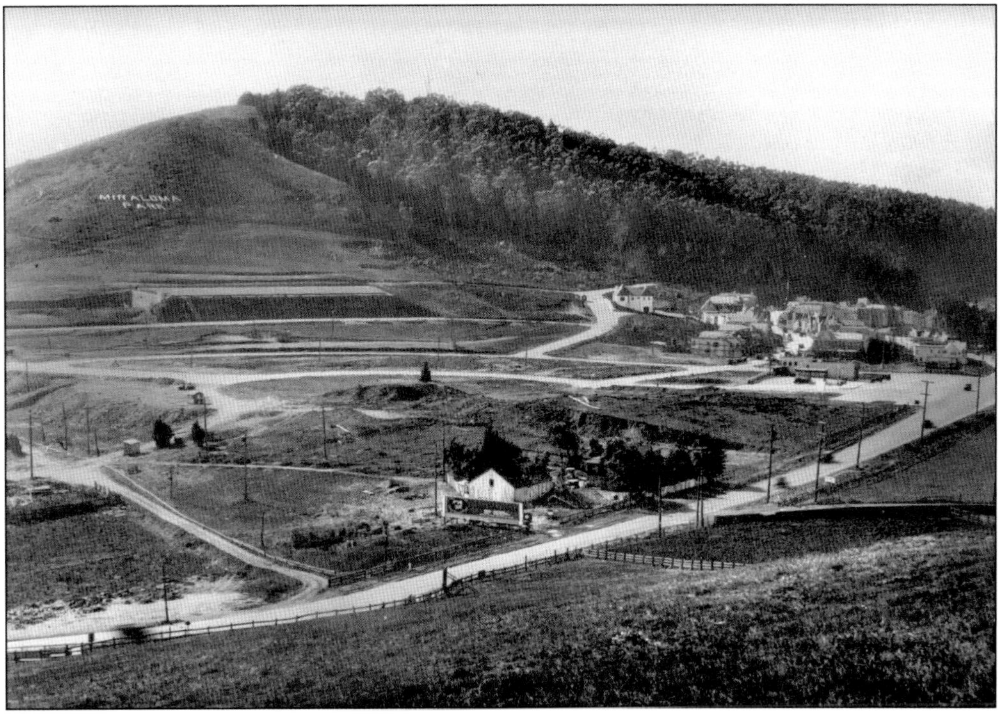

Even with land marked by painted hillside letters instead of the grand entrance gates of earlier subdivisions, Miraloma Park still incorporated City Beautiful features. The streets were wide and curved to take full advantage of the contours of Mount Davidson. Rear yard easements eliminated unsightly power poles on the street to take advantage of the panoramic views. Landscaped front yards and deep backyards created a greenbelt for urban farmers and gardeners. (Author's collection.)

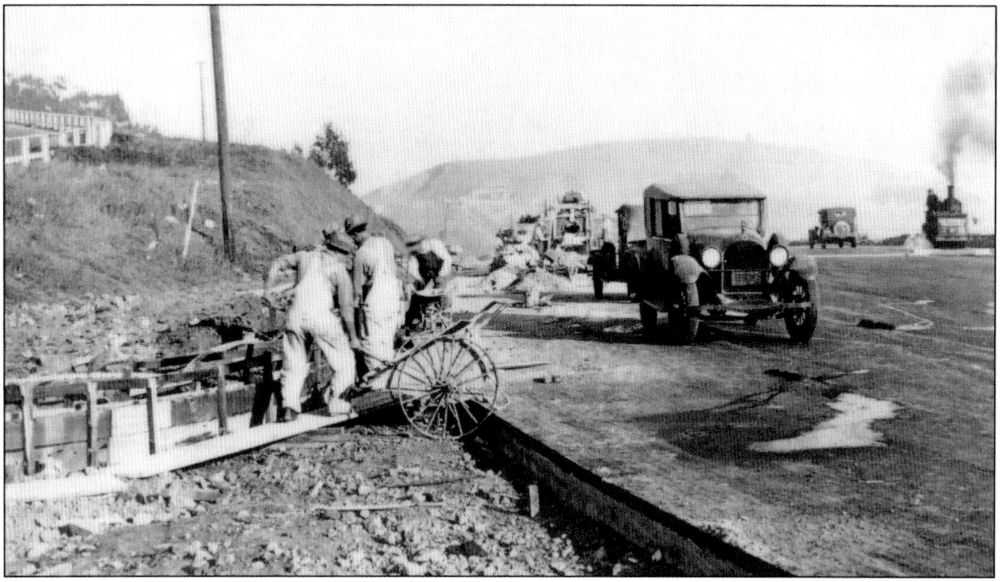

With the latest type homes combining city and country life, Miraloma Park was advertised as "far more quiet and restful than I had imagined anything so close to San Francisco could be." The wooded slopes of Mount Davidson were noted for adding beauty to the rural setting. This widening of Portola Drive west from Twin Peaks Boulevard in 1929 provided easier automobile and bus access to the homes being built west of Twin Peaks. (Courtesy John Pommon.)

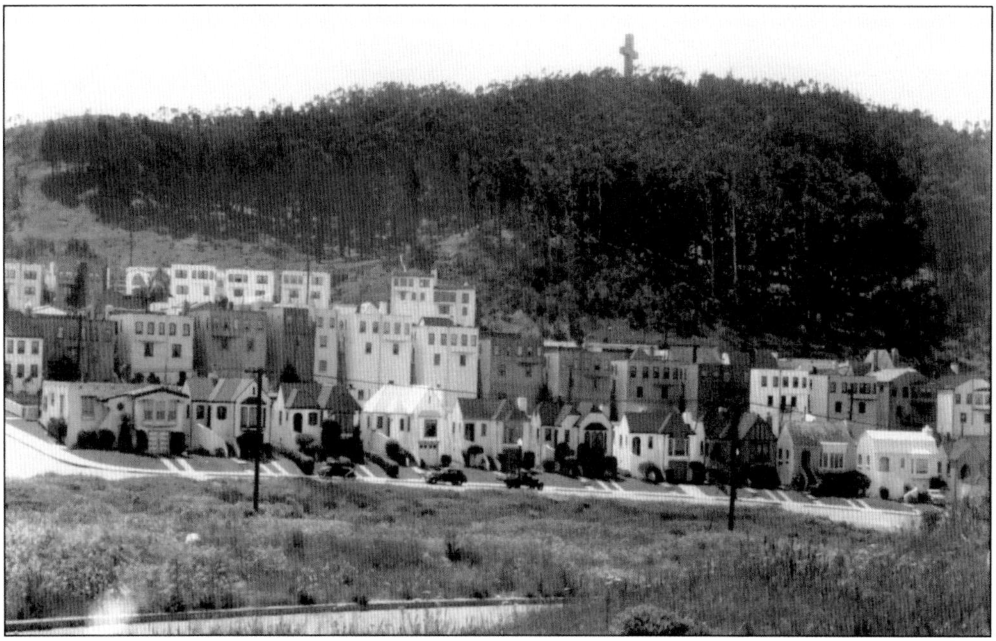

Miraloma Park, pictured here along Portola Drive, was described as having "scores of charming homes." With English and Spanish dwellings on large lots, prices were said to be as low as $7,500 with payments of $65 a month in the 1920s. Features included Kohler electric dishwashers and a radio den in the Raleigh design. Other homes, such as the Spanish Miraloma, included beautiful furnishings, while the smaller Sunshine Gables and Portola provided compact convenience. (Courtesy private collection.)

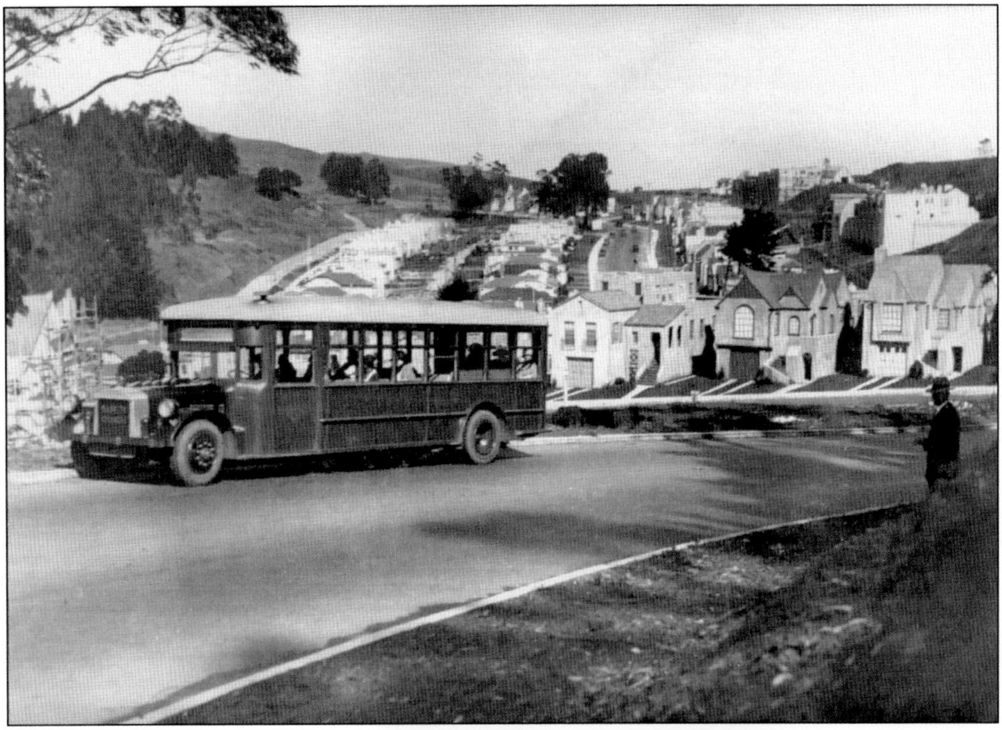

In 1926, this was one of the early bus routes in San Francisco. The Route No. 1 Line crossed the Richmond District and Golden Gate Park to Mount Davidson and Westwood Park. The middle street with seven automobiles is Portola Drive before it was widened in the 1950s. The homes on the north side were relocated. (Courtesy Ken and Kathy Hoegger.)

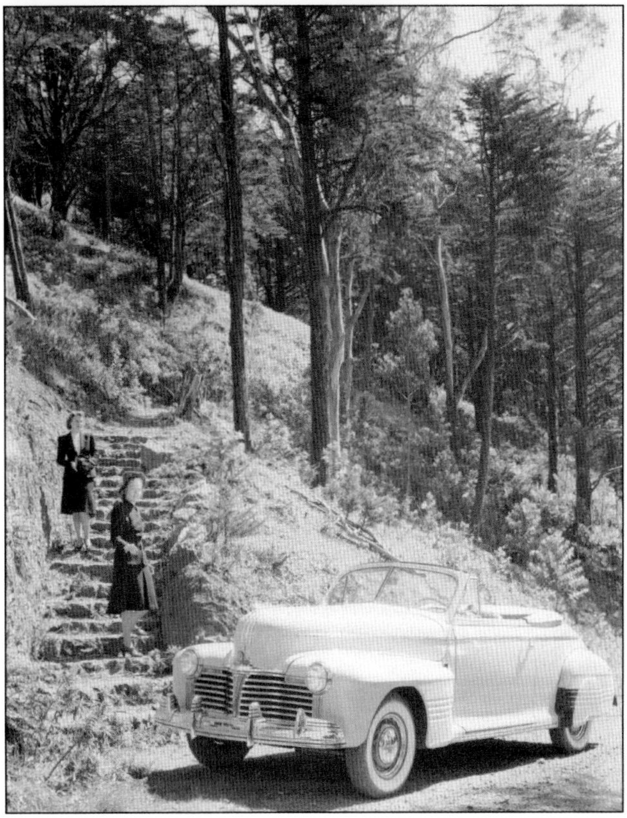

Developer A. S. Baldwin spent $2,000 to build hiking trails up Mount Davidson for the public's pleasure. YMCA director George Decatur later wrote that his hike to the top and view of "tall monuments of steel and concrete wherein were housed thousands of busy minds" inspired him to organize the city's first Easter sunrise service on its highest point in 1923. (Courtesy private collection.)

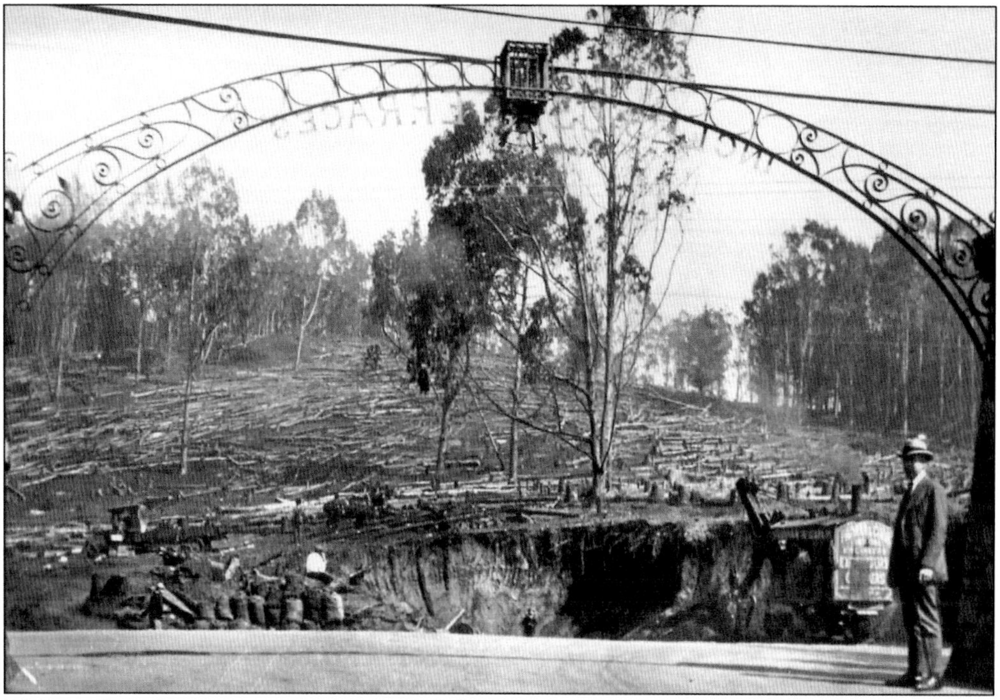

William Benedict, secretary to Mayor Rolph, wrote, "Women's active association with Mount Davidson history did not begin until 1926 when the subdivider's axe and steam shovel were heard on its lower slopes, destroying in ruthless fashion the beauties of nature." Here Fernando Nelson is cutting down thousands of trees for construction of the Mount Davidson Manor subdivision across Ocean Avenue from Ingleside Terraces at Victoria Street. (Courtesy Ken Hoegger.)

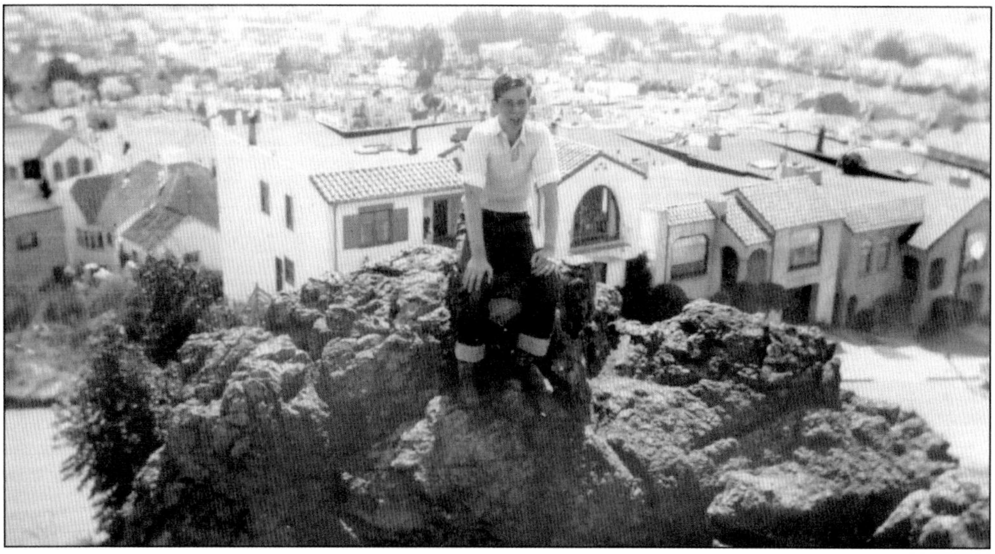

Fernando Nelson built his first San Francisco Victorian-style home in 1876 when he just 16. To produce homes that working families could afford, he bought whole blocks, or in this case 50 acres, where he built similar houses of a single popular style. He also developed the streets, sewer systems, and other facilities for Mount Davidson Manor pictured here below Tom O'Neill on the Big Red Rock in the 1930s. (Courtesy Tom O'Neil.)

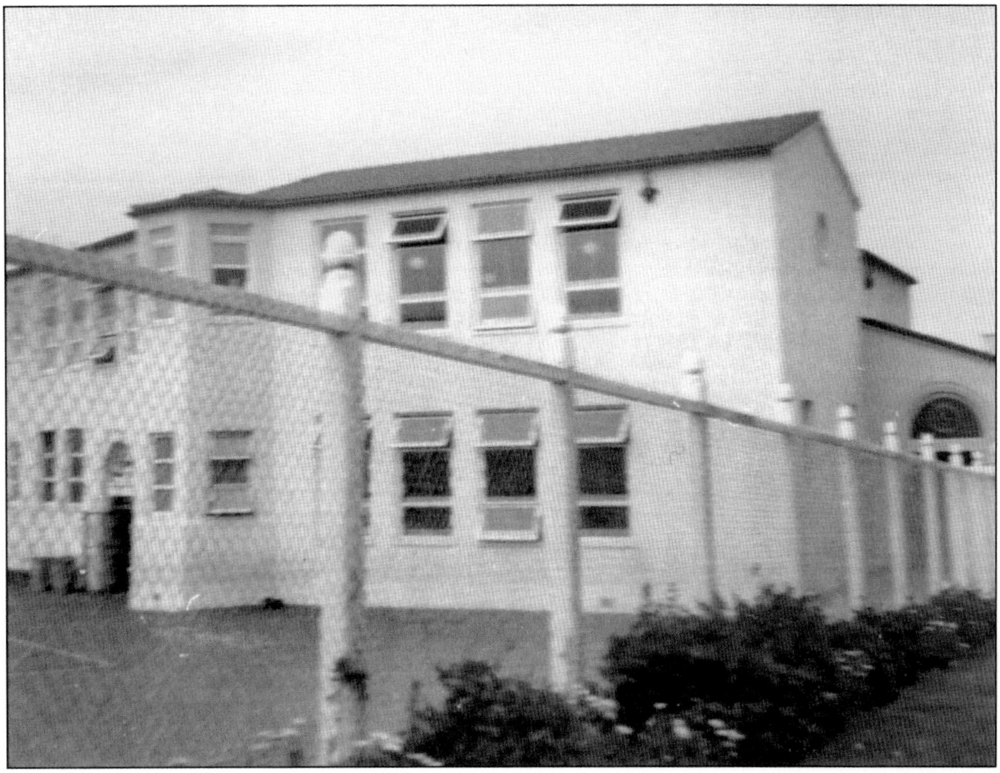

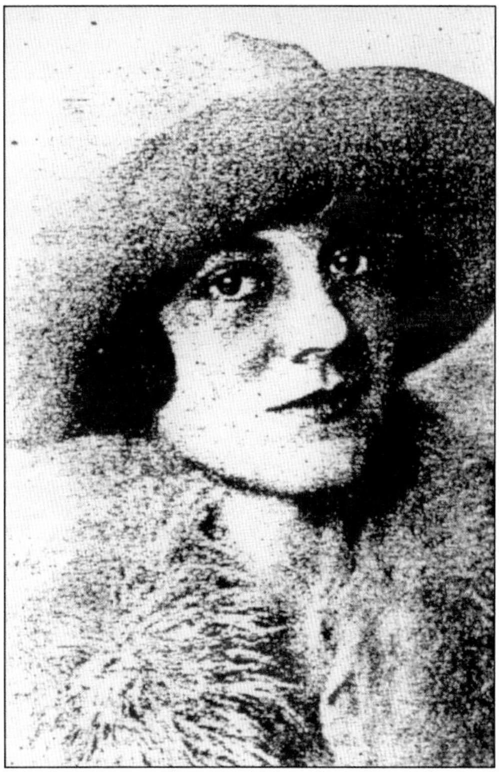

"An ardent nature lover, Mrs. Edmund N. 'Madie' Brown, was aroused over the destruction and made a plea at the Commodore Sloat Parent-Teacher Association on April 12, 1926, for the preservation of Mt. Davidson," according to William Benedict. She was appointed chair of a Mount Davidson conservation committee to gather historical data, maps, and property cost. (Courtesy Margie Whitnah.)

Madie Brown also obtained the support of the 15,000-member City and County Federation of Women's Clubs. For three years, they interviewed prominent citizens, wrote letters to individuals and to organizations asking for support, and sought "publicity through press and screen." Mount Davidson wildflowers were sent to individuals as pleas for support, and exhibits were arranged for flower shows and schools. (Author's collection.)

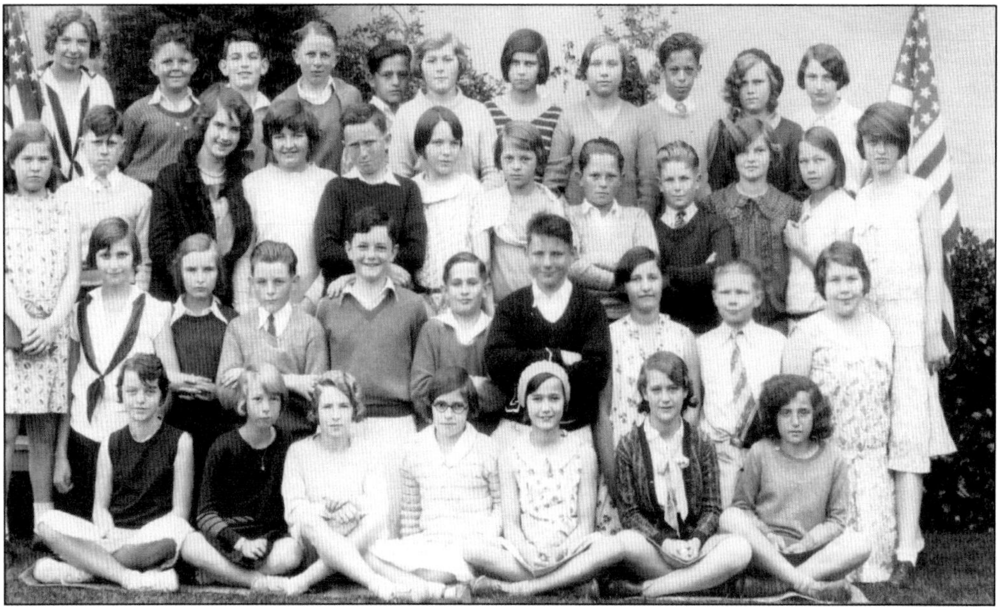

Betty Kern (third row, far right) and John Bryan (second row, third from left) are among the Commodore Sloat School students pictured here in 1930. Originally Ocean Road School in the 1880s, the school was named in honor of Commo. John Drake Sloat. On July 7, 1846, during the war with Mexico over ownership of California, he landed a detachment of Marines in Monterey, the capital of California at the time, and claimed it for the United States. (Courtesy Corinne Bryan.)

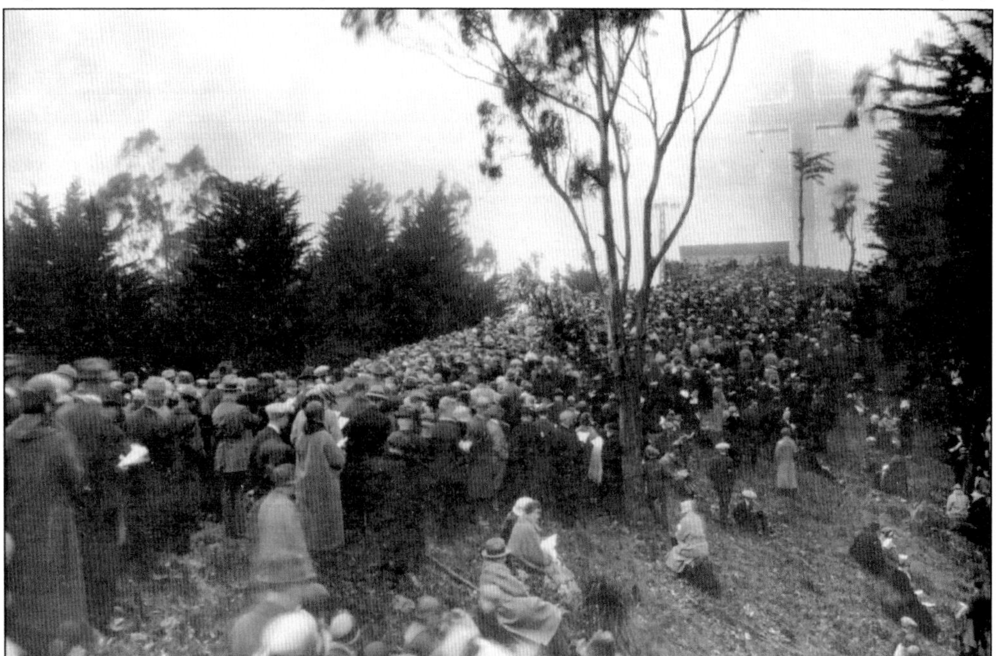

This 1930 sunrise event was the first on 20 acres purchased by the City of San Francisco in 1929 for a park described as providing children a place for nature study, Boy Scouts an area for hikes and overnight camping, Easter pilgrims a place of worship, and visitors unsurpassed views from the highest point in the city. (Courtesy Ken Hoegger collection.)

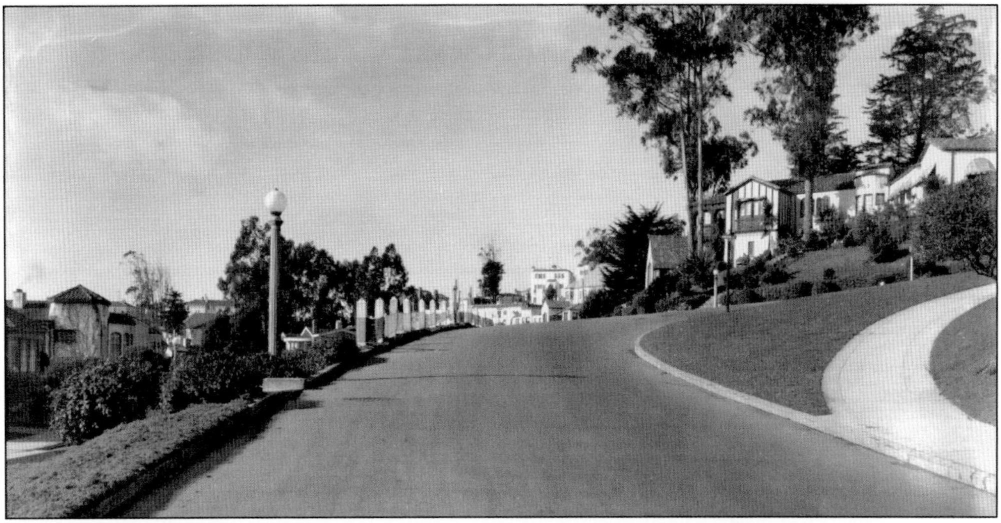

The Monterey Heights neighborhood at Monterey Boulevard and Yerba Buena Avenue is pictured here in the 1920s. In order to generate the sum of $130,000 to construct the present-day St. Emydius Church, the pastor raffled off a new house at 245 Brentwood in 1927. The contest for the Spanish-style bungalow Casa Emydio—complete with interior furnishings—was a notable success, with Mayor Rolph attending its dedication. (Courtesy Ken and Kathy Hoegger.)

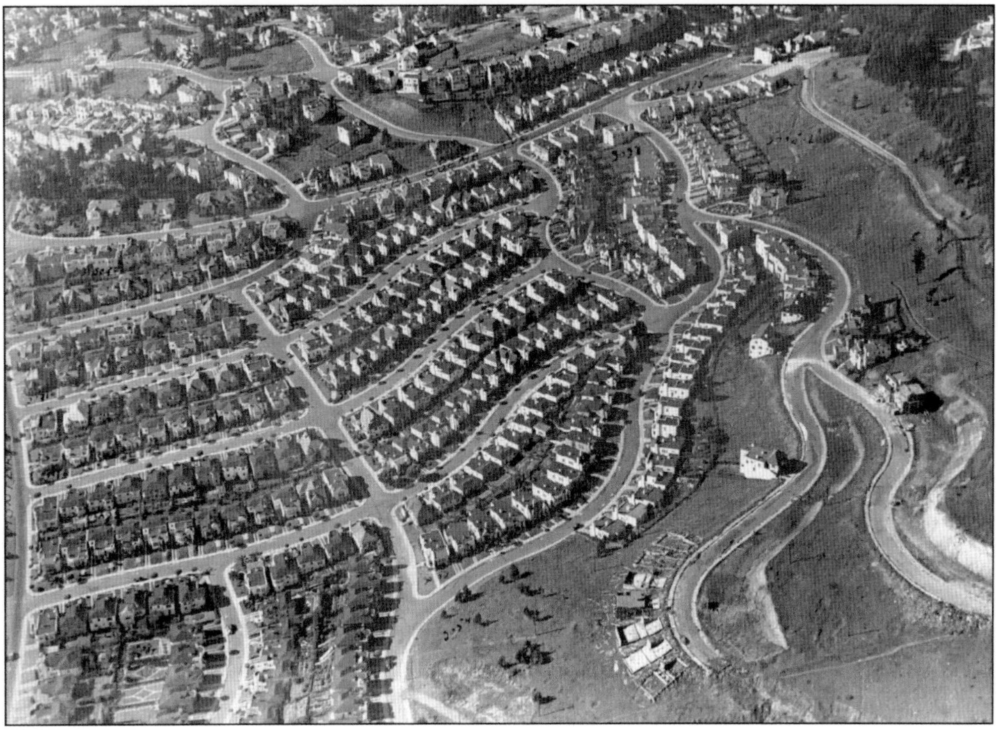

This aerial view shows Monterey Heights at the top with Westwood Highlands under construction in the foreground. All 283 custom-built, detached single-family homes of the original Westwood Highlands tract were constructed from 1924 to 1929, with each one a different architectural design from its neighbor. The last original streetlight is still in place at 345 Valdez Avenue. (Courtesy private collection.)

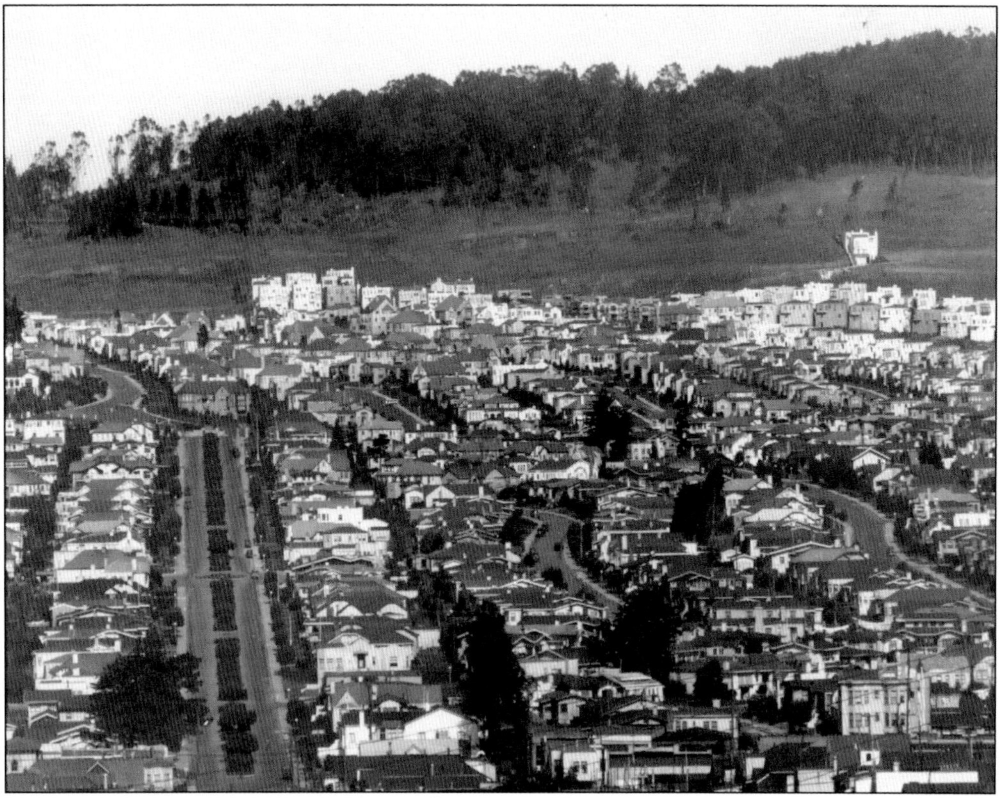

This is another view of Baldwin and Howell's Westwood Highlands subdivision under construction north of the now-completed Westwood Park. The neighborhood was described by a local newspaper as a place "where the higher you go up, the grander the dwelling," with homes boasting nice gardens and tiled roofs colored orange, yellow, or white. Designs included an "Englishy house with small, leaded windows" and "stuccoed pink with a tiled cupola." (Courtesy private collection.)

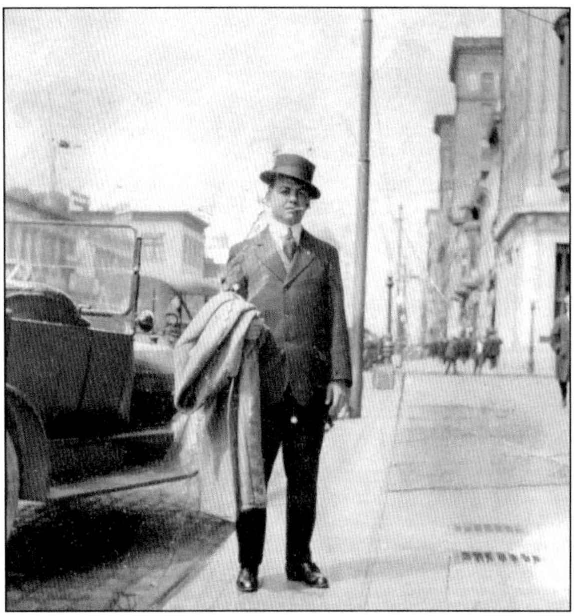

Joseph R. Bisho, the grandfather of Westwood Highlands president David Bisho, is pictured here on a visit to San Francisco. The son of Portuguese immigrants, he was a home builder in Hawaii and a lithographer for the *Honolulu Advertiser*. He brought Rose Azevedo to the city to marry her at Old St. Mary's Cathedral in 1923. After Joe's death in 1931, Rose and her young son Joseph Jr. came to live in San Francisco. (Courtesy Dave Bisho.)

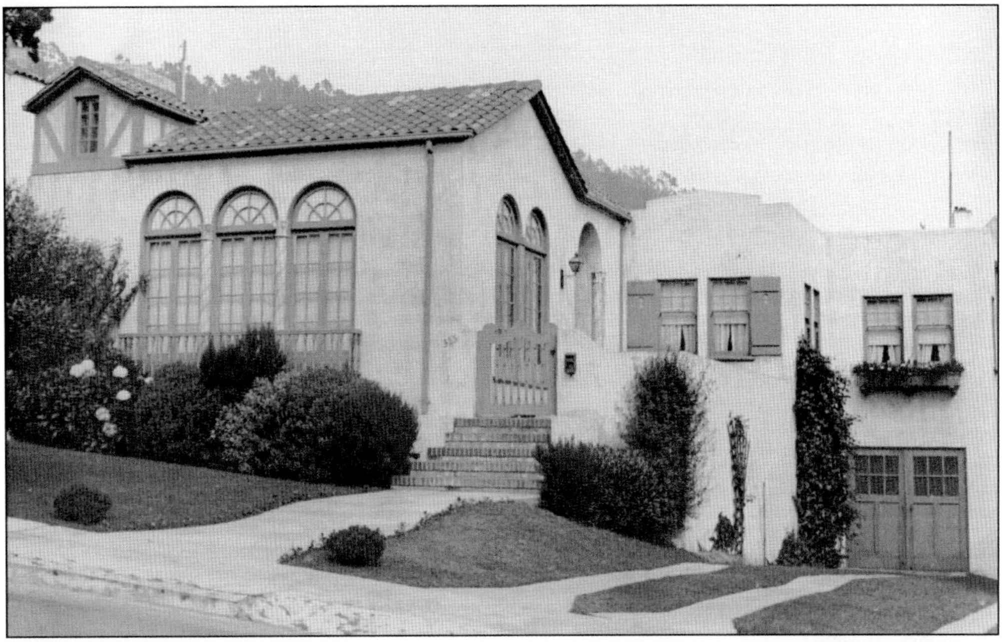

This is a close-up view of a Westwood Highlands home owned by James Coughlin at 325 Yerba Buena Avenue. A 1927 advertisement noted how the distinctive individual character of these homes added to their investment value and that owners would be proud to invite friends over. Prices started at $8,950 with payments of $65 a month. (Courtesy Beverly Coughlin.)

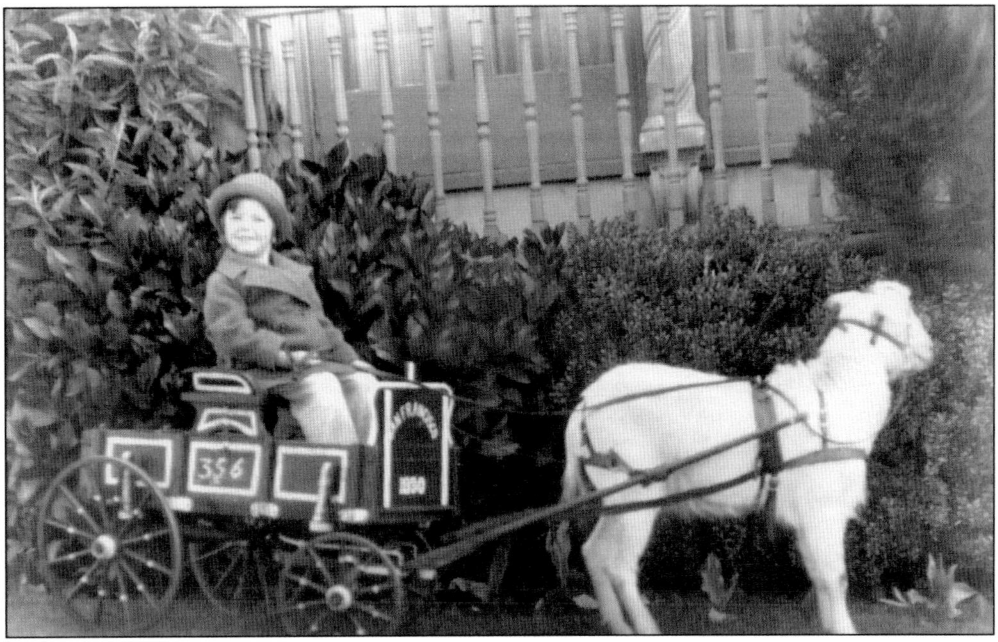

Warren Coughlin (future owner of Willig Truck Lines) is photographed receiving a country ride in his front yard. With the construction of Westwood Park and Highlands, Hamburg Street (named by Behrend Joost for a city in his native Germany) was changed to Ridgewood Avenue in 1930. This also changed the east-to-west alphabetical progression of street names in the neighboring Sunnyside District. (Courtesy Beverly Coughlin.)

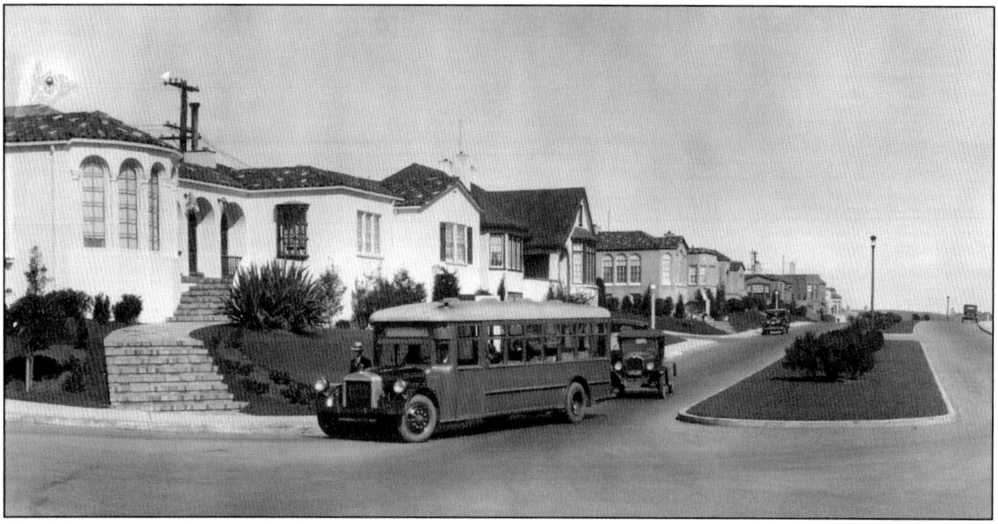

In 1927, Route 1 transportation to Westwood Highlands and Park ran from Tenth Avenue and California Street, through Golden Gate Park, to Forest Hill Station and Twin Peaks Tunnel, along Portola and Miraloma Drives, to Yerba Buena Avenue. It is pictured here at Monterey Boulevard coming back from the end of the line at Edna Street. (Courtesy Ron Davis.)

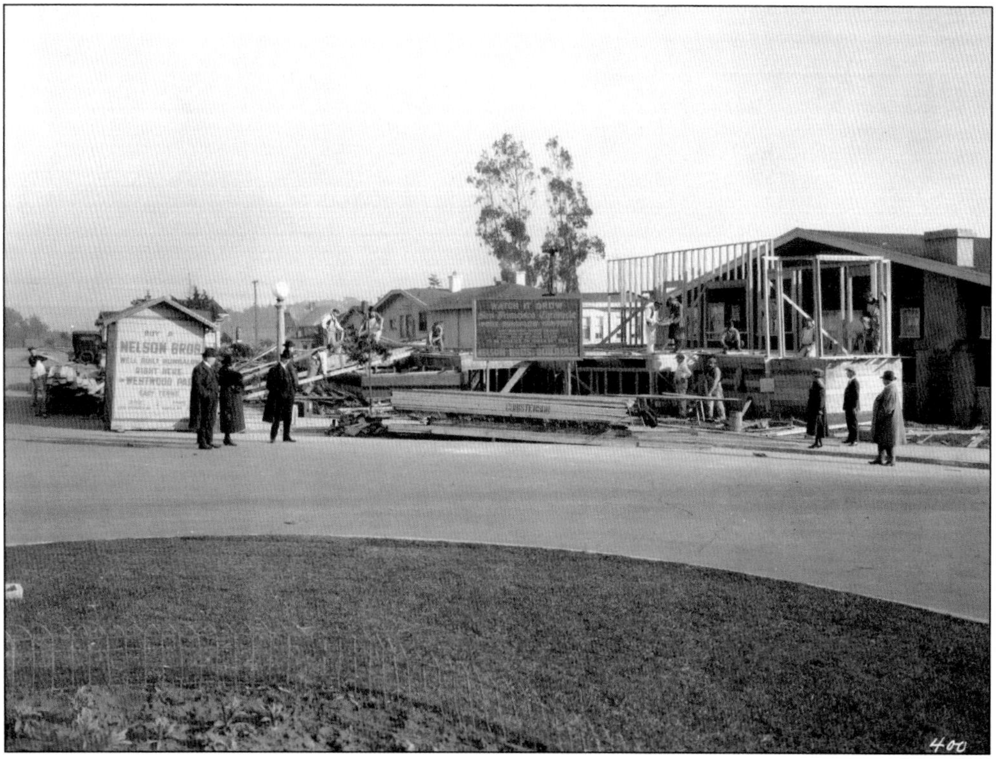

The Watch it Grow—Prize Bungalow Contest was offered in 1922 by the *San Francisco Chronicle* for this $15,000 home in Westwood Park, along with $2,500 worth of furniture. Designed by Charles Strothoff at 598 Miramar Avenue, it was given to the person who secured the highest number of votes. "Every $30 club of new subscriptions will bring a bonus of 75,000 votes in addition to the regular votes," the paper stated. (Courtesy Westwood Park Association.)

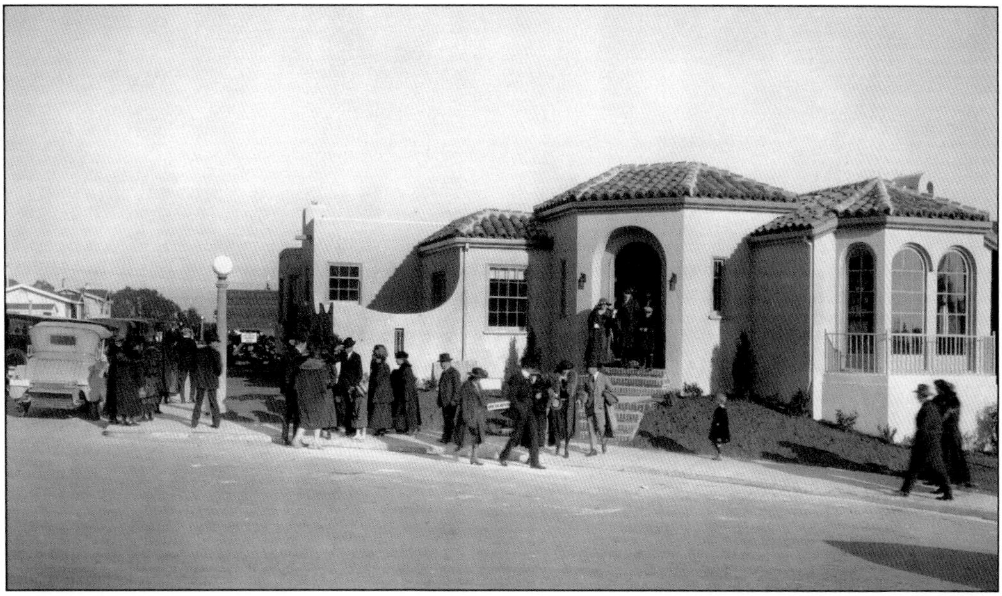

The home was described as "sure to be the envy of those who must be content with homes less modern." Offering electrical outlets in all rooms, "The lucky housewife can use her electrical appliances with perfect comfort." She would not have to "climb upon a chair to connect her vacuum cleaner or on the breakfast table to plug a toaster into a lighting fixture." (Courtesy Westwood Park Association.)

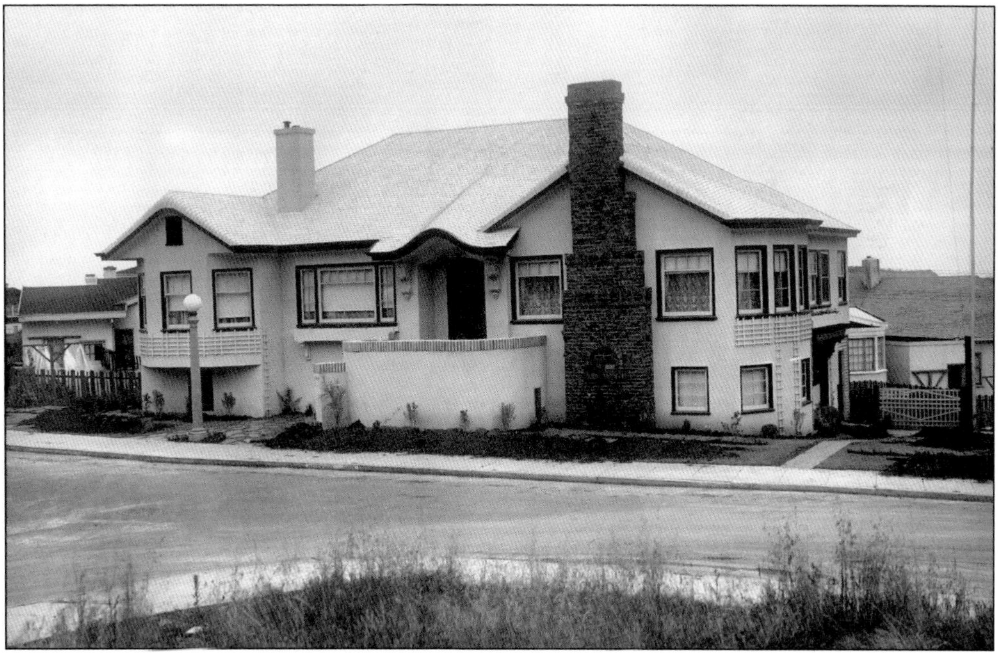

Architect Ida McCain designed this home at 180 Westwood Drive and others in Westwood Park and Monterey Heights. Historian Inge Horton writes about how she used her shoe to break through any knot-ridden planks so as to ensure their replacement. When her heel came off in the process, she said, "The carpenter very kindly brought me a hatchet . . . and in true 'Carrie Nation' style we knocked the knots out." (Courtesy Westwood Park Association.)

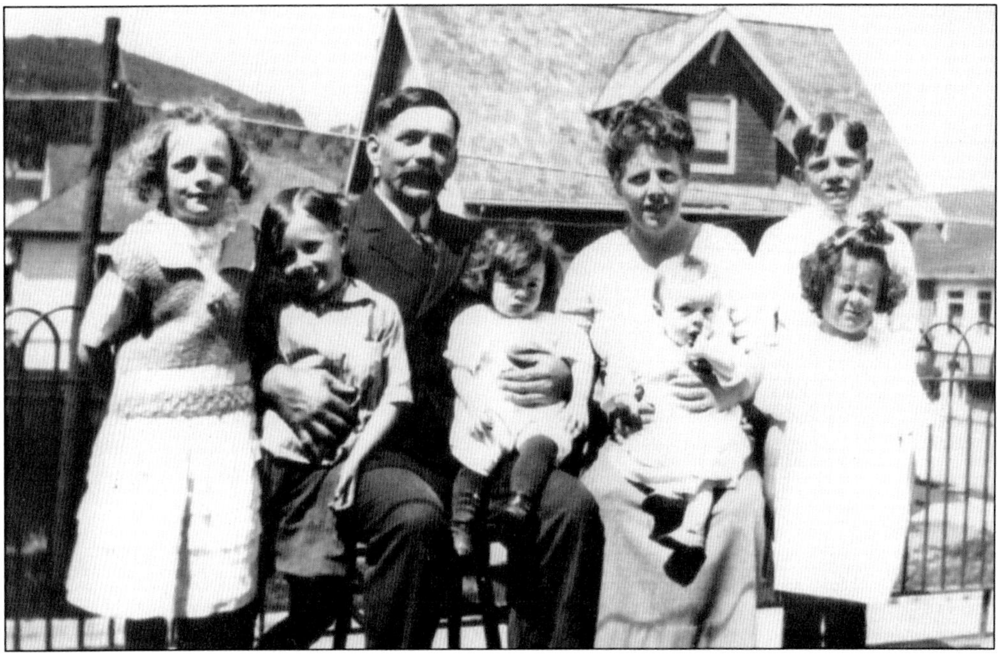

This is Peter Ward with his family on the roof of his 199 Gennessee Street market in the early 1920s, with Mount Davidson in the background. Pictured, from left to right, are little Mary, Dan, Peter, Sheila, Mary (Peter's wife, holding Mike), William, and Nora. Sheila grew up to marry Glenn Wade and moved across the street to raise their daughter Carolyn, who still lives in the same Sunnyside neighborhood house. (Courtesy Carolyn Wade.)

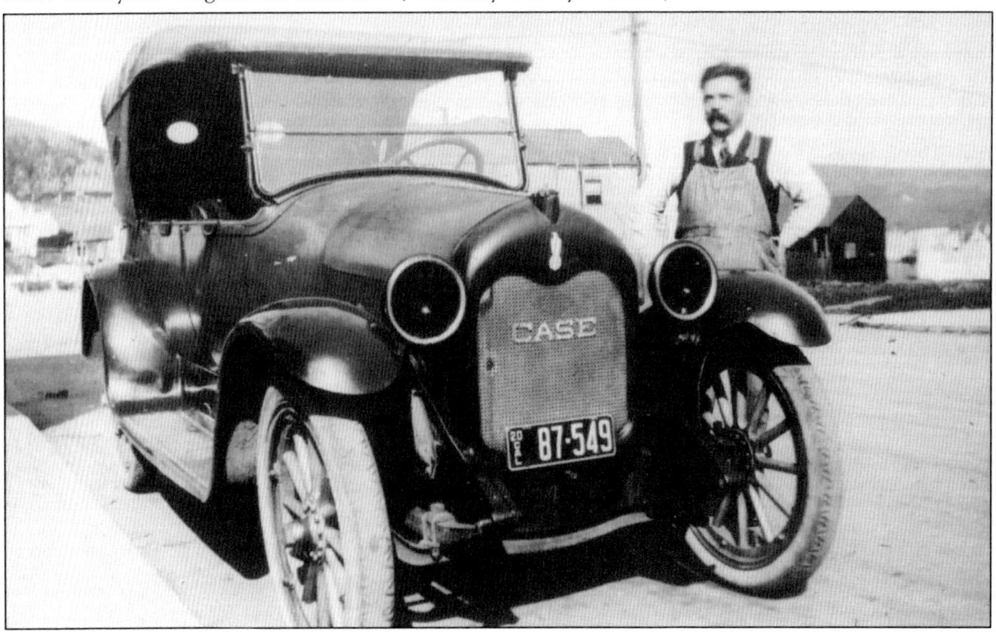


Peter Ward, next to his Case automobile, opened what eventually became Prosperity Market in the early 1900s. He sold vegetables and other grocery items with a butcher section in the back. Peter's house was built in 1909. He added a barn made from large beams, hauled by their horse all the way from the shipyards in Hunter's Point, with his son Will. (Courtesy Ron Davis.)

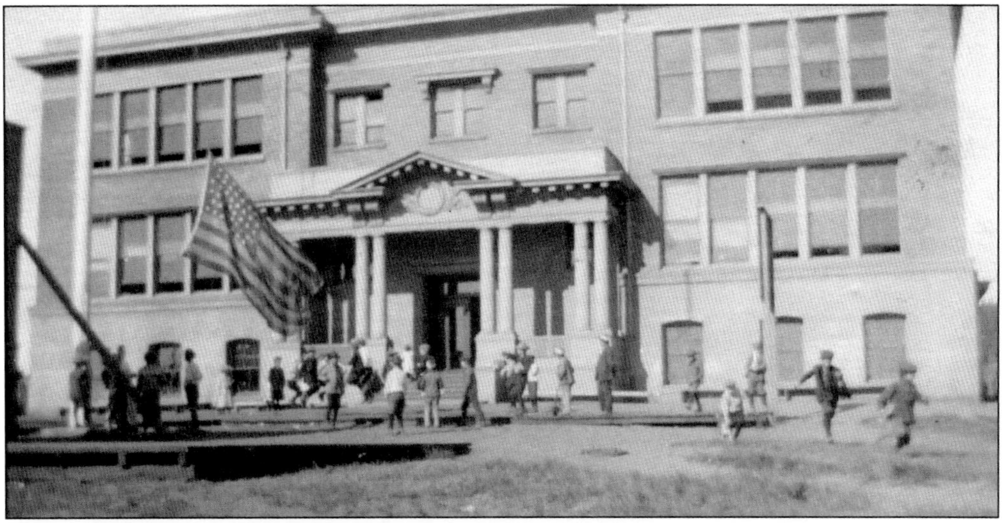

Here is old Sunnyside School before it was enlarged at 250 Foerster Street. While the children of Sunnyside had the advantage of country living, their school was so overcrowded a 1904 newspaper reported that the "children are practically herded into it like sheep in a pen." The 1920s brought Sunnyside its own park and playground, which was dedicated by Mayor James Rolph Jr. where the City College Student Health Center was later built. (Courtesy Ron Davis.)

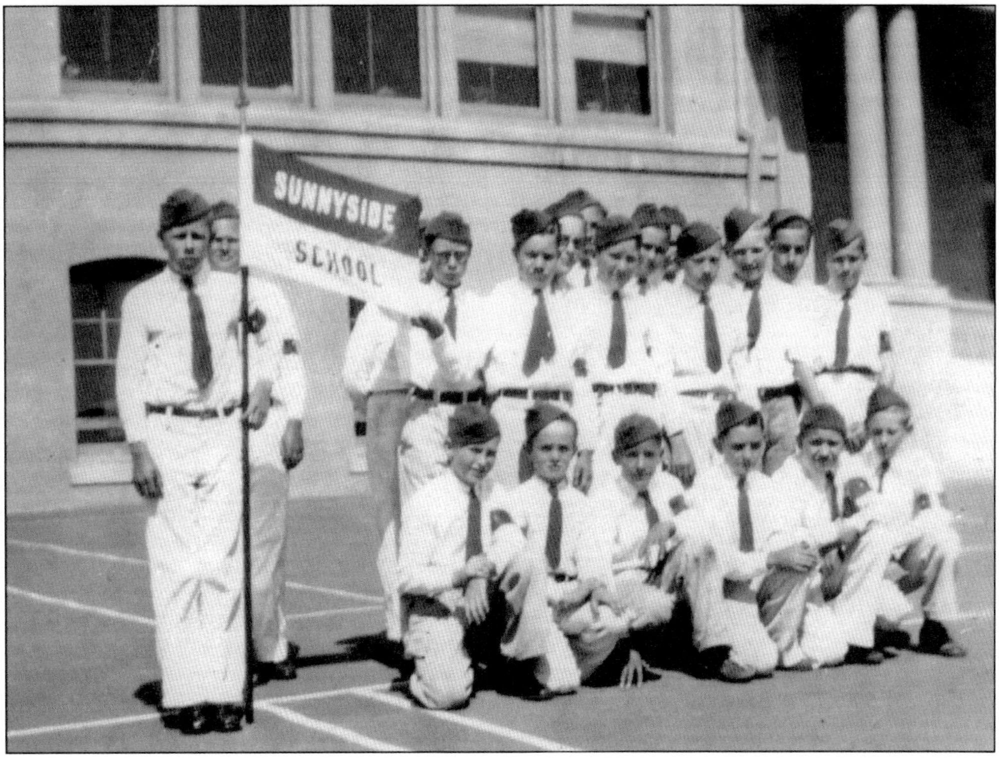


The Sunnyside School traffic patrol is lined up with Mike Ward (front row, second from left) in the 1920s. Early residents say the neighborhood had a pronounced Irish and Italian flavor, where O'Learys and Mahoneys lived beside DeLucchis and Molinaris. There were also a number of English, German, and Mexican families. (Courtesy Carolyn Wade.)

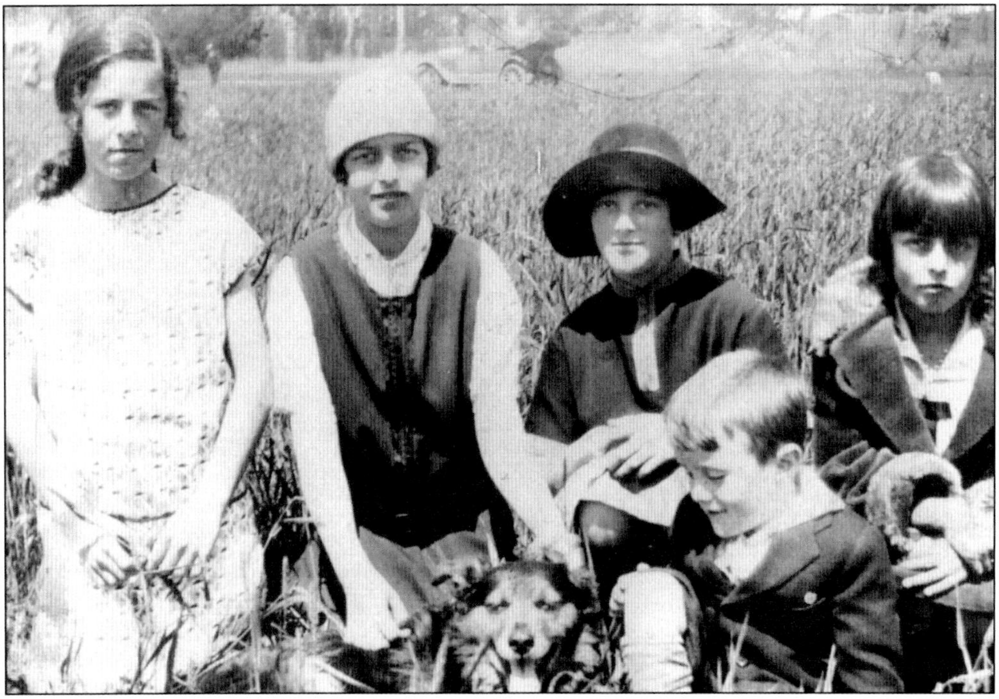

Jean Ward and her friends are pictured here in the 1920s enjoying the country atmosphere along Judson Avenue at Gennessee Street. According to Thomas Malim, with Sunnyside being sparsely settled, it became a bootleggers' paradise during Prohibition. Stills at 327 Staples Avenue and in other homes made the air "redolent with the odors of fermenting corn, and all the other goodies that go into the making of a prime batch of Grog," Malim wrote. (Courtesy Carolyn Wade.)

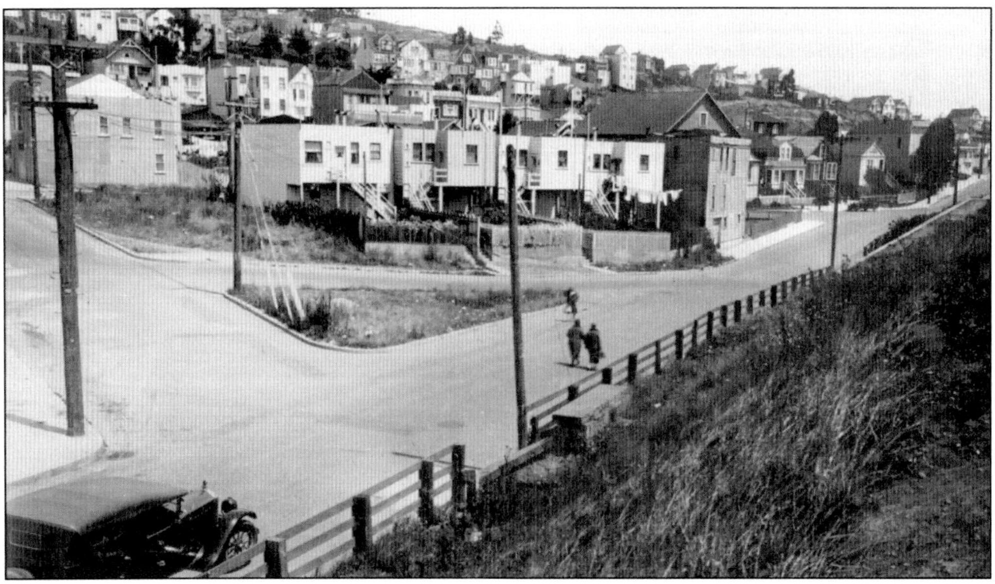

This is the view from Sunnyside's Santa Rosa Bridge in 1927, when Malim says the bean and rice sacks of the friendly neighborhood grocers were well stocked on Saturday nights with bottles of the local product. This method of supply was for the workingmen, who, according to Malim, "needed a little relaxation after six days of hard work." (Courtesy Ken Hoegger.)

# *Four*

# THE DEPRESSION

## PUBLIC WORKS PROJECTS KEEP THE DREAM ALIVE

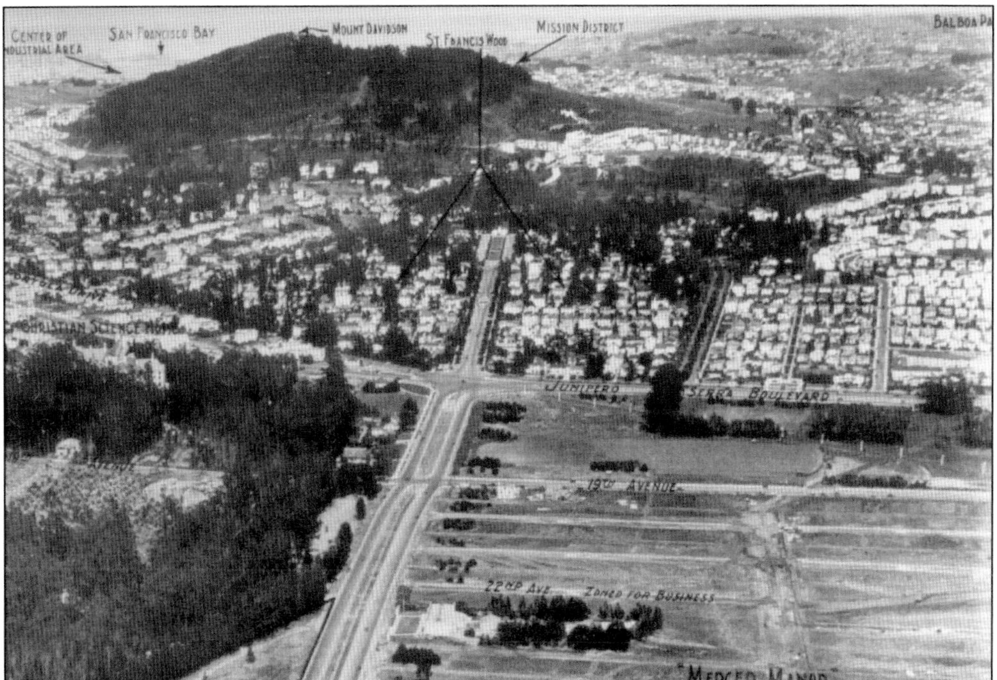


This 1930 aerial view of the neighborhoods west of Twin Peaks, running east from Sloat Boulevard (center), shows a still tree-covered Mount Davidson. (Courtesy Ken and Kathy Hoegger.)

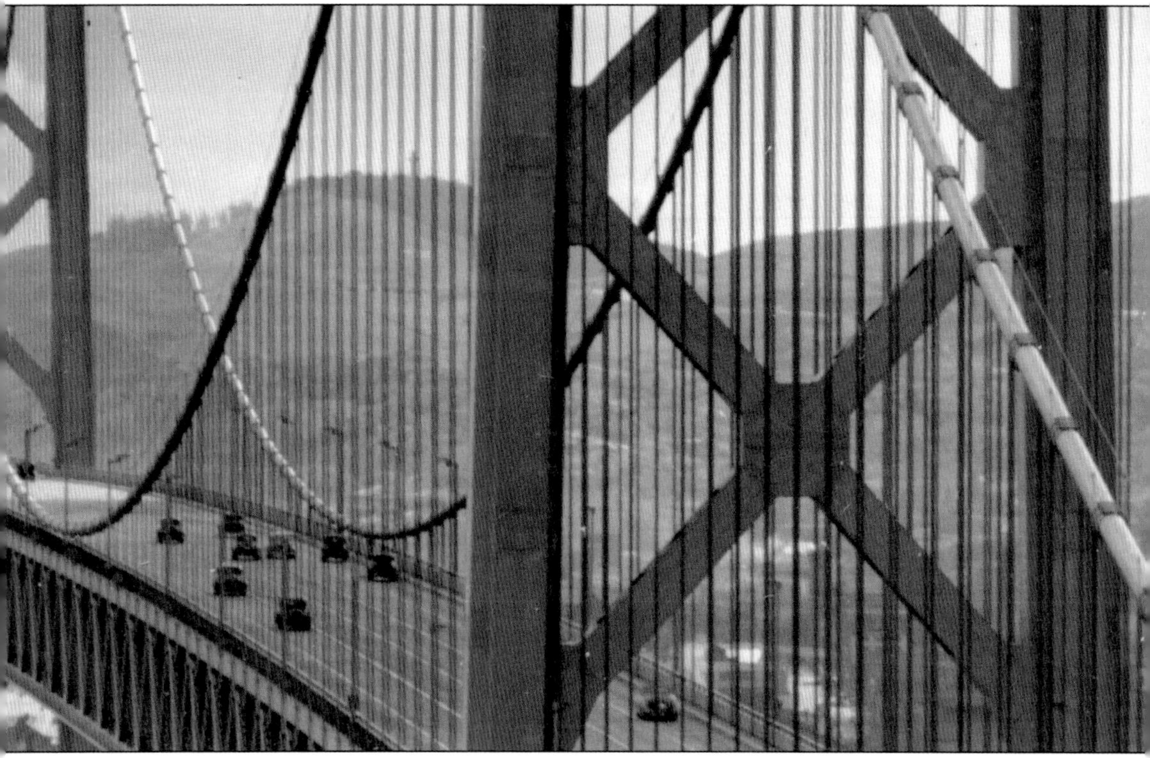

Historian Kevin Starr documents how Californians managed, amidst some "social misbehavior," to accomplish one of the most creative decades in the history of any American state during the 1930s. The San Francisco–Oakland Bay Bridge, pictured here, was built along with serviceable and architecturally significant schools, armories, libraries, and airports. Paths and trails were added to Mount Davidson (visible through the bridge) and other public parks and wilderness preserves that are still in use today. He writes, "Despite clashes of Left and Right, despite horrendous suspension of civil liberties—they never completely detached themselves from the American tradition of constitutional law and fair play. Nor did they abandon the public realm; indeed, in their politics and their public works, their literature and art, they brought public values into a golden age of expression." (Courtesy Ron Davis.)

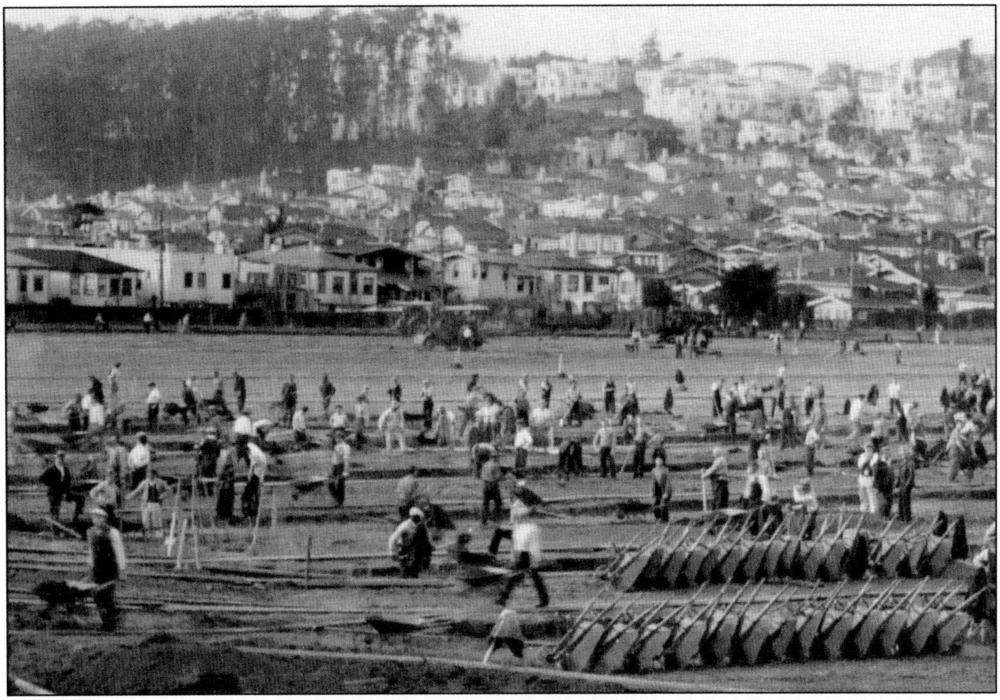

Kevin Starr also documents how much California benefited from federally financed public works projects during the Great Depression, resulting in his words, "An epic of construction without precedent in the history of the state." In addition to the Hetch Hetchy Aqueduct and Golden Gate Bridge, there were countless flood-control and urban-improvement projects, such as this labor-intensive construction of a never-to-be-filled Balboa Park Reservoir east of Westwood Park in 1933. (Courtesy private collection.)

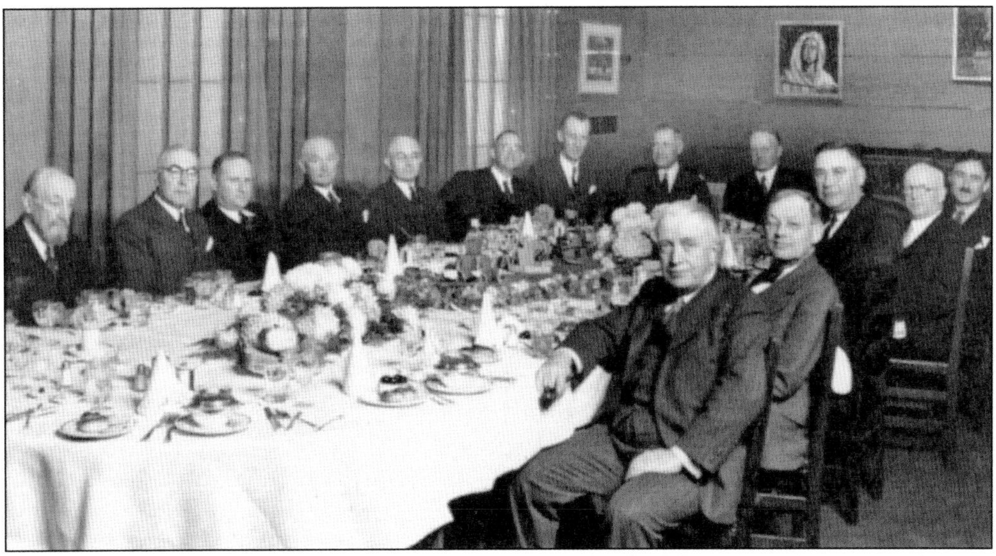

West of Twin Peaks resident and construction engineer for the Mount Davidson Cross Henry J. Brunnier (seventh from left) is among the guests at this luncheon given by Timothy Pflueger (third from left), the chairman of the Consulting Board of Architects for the engineers and architects of the San Francisco–Oakland Bay Bridge. (Courtesy John Pflueger.)

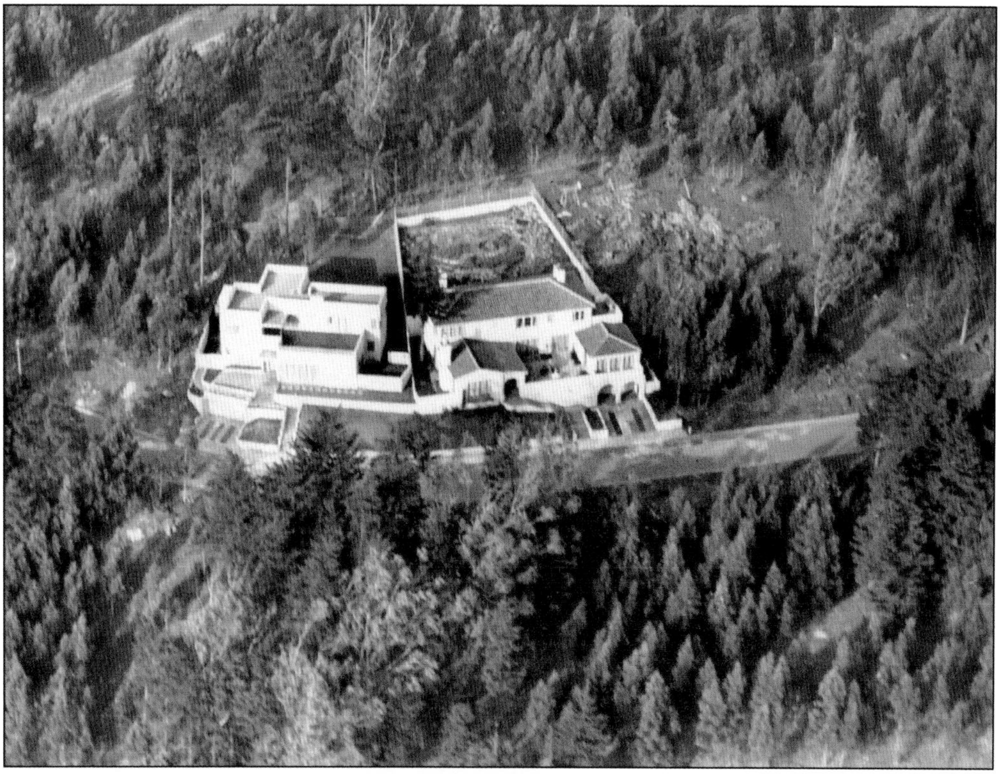

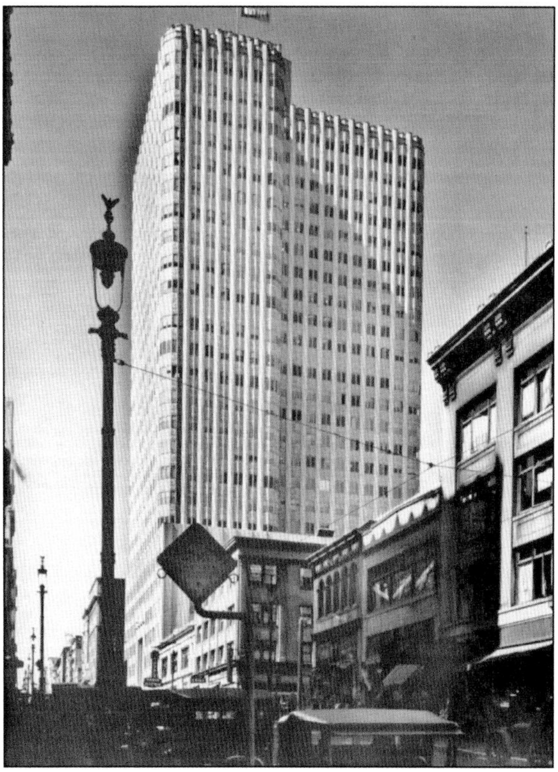

Timothy Pflueger was one of the most significant architects in San Francisco, designing many familiar landmarks, including the Top of the Mark and Castro Theater. He designed these two houses in Sherwood Forest for Drs. Vollmer and Delprat. Both physicians had offices at 450 Sutter Street. The art deco– and Spanish-style houses were built on Lansdale Avenue. (Courtesy Denis Pinto.)

The art deco Medical and Dental Building at 450 Sutter Street was the second of San Francisco's two earliest skyscrapers (Pacific Telephone and Telegraph Building was the other) Timothy Pflueger designed in the 1920s, and it was the last to be built until after the end of World War II. He also designed the Union Square Garage, which was the first of its kind, and the I. Magnin Department Store before his untimely death in 1946. (Courtesy John Pflueger.)

This statue facing west to a panoramic view of the Pacific Ocean anchors the entrance to the streamline moderne-style home built in 1936 for Drs. Delprat. A derivative of art deco, the horizontal and rectangular design utilizes concrete, stucco, and metal surfaces and was featured at the 1939–1940 Golden Gate International Exposition, according to the *San Francisco Chronicle*, as "embodying both a futuristic vision and paean to the past." (Courtesy Denis Pinto.)

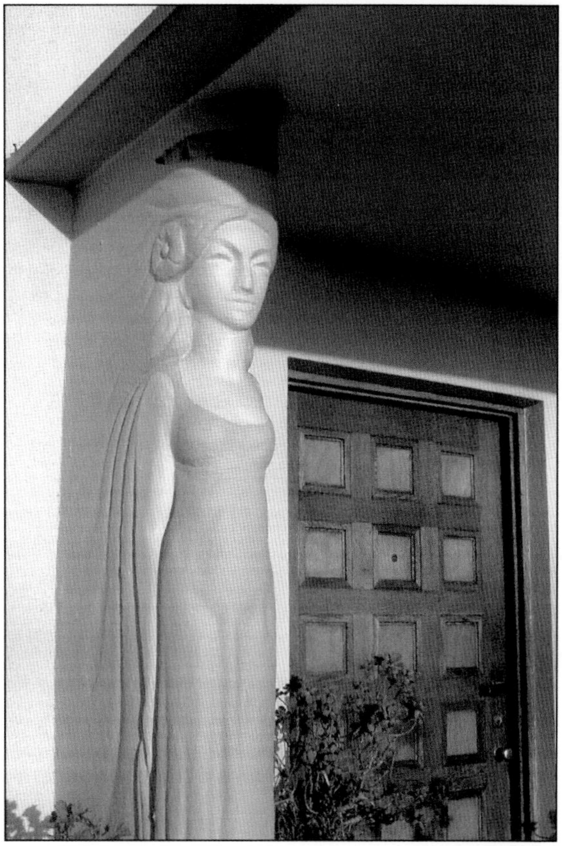

To keep selling houses at 1920s prices during the Depression, the lots became smaller and the houses were no longer detached as they progressed down Teresita Boulevard in Miraloma Park by 1939. The side of the street with a view was developed first. Art deco architecture (below center) was added to the exterior styles available. Unemployed homeowners managed to keep their house under a federal agency, which extended mortgage payments. (Courtesy John Pinkerton and David Atkins.)

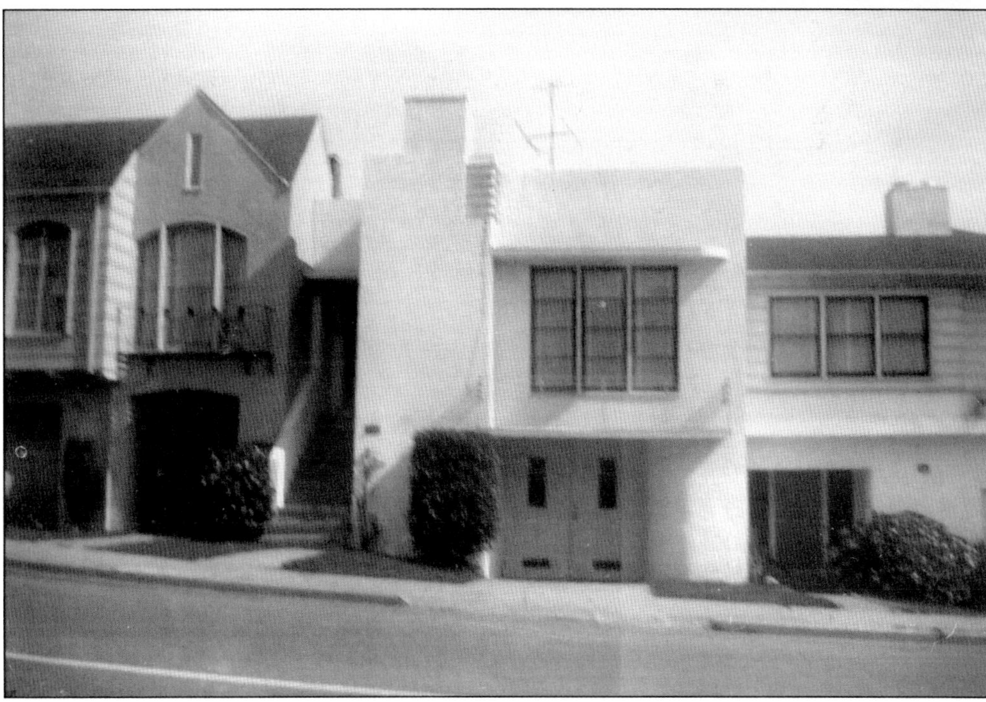

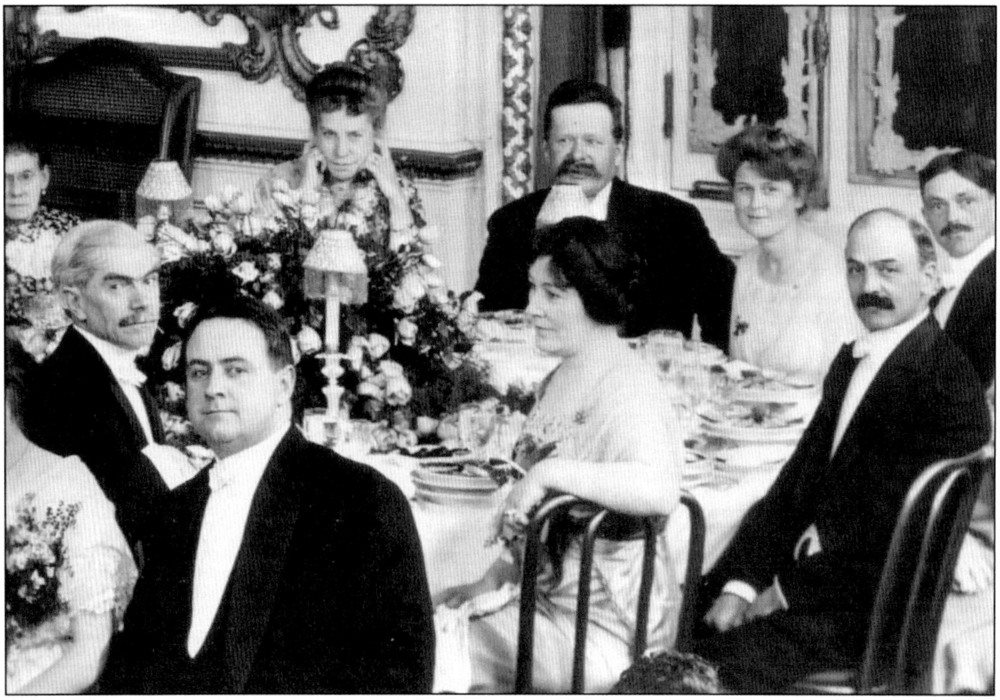

Pictured in 1914 at the Horticultural Society Annual Banquet at the Fairmont Hotel, Elizabeth Fotheringham (center, front) encouraged her daughter to buy a house in Miraloma Park in 1940, when Angelo J. Rossi (at Elizabeth's right) was mayor. He is credited for helping San Francisco become one of the first cities to receive Works Progress Administration funding during the Depression, as well as receiving employment for all residents eligible for the program. (Courtesy Elizabeth Mettling.)

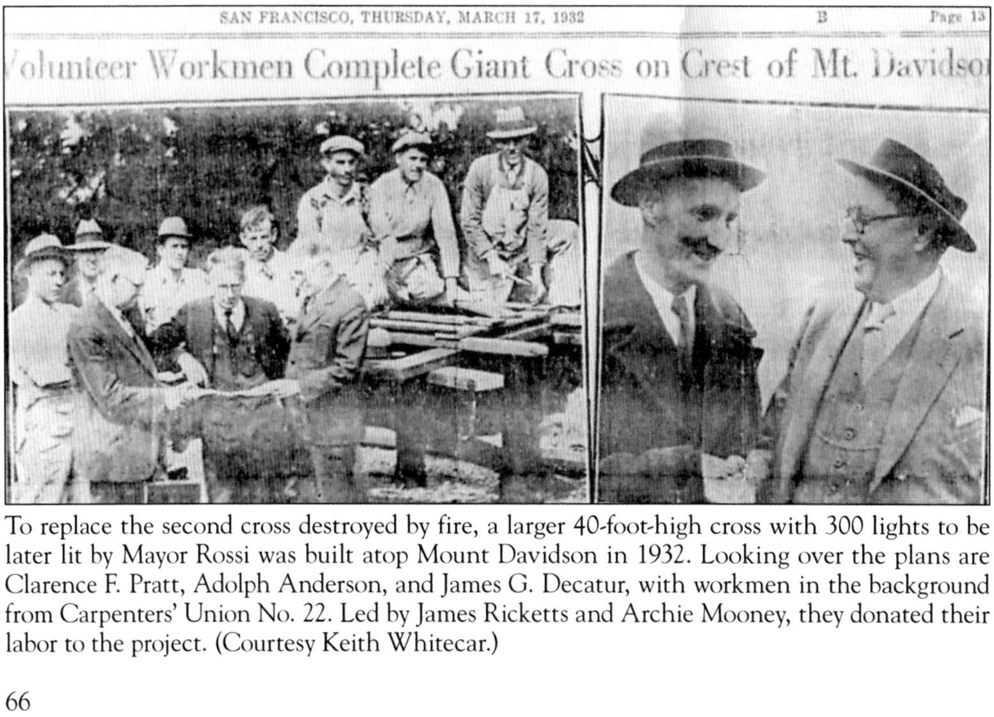


To replace the second cross destroyed by fire, a larger 40-foot-high cross with 300 lights to be later lit by Mayor Rossi was built atop Mount Davidson in 1932. Looking over the plans are Clarence F. Pratt, Adolph Anderson, and James G. Decatur, with workmen in the background from Carpenters' Union No. 22. Led by James Ricketts and Archie Mooney, they donated their labor to the project. (Courtesy Keith Whitecar.)

With 32,000 attending the 1932 Easter sunrise event that was broadcast coast-to-coast on CBS radio, George Decatur starts a campaign to realize his dream of building a huge concrete, and therefore fireproof, cross atop Mount Davidson. Designed by George Kelham and Henry J. Brunnier, the fifth cross to be built on the site was the world's largest at the time. (Author's Collection.)

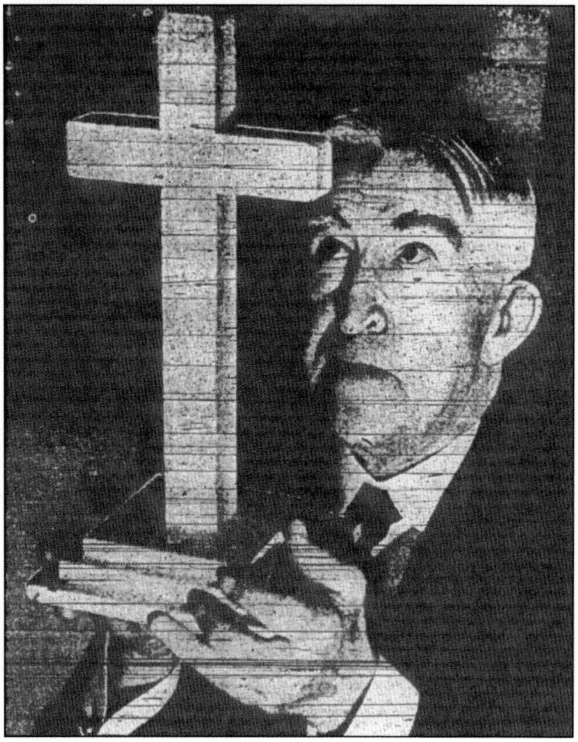

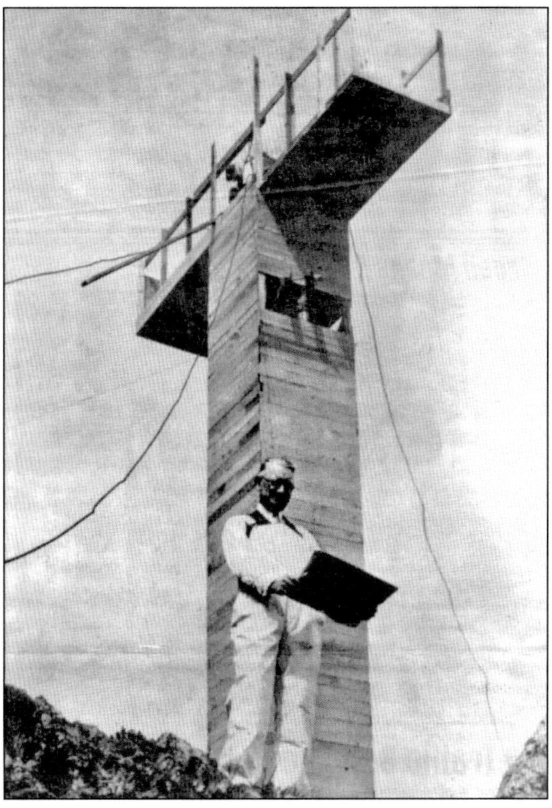

Clarence F. (Sandy) Pratt, director of Pacific Coast Aggregates and chairman of the Sunrise Easter Service Committee since 1927, is believed to be the person pictured here in front of the 103-foot-high cross under construction in 1934. Built with $20,000 donated by subscribers and schoolchildren, 30,000 feet of lumber was used to form the 750 cubic yards of concrete around 30 tons of reinforced steel. It would be visible from most parts of San Francisco by day, and up to 75 miles away when illuminated at night. (Courtesy Glenn Gullmes.)

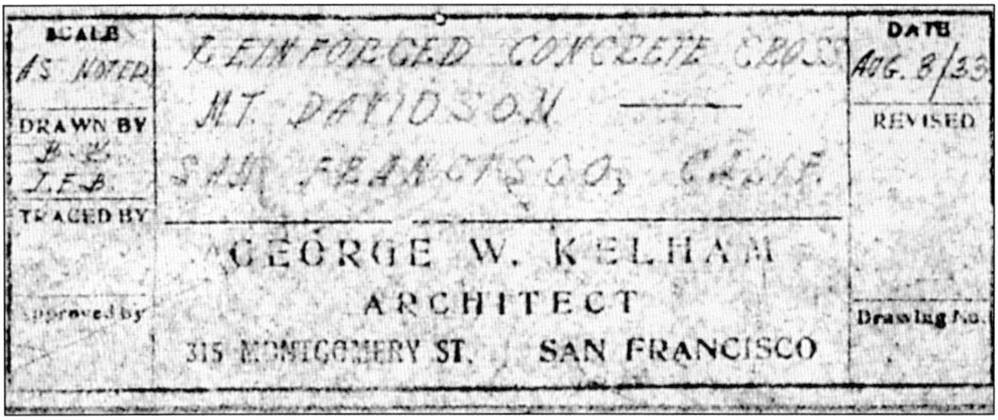


Architect and historian Patrick McGrew describes the monument as an object lesson in design purity: "The unadorned cross itself is expressed in complete simplicity, a style that is at once both contemporary, and timeless." He further points out how the art deco styling of the podium was being explored by its designer George Kelham as early as 1928. McGrew describes Kelham's Shell Oil Building as "an art deco tour de force." (Courtesy Bob DeLiso.)

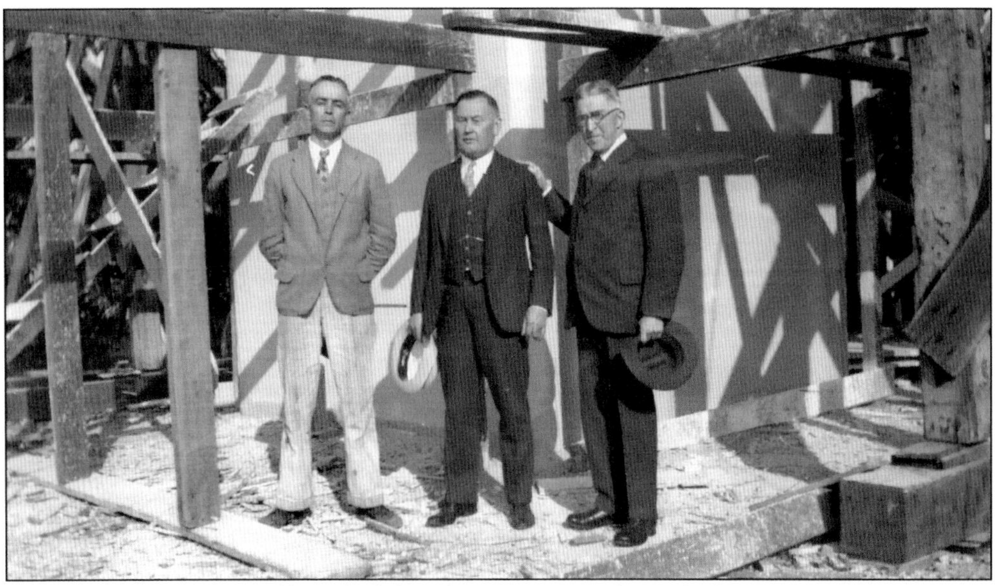

George Decatur is pictured here (right) with J. O. Munson (center), the construction contractor who built the cross. The monument was the only one Kelham ever designed and was among his final projects. (Courtesy Glenn Gullmes.)

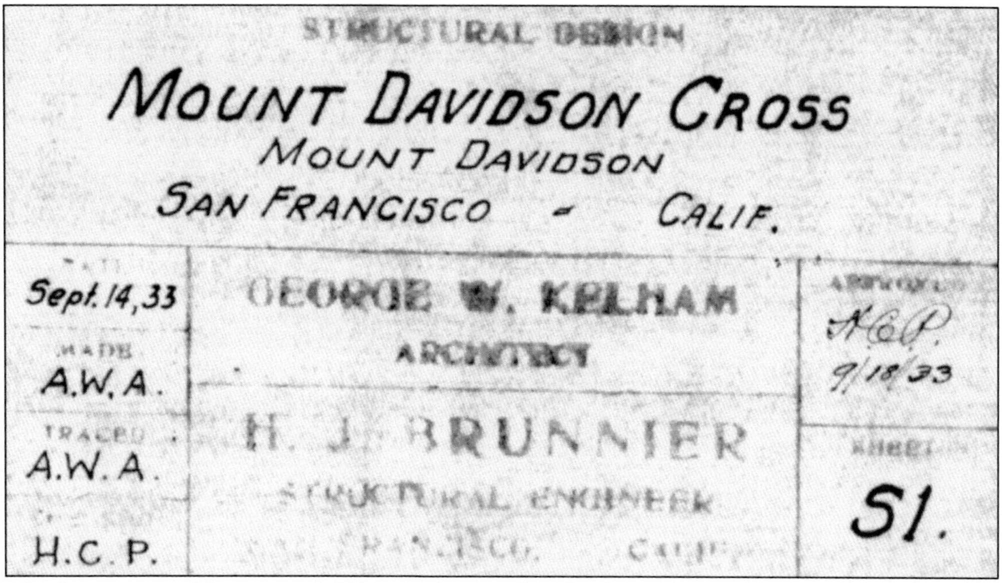


The dimensions of the cross would be as substantial as the skyscrapers and bridges Henry Brunnier engineered. Its foundation goes 16 feet into solid rock and consists of a cylindrical block of concrete 18 feet in diameter at the bottom and 14.5 feet at the top. Upon the foundation, there is a 62-foot-diameter platform with seven 35-foot-wide steps. (Courtesy Bob DeLiso.)

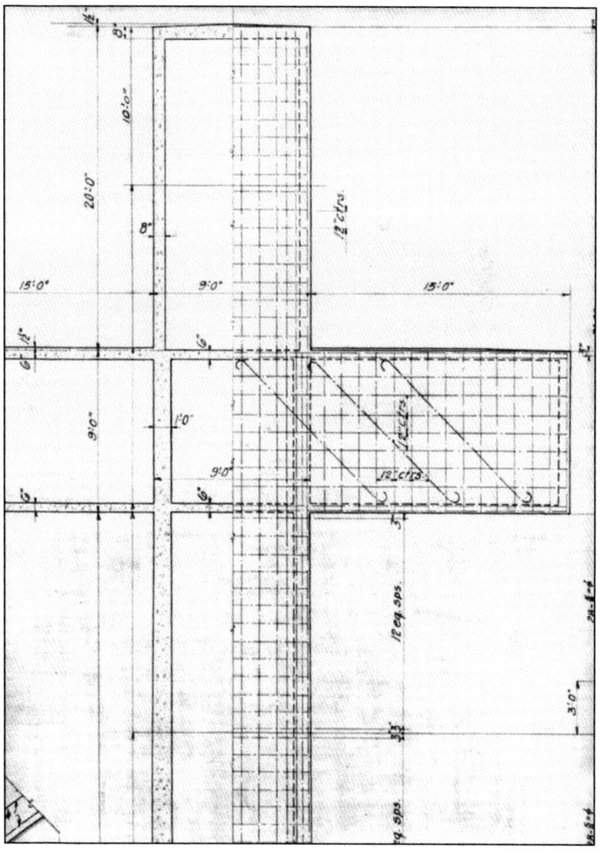


The east-facing cross is 10 square feet at the base and tapers to 9 feet at the top. Henry Brunnier teamed up with George Kelham on over 20 significant projects, including the Russ Building in 1927, which is described by historian Kevin Starr as a "skyscraper which asserted (and perhaps brought to conclusion) the preeminence of San Francisco as the business and financial capital of the Far West." (Courtesy Bob DeLiso.)

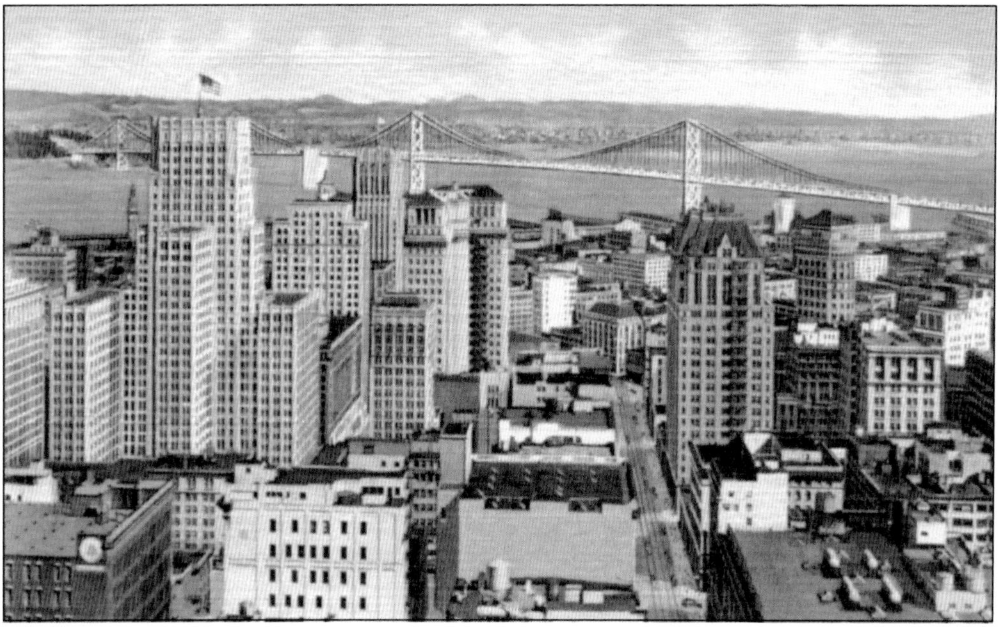

The 31-story Russ Building (with the flag), located at 235 Montgomery Street, was the tallest building on the West Coast until 1964. Randolph Delehanty describes it as a marvel of its day with 1,370 offices and every conceivable service. The first downtown building to accommodate the automobile with a 400-car garage built beneath its Gothic exterior, its E-shape with three wings to the west utilized natural light and ventilation. (Author's collection.)

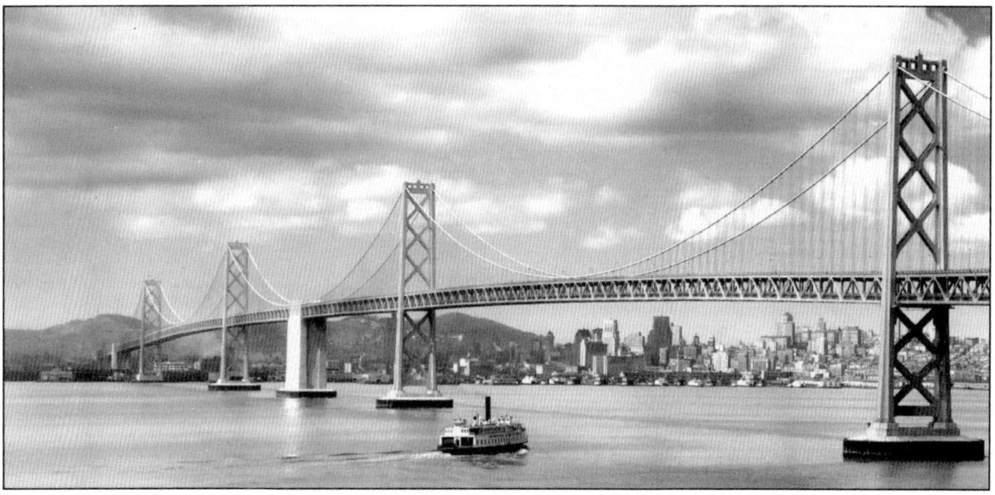

Completed in 1936, the San Francisco–Oakland Bay Bridge is the longest steel high-level bridge in the world. The Yerba Buena Tunnel has a diameter of 58 feet, which is the tallest bore in the world. Its foundations go deeper than any other bridge—to 242 feet, which is bigger than the largest of the Great Pyramids. Mount Davidson is visible to left of the bridge. (Courtesy Ron Davis.)

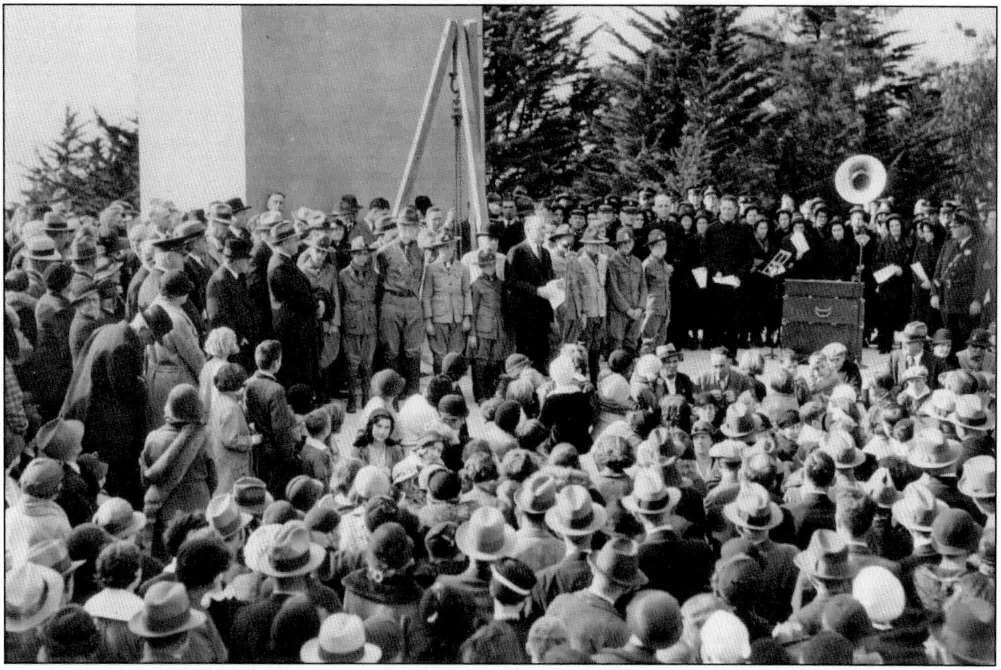

Mayor Angelo Rossi addressed the crowd at the cross dedication ceremony on March 4, 1934, after charging the San Francisco Boy Scouts with guardianship of the record box. J. O. Munson presented the sand and cement mixed by Native Sons and Daughters with water from the River Jordan. John McLaren, superintendent of parks, placed two rocks from Gethsemane in the vault and Henry Brunnier sealed the cornerstone. (Courtesy Glenn Gullmes.)

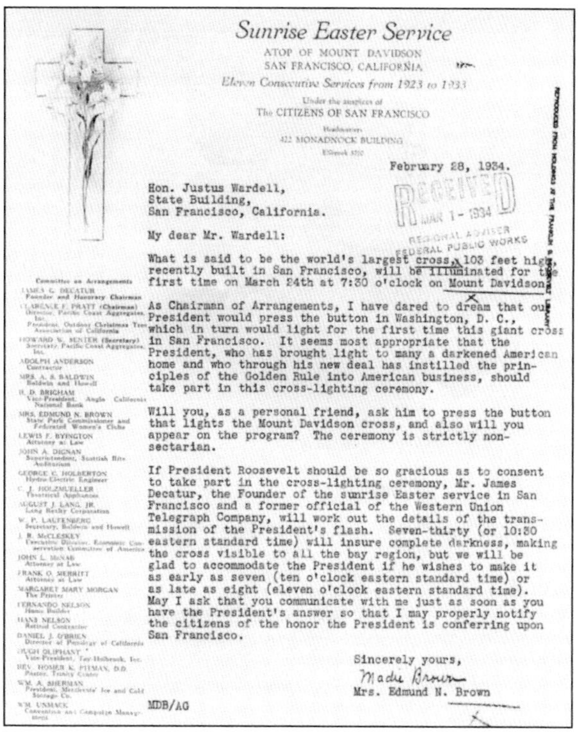

*Sunrise Easter Service*

ATOP OF MOUNT DAVIDSON
SAN FRANCISCO, CALIFORNIA

*Eleven Consecutive Services from 1923 to 1933*

Under the auspices of
The CITIZENS OF SAN FRANCISCO

Headquarters
422 MONADNOCK BUILDING

Committee on Arrangements

JAMES G. DECATUR, Founder and Honorary Chairman
CLARENCE F. PRATT (Chairman)
HOWARD W. SENTER (Secretary)
ADOLPH ANDERSON
MRS. A. S. BALDWIN
H. D. BRIGHAM
MRS. EDMUND N. BROWN
LEWIS F. BYINGTON
JOHN A. DIGNAN
GEORGE C. HOLBERTON
C. J. HOLZMUELLER
AUGUST J. LANG, JR.
W. P. LAUFENBERG
J. R. McCLESKEY
JOHN L. McNAB
FRANK O. MERRITT
MARGARET MARY MORGAN
FERNANDO NELSON
HANS NELSON
DANIEL J. O'BRIEN
HUGH OLIPHANT
REV. HOMER K. PITMAN, D.D.
WM. A. SHERMAN
WM. UNMACK

February 28, 1934.

RECEIVED MAR 1 - 1934 REGIONAL ADVISER FEDERAL PUBLIC WORKS

Hon. Justus Wardell,
State Building,
San Francisco, California.

My dear Mr. Wardell:

What is said to be the world's largest cross, 103 feet high, recently built in San Francisco, will be illuminated for the first time on March 24th at 7:30 o'clock on Mount Davidson.

As Chairman of Arrangements, I have dared to dream that our President would press the button in Washington, D. C., which in turn would light for the first time this giant cross in San Francisco. It seems most appropriate that the President, who has brought light to many a darkened American home and who through his new deal has instilled the principles of the Golden Rule into American business, should take part in this cross-lighting ceremony.

Will you, as a personal friend, ask him to press the button that lights the Mount Davidson cross, and also will you appear on the program? The ceremony is strictly non-sectarian.

If President Roosevelt should be so gracious as to consent to take part in the cross-lighting ceremony, Mr. James Decatur, the Founder of the sunrise Easter service in San Francisco and a former official of the Western Union Telegraph Company, will work out the details of the transmission of the President's flash. Seven-thirty (or 10:30 eastern standard time) will insure complete darkness, making the cross visible to all the bay region, but we will be glad to accommodate the President if he wishes to make it as early as seven (ten o'clock eastern standard time) or as late as eight (eleven o'clock eastern standard time). May I ask that you communicate with me just as soon as you have the President's answer so that I may properly notify the citizens of the honor the President is conferring upon San Francisco.

Sincerely yours,
Madie Brown
Mrs. Edmund N. Brown

MDB/AG

In this letter dated February 28, 1934, Madie Brown asked President Roosevelt to light the Mount Davidson Cross just before one of the most historic events of the decade. A coast-wide maritime strike, headquartered in San Francisco, writes Kevin Starr, "played out a powerful scenario of Left versus Right in Depression America. July erupted in fistfights, gunfire, and blood; and the National Guard marched into the city." (Author's collection.)

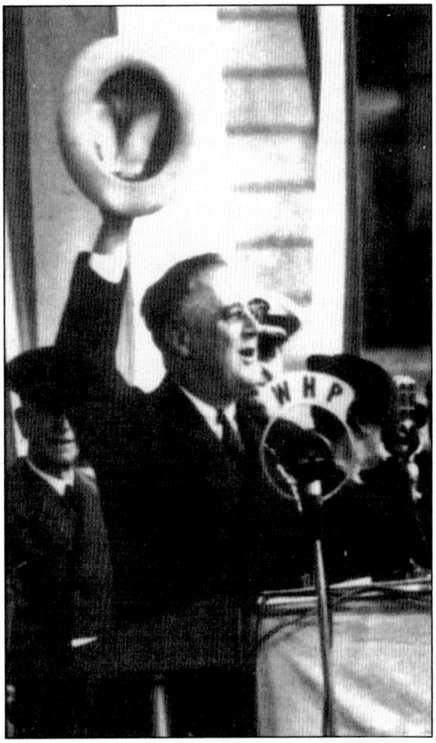


Elected in 1932, Roosevelt got his New Deal approved in the first 100 days that included Social Security, minimum wage, insured bank deposits, and the right to join a union. A week after Madie wrote to him, the International Longshoremen Union voted to strike on March 23, 1934—the day before the cross-lighting event. Roosevelt appointed a fact-finding commission and the union postponed their walkout just two days before the ceremony. (Author's collection.)

President Roosevelt pressed a gold telegraph key from the White House, sending electricity over the wires to turn on the twelve 1,000-watt floodlights (three each on four poles concealed among the trees) surrounding the Mount Davidson Cross on March 24, 1934 at 7:30 p.m. Three years later, Roosevelt would again press a telegraph key to officially open the Golden Gate Bridge. (Courtesy Ron Davis.)

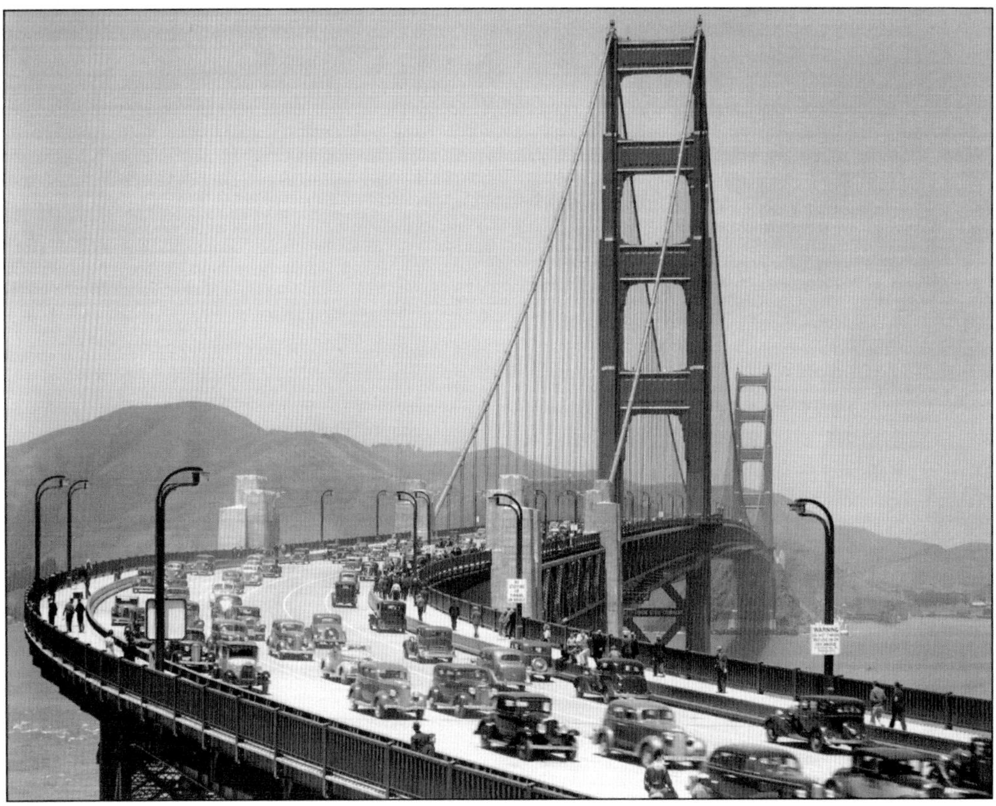

The program for the first sunrise service at the 103-foot-high cross on April 1, 1934, shows the Committee of Arrangements included Mrs. A. S. Baldwin; Madie Brown; Hans Nelson, retired builder of Westwood Park; August L. Lang, Balboa Terrace realtor; Fernando Nelson, builder of Mount Davidson Manor; and Margaret Mary Morgan, printer and the first woman elected to the San Francisco Board of Supervisors. Over 50,000 attended the event that year. (Author's collection.)

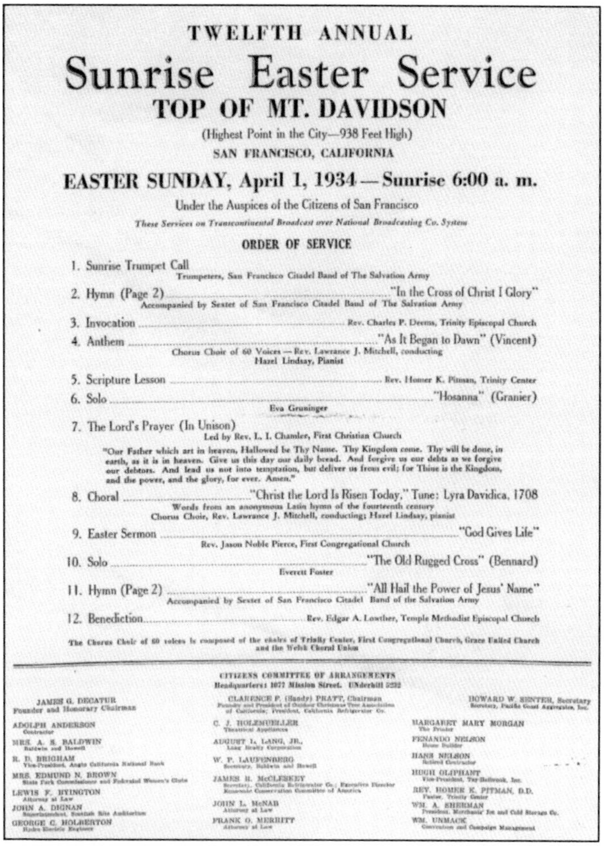

TWELFTH ANNUAL

Sunrise Easter Service

TOP OF MT. DAVIDSON

(Highest Point in the City—938 Feet High)

SAN FRANCISCO, CALIFORNIA

EASTER SUNDAY, April 1, 1934—Sunrise 6:00 a. m.

Under the Auspices of the Citizens of San Francisco

*These Services on Transcontinental Broadcast over National Broadcasting Co. System*

ORDER OF SERVICE

1. Sunrise Trumpet Call
   Trumpeters, San Francisco Citadel Band of The Salvation Army
2. Hymn (Page 2) ........ "In the Cross of Christ I Glory"
   Accompanied by Sextet of San Francisco Citadel Band of The Salvation Army
3. Invocation ........ Rev. Charles P. Deems, Trinity Episcopal Church
4. Anthem ........ "As It Began to Dawn" (Vincent)
   Chorus Choir of 60 Voices — Rev. Lawrance J. Mitchell, conducting
   Hazel Lindsay, Pianist
5. Scripture Lesson ........ Rev. Homer K. Pitman, Trinity Center
6. Solo ........ "Hosanna" (Granier)
   Eva Gruninger
7. The Lord's Prayer (In Unison)
   Led by Rev. L. I. Chamlee, First Christian Church
   "Our Father which art in heaven, Hallowed be Thy Name. Thy Kingdom come. Thy will be done, in earth, as it is in heaven. Give us this day our daily bread. And forgive us our debts as we forgive our debtors. And lead us not into temptation, but deliver us from evil; for Thine is the Kingdom, and the power, and the glory, for ever. Amen."
8. Choral ........ "Christ the Lord Is Risen Today," Tune: Lyra Davidica, 1708
   Words from an anonymous Latin hymn of the fourteenth century
   Chorus Choir, Rev. Lawrance J. Mitchell, conducting; Hazel Lindsay, pianist
9. Easter Sermon ........ "God Gives Life"
   Rev. Jason Noble Pierce, First Congregational Church
10. Solo ........ "The Old Rugged Cross" (Bennard)
   Everett Foster
11. Hymn (Page 2) ........ "All Hail the Power of Jesus' Name"
   Accompanied by Sextet of San Francisco Citadel Band of the Salvation Army
12. Benediction........ Rev. Edgar A. Lowther, Temple Methodist Episcopal Church

The Chorus Choir of 60 voices is composed of the choirs of Trinity Center, First Congregational Church, Grace United Church and the Welsh Choral Union

CITIZENS COMMITTEE OF ARRANGEMENTS
Headquarters: 1077 Mission Street. UNderhill 5232

JAMES G. DECATUR
Founder and Honorary Chairman

CLARENCE F. (Sandy) PRATT, Chairman
Founder and President of Outdoor Christmas Tree Association of California; President, California Refrigerator Co.

HOWARD W. SENTER, Secretary
Secretary, Pacific Coast Aggregates, Inc.

ADOLPH ANDERSON
Contractor

MRS. A. S. BALDWIN
Baldwin and Howell

R. D. BRIGHAM
Vice-President, Anglo California National Bank

MRS. EDMUND N. BROWN
State Park Commissioner and Federated Women's Clubs

LEWIS F. BYINGTON
Attorney at Law

JOHN A. DIGNAN
Superintendent, Scottish Rite Auditorium

GEORGE C. HOLBERTON
Hydro Electric Engineer

C. J. HOLZMUELLER
Theatrical Appliances

AUGUST L. LANG, JR.,
Lang Realty Corporation

W. P. LAUFENBERG
Secretary, Baldwin and Howell

JAMES R. McCLESKEY

JOHN L. McNAB
Attorney at Law

FRANK O. MERRITT
Attorney at Law

MARGARET MARY MORGAN
The Printer

FENANDO NELSON
Home Builder

HANS NELSON
Retired Contractor

HUGH OLIPHANT

REV. HOMER K. PITMAN, D.D.
Pastor, Trinity Center

WM. A. SHERMAN

WM. UNMACK
Convention and Campaign Management

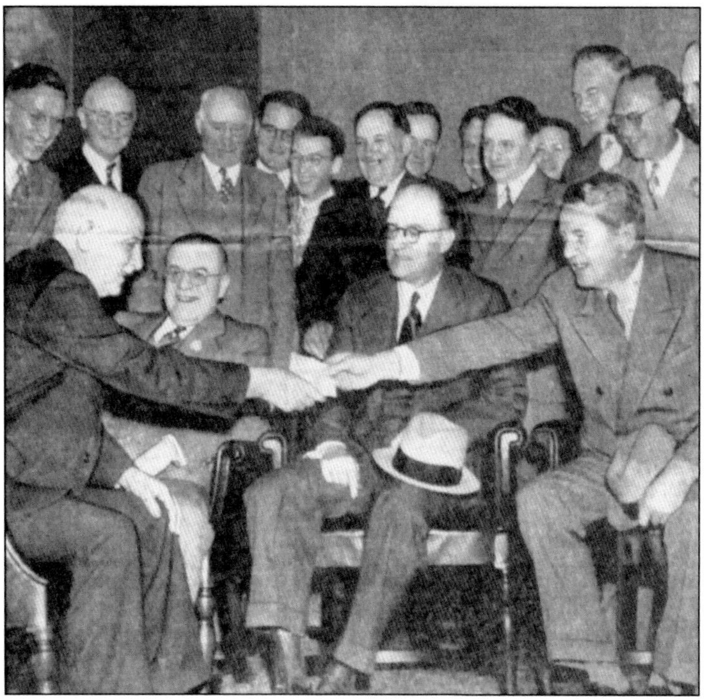

The West of Twin Peaks Central Council was organized in 1936 to bring about united action among local home, civic, and improvement organizations. Opposed to the proliferation of gas stations in the residential area, John S. Curran told Mayor Rossi in straightforward language that continued efforts to rezone the district were sources of constant irritation and would ultimately mean breakup of the district and destruction of its beauty. (Courtesy MPIC.)

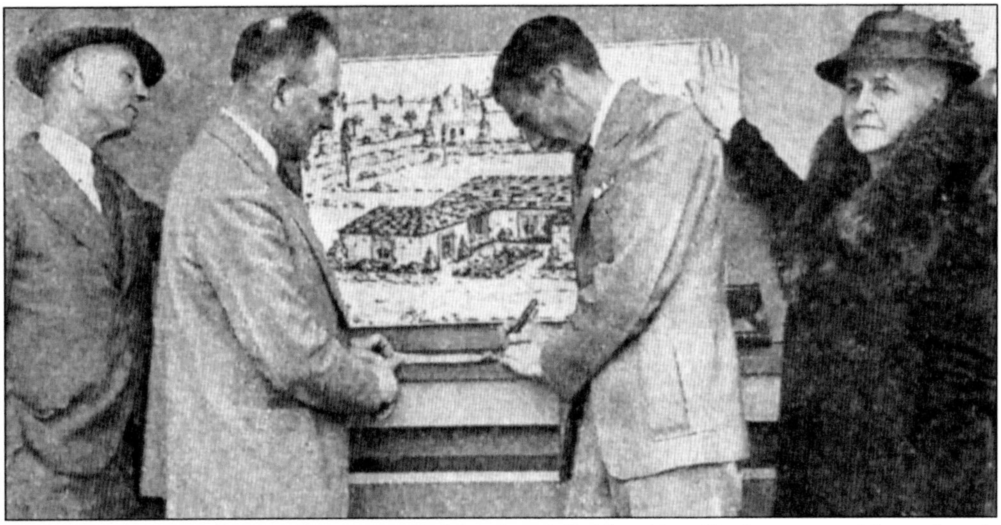

The completion of the San Francisco–Oakland and Golden Gate Bridges was celebrated with the Golden Gate International Exposition on Treasure Island. Emma, the wife of developer A. S. Baldwin, who donated the crest of Mount Davidson, is in front of a model home built for the exposition in this 1939 photograph. At the time of his death in 1936, George Kelham was the exposition's chairman of the architectural committee. (Courtesy California Association of REALTORS®.)

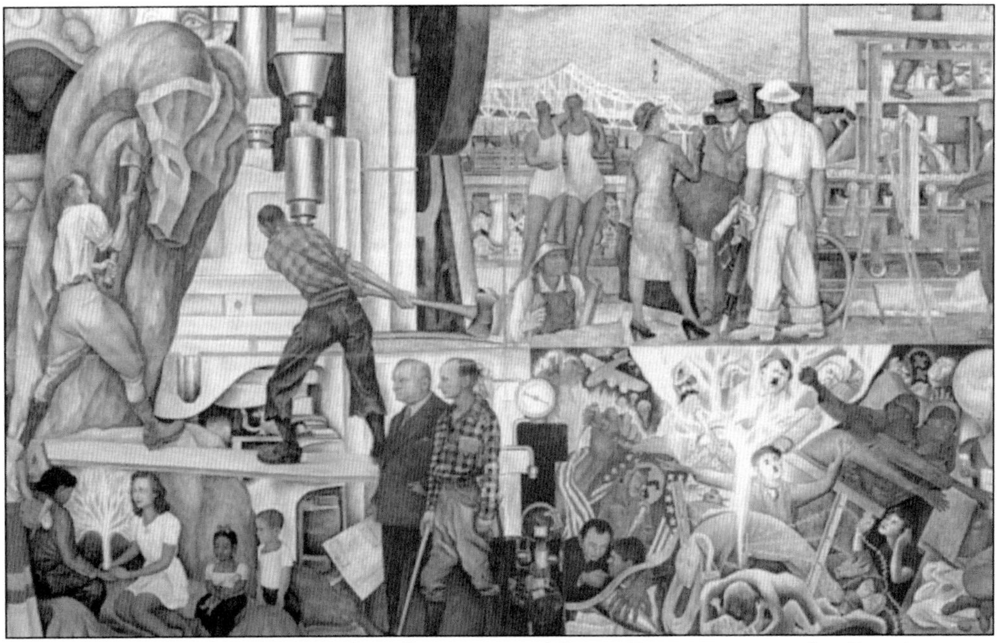

Vice chairman of fine arts Timothy Pflueger invited Diego Rivera to create this *Pan American Unity* mural at the exposition for the new junior college library. His design was never built, and the mural went into storage. In 1961, Timothy's brother Milton Pflueger convinced the college to display the mural in the campus theater. The college mascot, *Big Horn Mountain Redwood Ram*, by Dudley Carter, is pictured in the mural. (Author's collection.)

Ingleside Terraces teenager Esperanza "Espie" Lupe Puente worked at the 1939 exhibition's Mexican Arts and Crafts Pavilion. Espie came from Mexico with her family in 1923 when her father became manager of the National Railways of Mexico's San Francisco office. In 1939, a household of mostly boys moved in by the Puentes, singing from a panel truck as Bill Brown played "Beer Barrel Polka" on their piano. (Courtesy Margie Whitnah.)

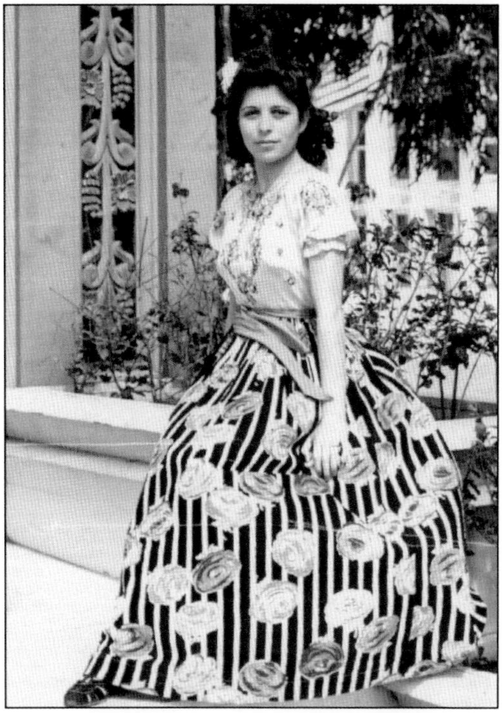

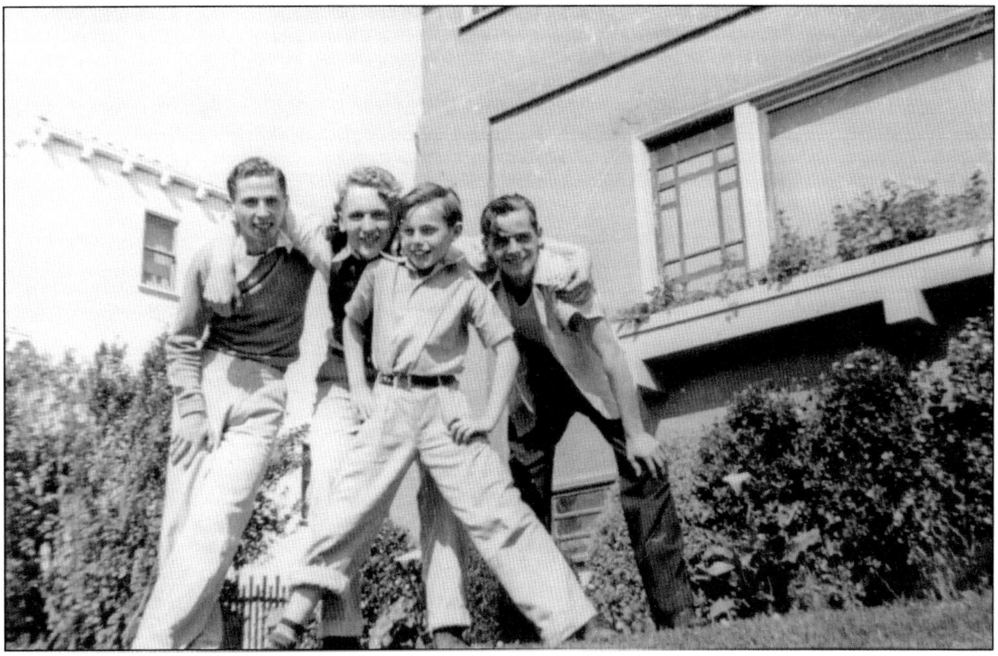

During those fun times, the Brown-Hancock boys of 245 Moncada Way liked showing off for the five Puente sisters living across the street. During wartime, Bill Brown's mother was honored for having three Army Air Force pilot sons, which was the most of any American family at one time during World War II. Two of those brothers, Dick Brown (left) and Victor Hancock (right), are pictured here with friends Paul (second to the left) and Jack Hancock (second to right). (Courtesy Margie Brown Whitnah.)

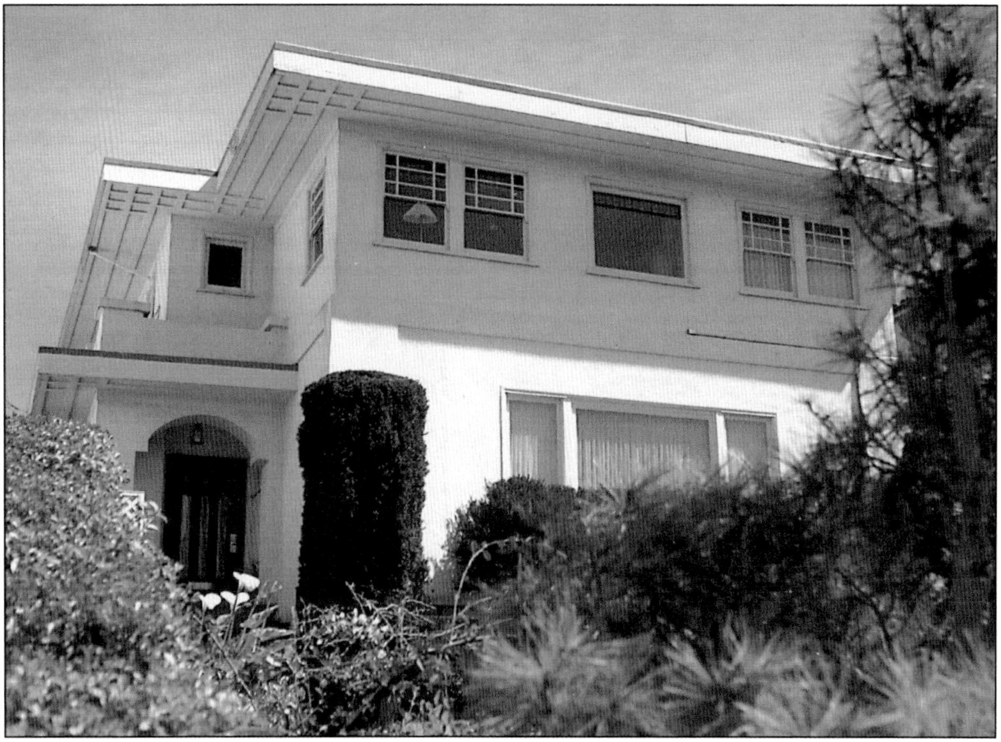

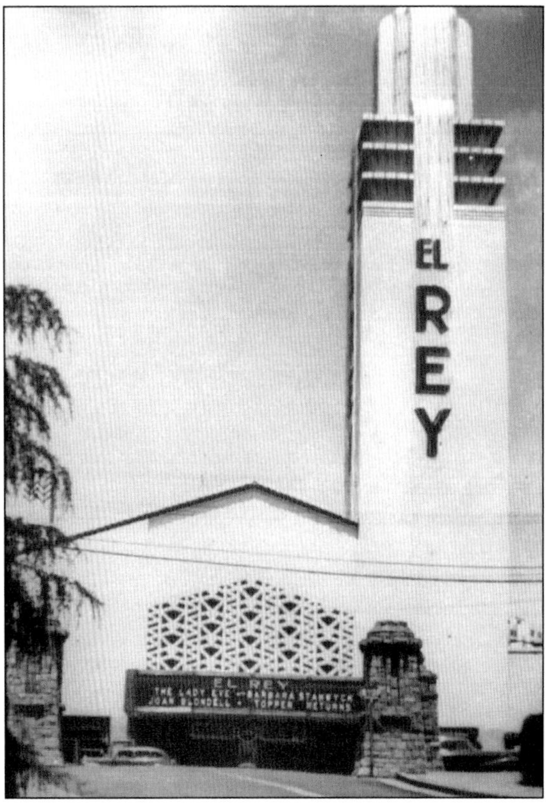


The Puentes lived at 262 Moncada Way. Father Felipe Puente was Pancho Villa's transportation general during the Mexican Revolution. In 1915, in Chihuahua, Mexico, Felipe met and married Tomasita Aquirre, the daughter of a cattle-ranching family whose haciendas were right across the road from Pancho Villa's home, which is now a museum. (Courtesy Margie Brown Whitnah.)

A site for a nickelodeon was reserved in Ingleside Terrace and became the El Rey Theatre, designed by Timothy Pflueger. With seating for 1,831 people, it opened in 1931, showing *The Smiling Lieutenant*, starring Maurice Chevalier. Espie Puente and her siblings spent many Saturday and Sunday afternoons watching movies there. Espie saved a tiny movie card from the theater with Rudolph Valentino's photograph on it for her entire life. (Courtesy J. E. Tillmany.)

# *Five*

# WORLD WAR II POPULATION GROWTH

## LIVING THE AMERICAN DREAM

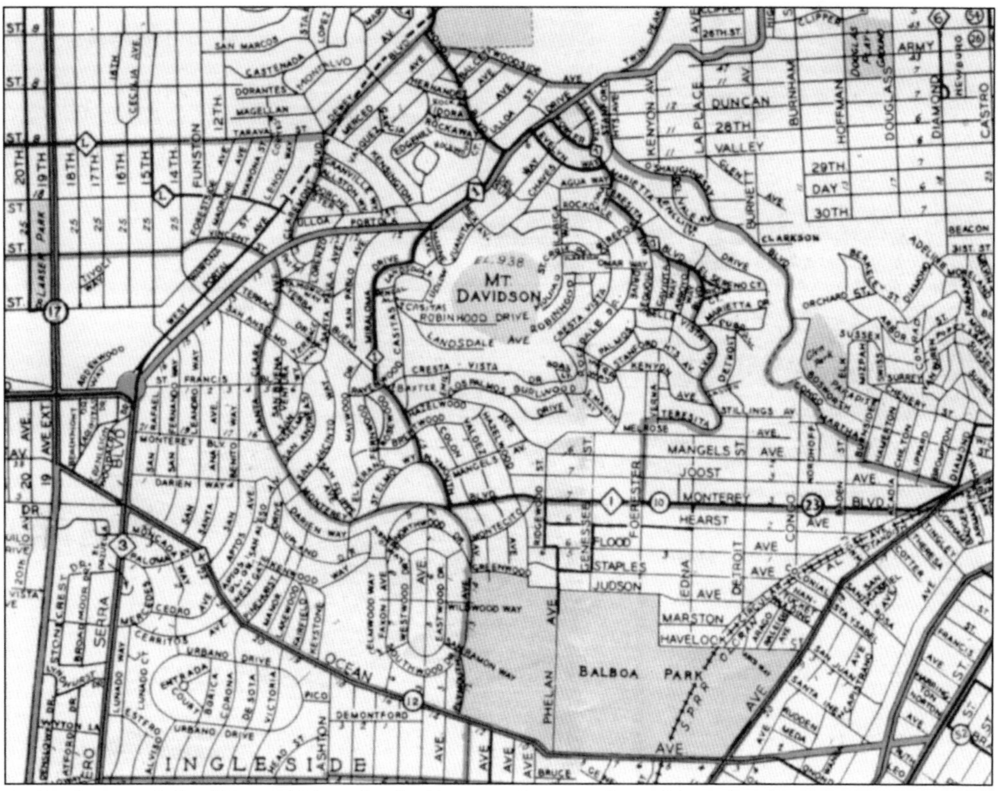


A 1940 map of the West of Twin Peaks District shows a dotted line for the new major arterial roadway, O'Shaughnessy Boulevard, under construction and named for the city's famous engineer. This map also depicts the 10 streetcar line on Monterey Boulevard before it was discontinued in 1942. At Balboa Park, a yet-to-be-completed San Francisco junior college has not made its mark. (Courtesy Ken and Kathy Hoegger.)

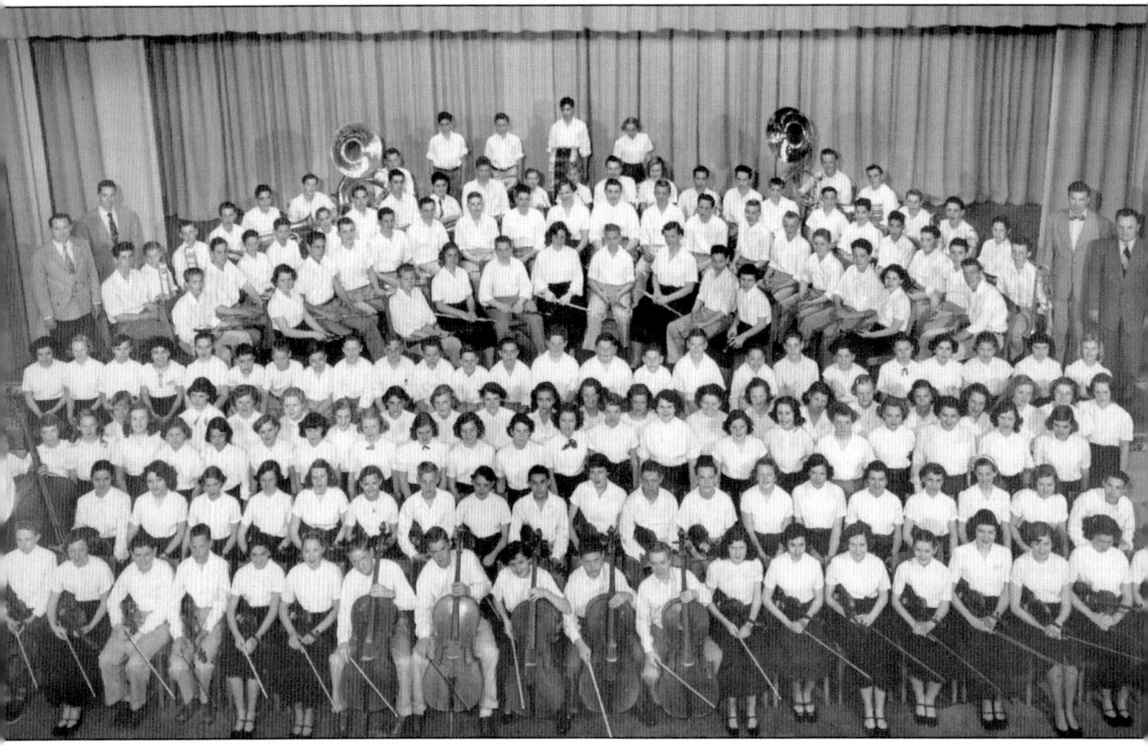

Historian Oscar Lewis wrote, "World War II had as great an impact on the city's economy as any event since the Gold Rush almost a century earlier." More than 1.5 million military personnel and 23 million tons of war supplies passed through the Golden Gate during the war. Already densely populated San Francisco was filled beyond capacity as the number of factories increased by a third and doubled the size of the industrial workforce. With the baby boom that followed, San Francisco's population peaked in 1950 and West of Twin Peaks grew—as illustrated by the size of the Aptos Middle School Orchestra and Band in 1952. (Courtesy Jeanne Davis MacKenzie.)

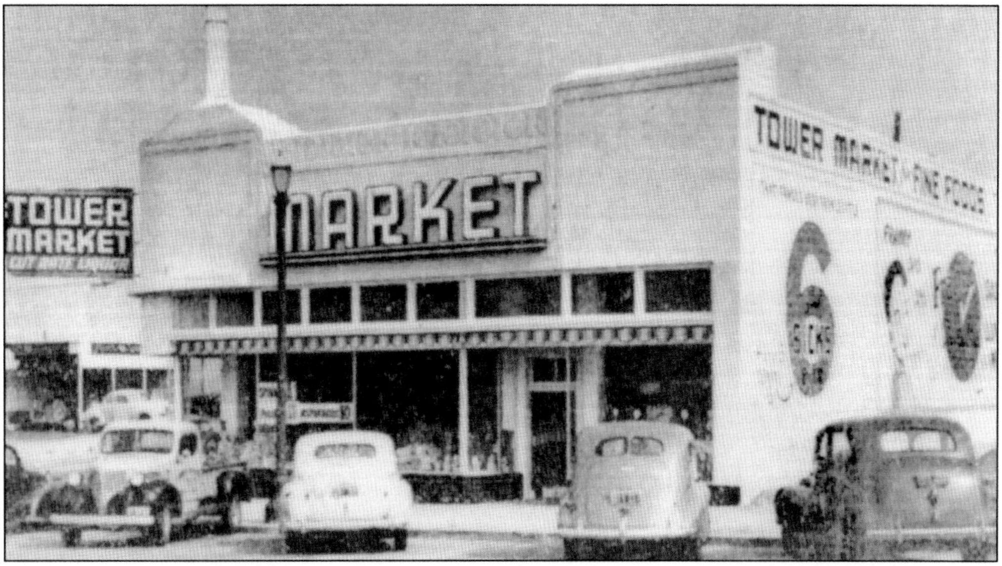

Mark Pommon saved up to build his 2,000-square-foot Tower Market on Portola Drive and opened it in 1942 despite the challenges of government-issued ration books during World War II. As Mark apologized to each customer for the lack of certain items, he was faced with filling out hundreds of their ration stamps to present to wholesalers in order to replenish his stock. (Author's collection.)

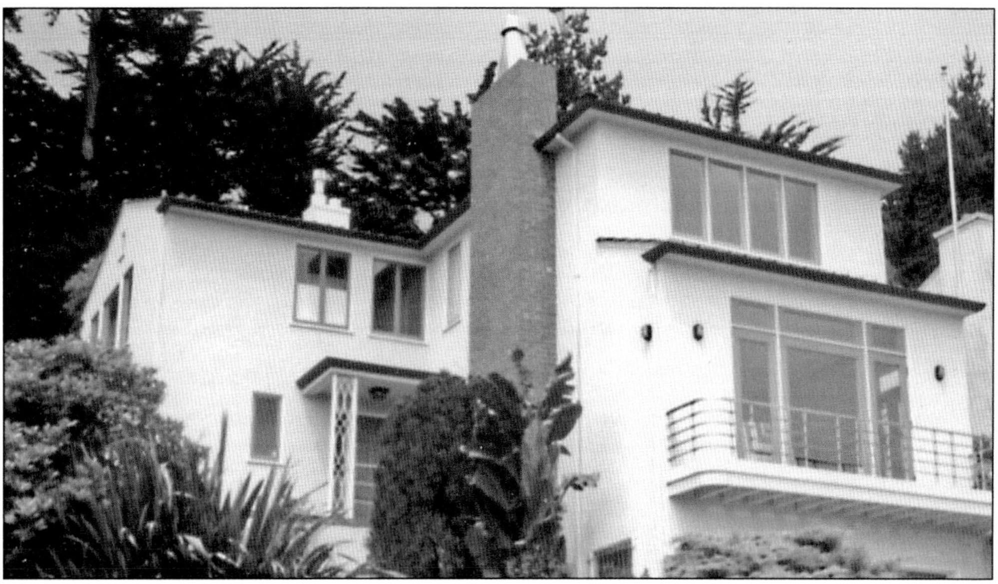
Baldwin and Howell built the KGO Radio "dream house" in Sherwood Forest at One Cresta Vista Drive for the well-known Edwards family radio show in 1941. While the fictional family discussed their design and wishes on the air the home was actually being built. Thousands toured the residence every Sunday. It was last open to the public on the day of Pearl Harbor's bombing. (Author's collection.)

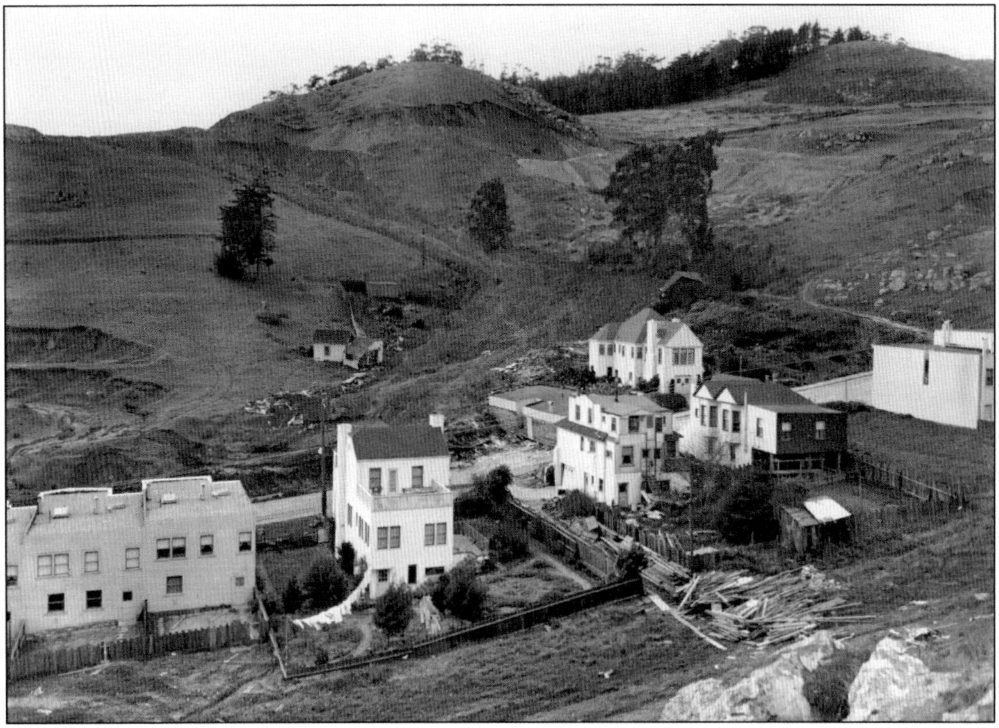

Madie Brown managed to keep the subdivider's axe from reaching the top of Mount Davidson, but the next major obstacle to its development came from the mountain itself. On February 6, 1942, after a rainy winter when construction crews busily cut new roads for more homes to be built on its southeastern slope, the entire hillside gave way and crashed down on the older homes below. (Courtesy private collection.)

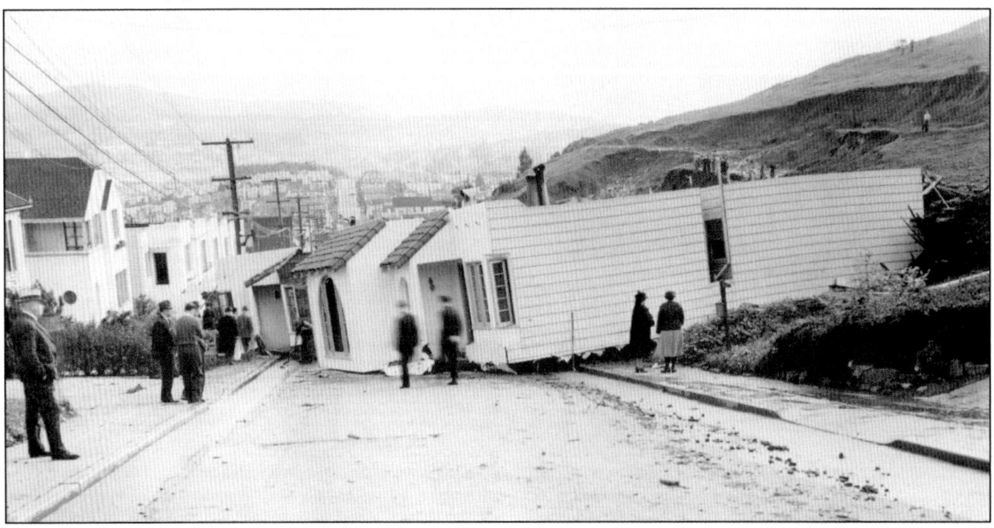

A river of mud a half-mile-long and 10 to 20 feet deep buried the 700 block of Foerster Street, trapping residents in their homes and killing Mrs. Dora Krammer. Nine subdivisions had been approved for building in Miraloma Park by 1931, but the Depression slowed down their completion. When the government stopped all home building in 1942, Meyer Brothers was dissolved. (Courtesy Kathy Rawlins.)

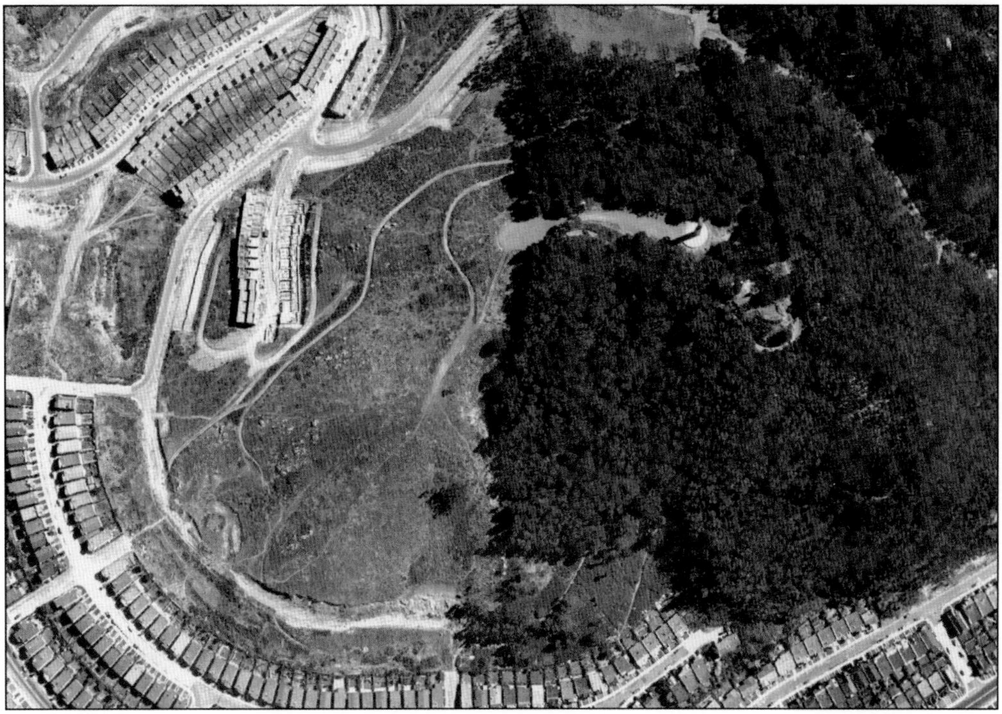

This 1948 aerial view of Mount Davidson Park shows that it is now surrounded by homes. To save the rest of the eastern slope named Inspiration Point by Mayor Rolph, former mayor Rossi convinced the City of San Francisco to purchase the seven-acre area in 1941. Five more acres on the southwest side of Mount Davidson were purchased in 1950, increasing the park to its present size of 38 acres. (Courtesy private collection.)

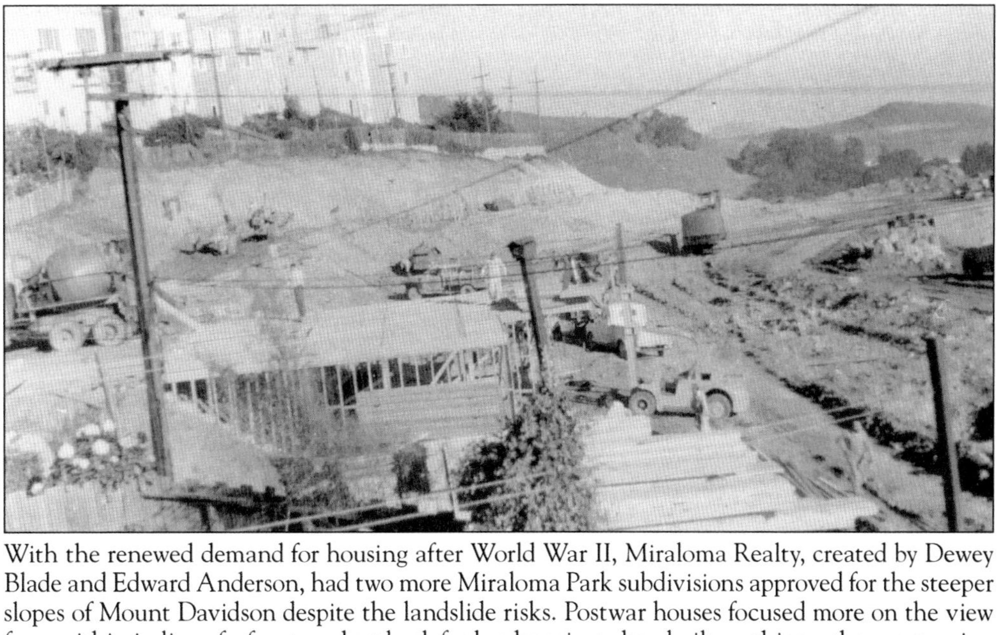

With the renewed demand for housing after World War II, Miraloma Realty, created by Dewey Blade and Edward Anderson, had two more Miraloma Park subdivisions approved for the steeper slopes of Mount Davidson despite the landslide risks. Postwar houses focused more on the view from within in lieu of a front yard set back for landscaping when built on this southern extension of Marietta Drive below Teresita Boulevard as pictured in 1958. (Courtesy Virginia Larribeau.)

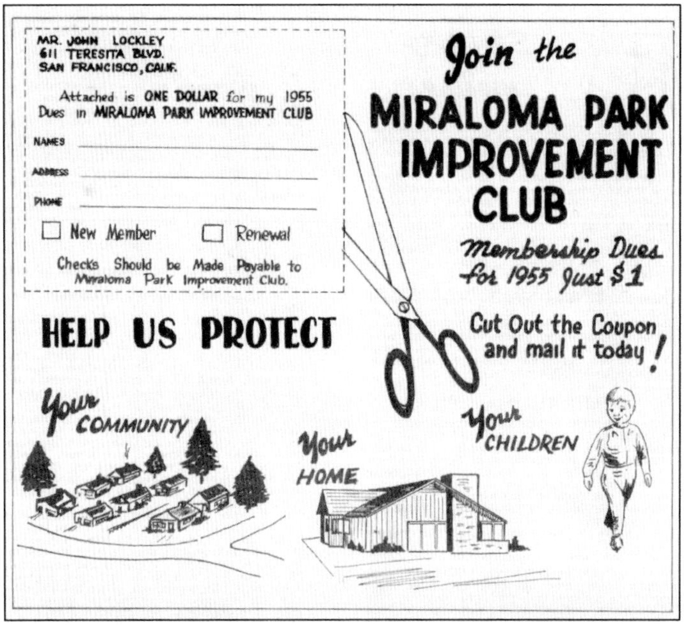


In 1940, Meyer Brothers built a clubhouse for Miraloma Park residents at Del Vale Avenue off O'Shaughnessy Boulevard on land leased from the San Francisco Water Department. The department of public works graded the parking lot in exchange for permission to store equipment during the construction of O'Shaughnessy Boulevard. By July 1946, the combined Miraloma Park Garden and Improvement Clubs had a membership of 1,000, an unequaled record in San Francisco. (Courtesy MPIC.)

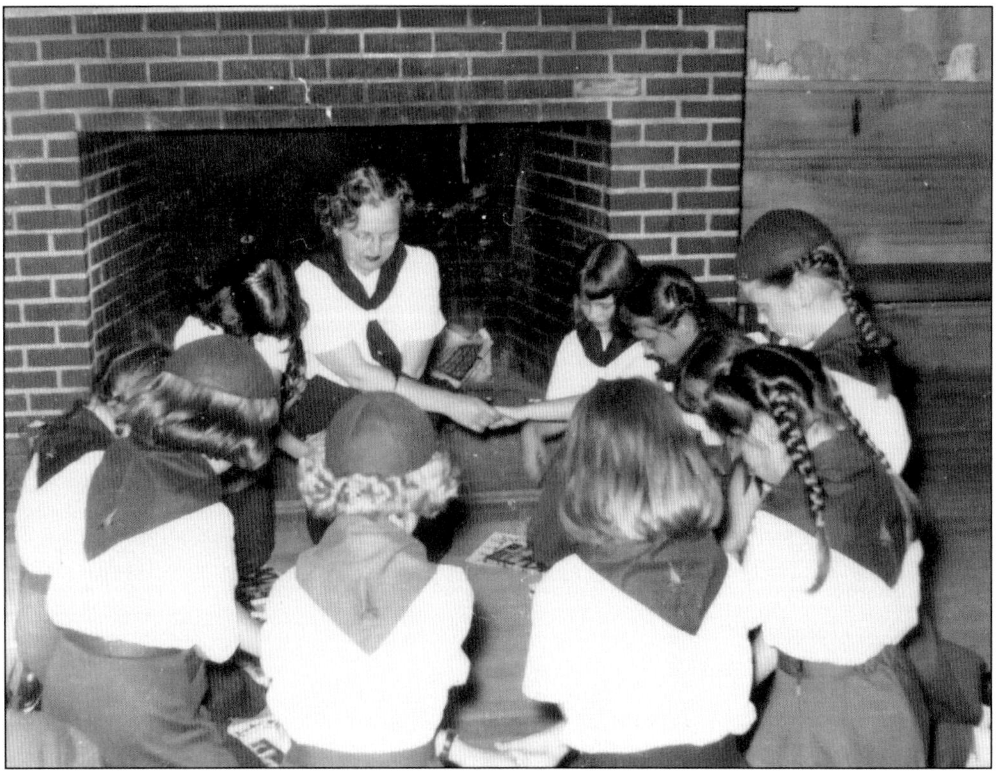

The clubhouse provided a place for residents to meet and work together to maintain the neighborhood character of Miraloma Park, the vitality of the neighboring commercial areas, and the open space in Mount Davidson Park. Funds to maintain the building as a community center for the Camp Fires Girls, led here by Bertha Jones in 1954, and other groups were raised voluntarily without the benefit of mandatory homeowner association dues. (Courtesy Bertha Jones.)

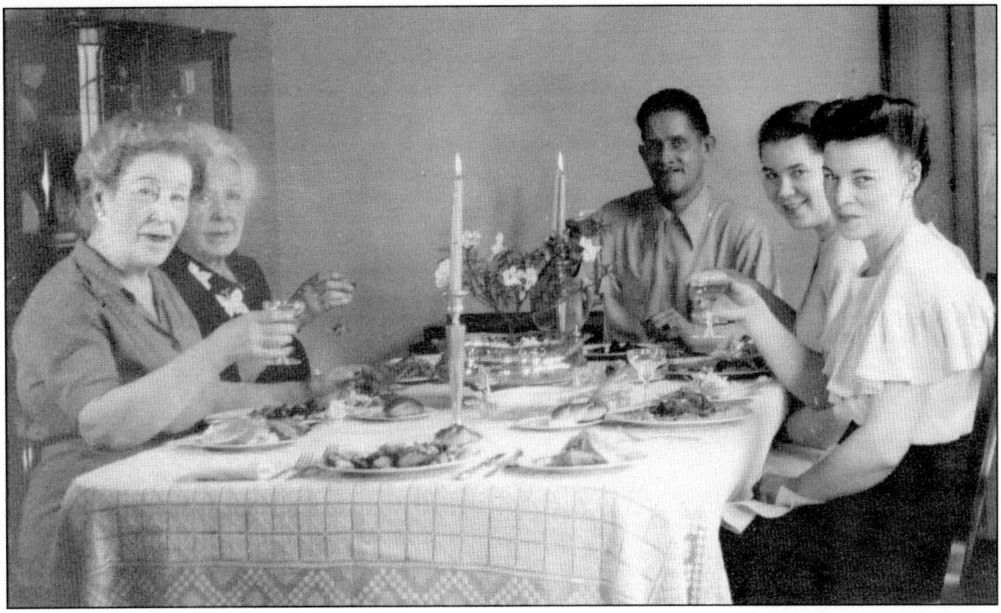

After her grandfather Weir came to San Francisco with Leland Stanford, Sally Shank Grusser lived on The Heights formerly owned by Stanford in Miraloma Park. Thirty-four years after surviving the 1906 earthquake together, Sally's mother said, "Buy this house—it has a dining room in it." Sally's mother, Elizabeth Fotheringham, aunt Charlotte, husband Gunnar Grusser, niece Elizabeth Mettling, and sister Charlotte are pictured dining in that home in 1945. (Courtesy Elizabeth Mettling.)

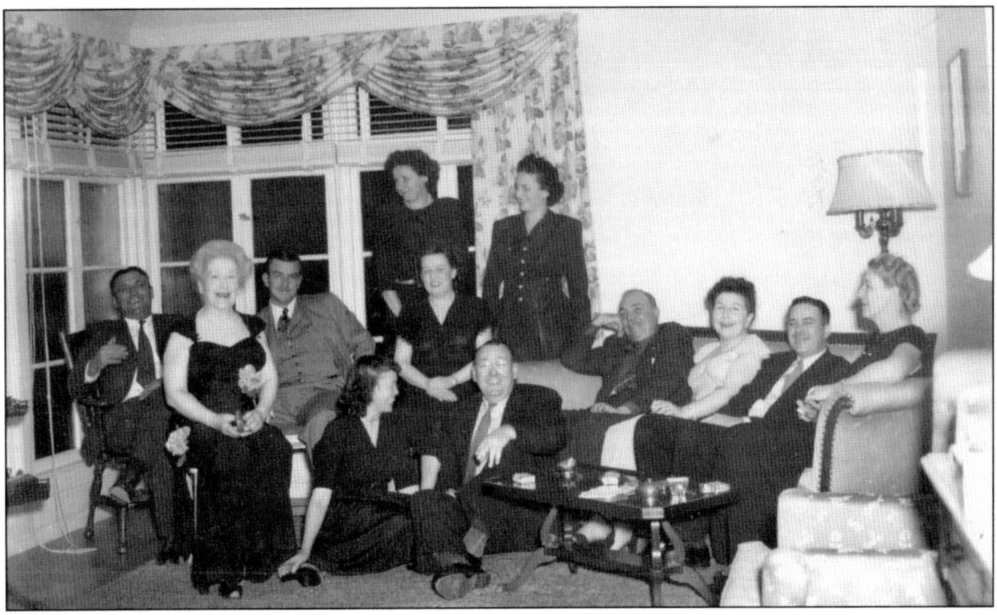

Sally and Gunnar entertain friends and neighbors (Charles and Francis DeRosier) after Gunnar returned from World War II service at New Caledonia. Charles Friscia (on the floor) was maître d' at DiMaggio's Restaurant and loved to tell how Joe brought his wife Marilyn Monroe over for dinner, stating, "She was absolutely charming. Wearing a beautiful white dress, she was just as pretty in life as on the screen." (Courtesy Elizabeth Mettling.)

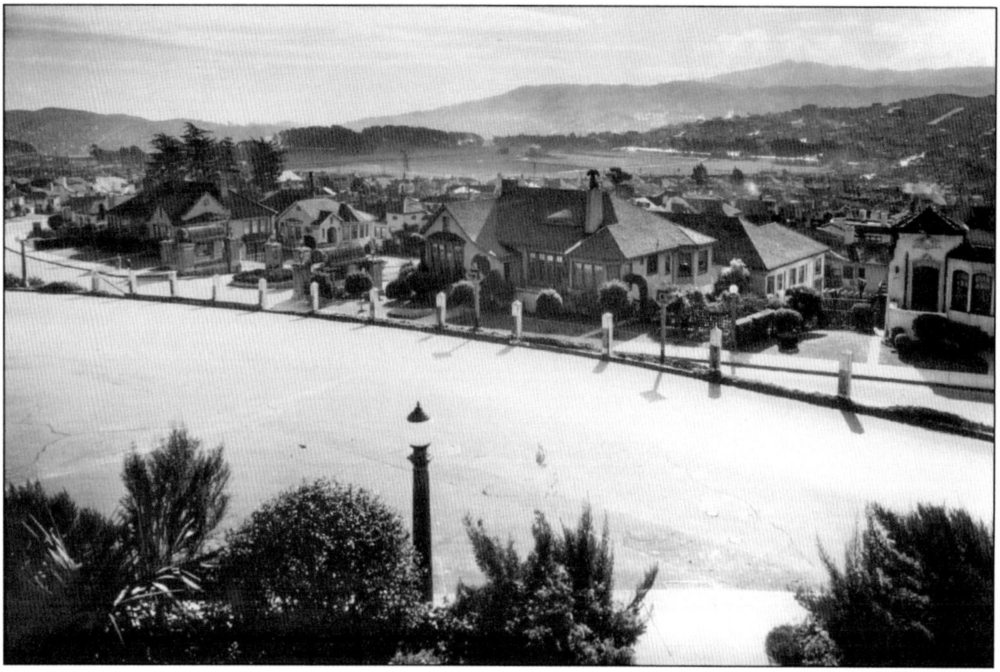

Westwood Park is pictured here from Monterey Boulevard at Yerba Buena Avenue. After World War II, homes in this area were being advertised for sale by Nelson Brothers for $8,950. The advertisement declared, "Buy now or pay more! The enormous demand for building materials already being ordered for the reconstruction of Japan's destroyed cities is bound to result in advanced prices. It will be impossible to duplicate the values we are now offering." (Courtesy Ken Hoegger.)

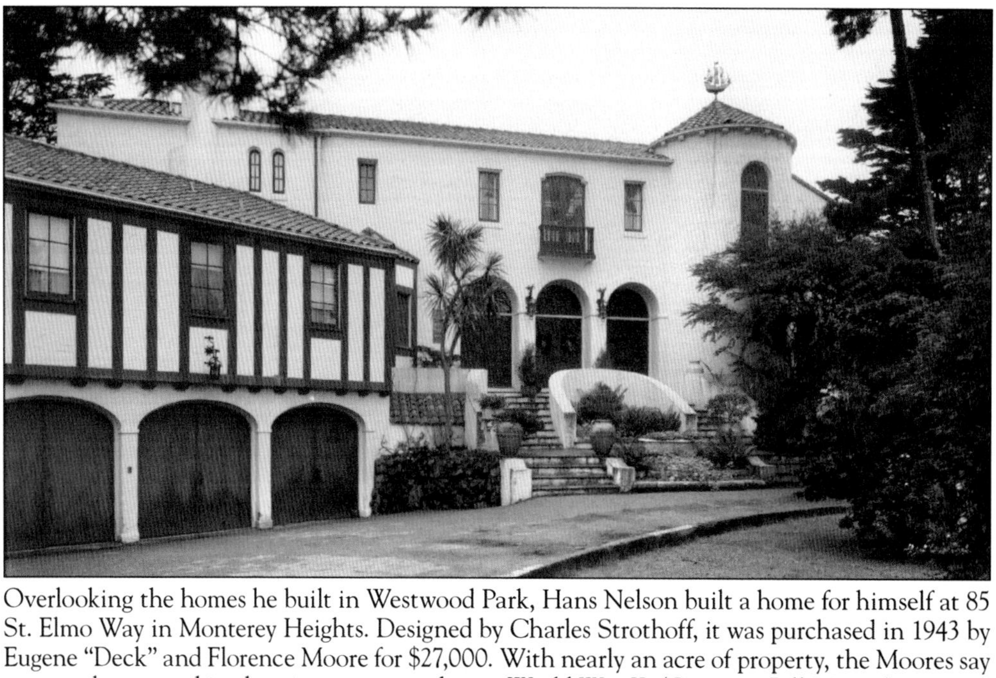

Overlooking the homes he built in Westwood Park, Hans Nelson built a home for himself at 85 St. Elmo Way in Monterey Heights. Designed by Charles Strothoff, it was purchased in 1943 by Eugene "Deck" and Florence Moore for $27,000. With nearly an acre of property, the Moores say no one else wanted it when it was vacant during World War II. (Courtesy Bill Moore.)

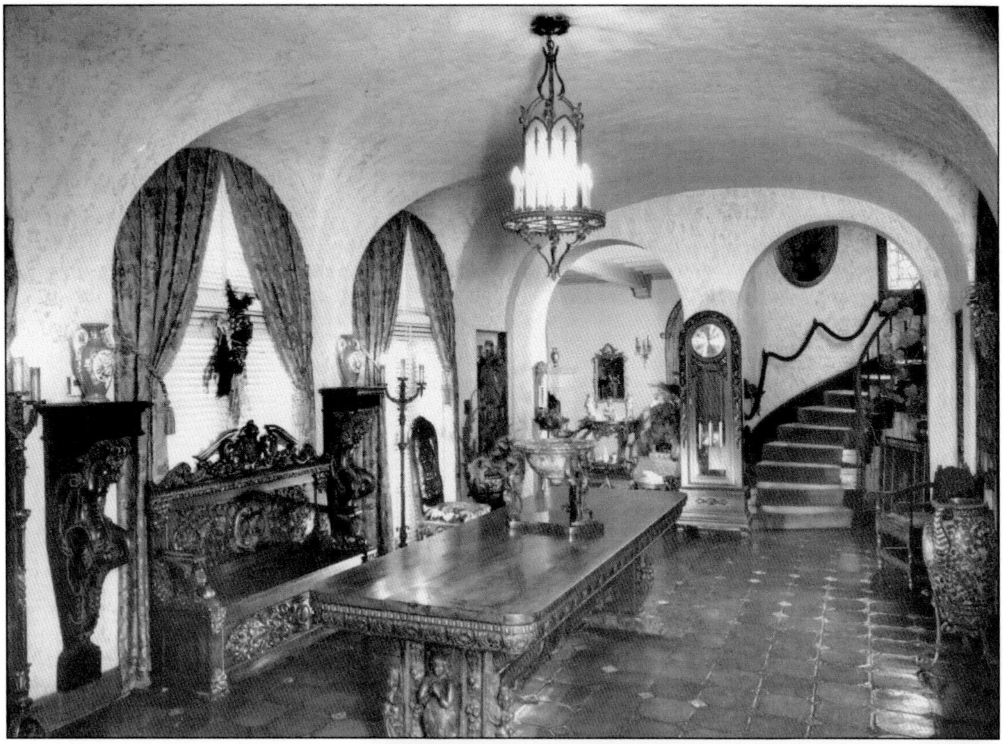

The entrance hall to 85 St. Elmo Way was decorated with a table from the Hearst Castle in 1943. Construction in Monterey Heights halted during the Depression until 1938 when split-level houses with garages were added through 1942. Located uphill from St. Francis Wood, it was described as having streets that swirl around a small peak and big houses with big dogs and big cars out front. (Courtesy Bill Moore.)

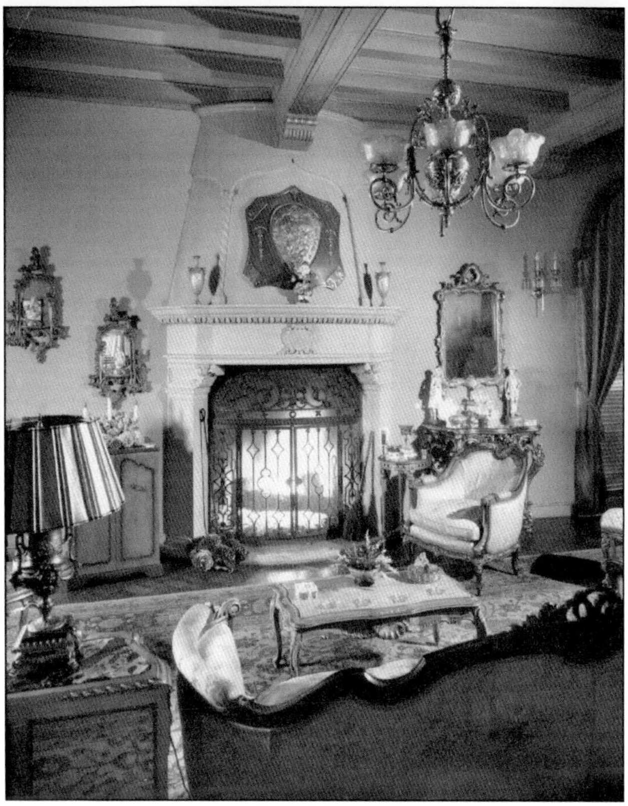

This is an interior view of the Moore's living room. The handsome Monterey Heights neighborhood was colorfully noted for having double-occupancy car shelters at a time when most San Francisco homes had room for just one automobile and front windows showing a striking preference for flouncy satin draperies. (Courtesy Bill Moore.)

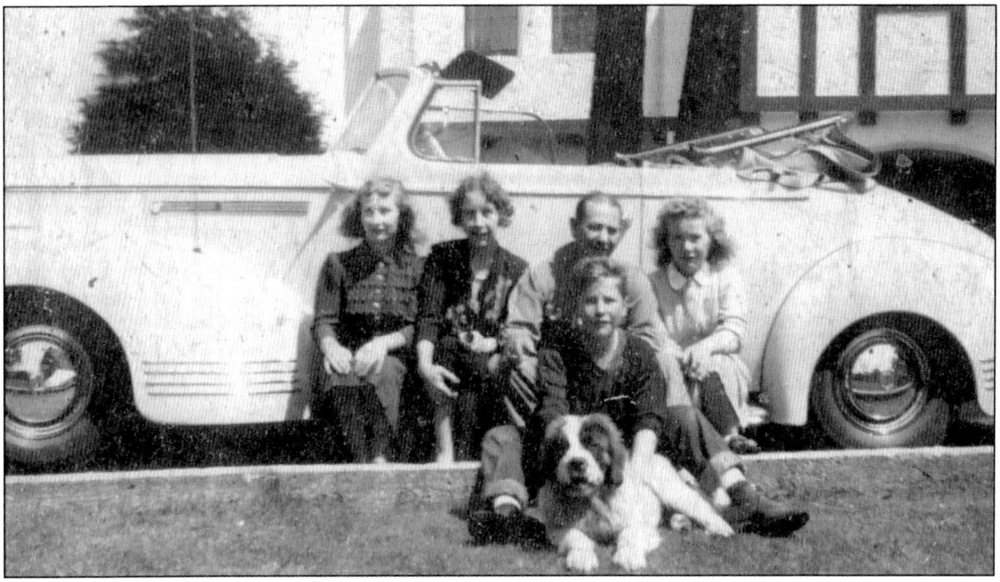

Evelyn, Florence, Deck, and Patsy Moore sit in front of their 1942 Packard, parked at their home on 85 St. Elmo Way in 1944. Bobby Moore is in front with the family's soon-to-be big Saint Bernard puppy, Duke. (Courtesy Bill Moore.)

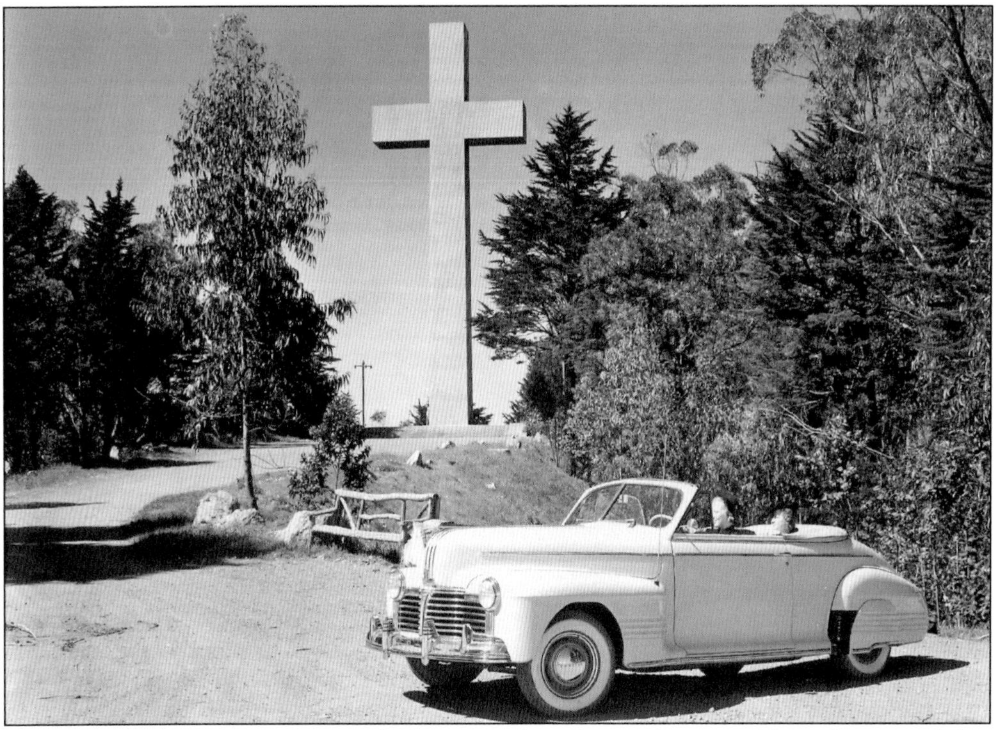

Attendance at the sunrise event peaked in 1941 when the *San Francisco Chronicle* reported that 75,000 "men, women, and children toiled up the slopes of the mountain in the early dawn to participate in this annual service." A few years later, the Mount Davidson Cross is the backdrop for the dawn of California's postwar car fervor in this photograph of two women enjoying the sun in their new chrome-covered deluxe Pontiac convertible. (Courtesy private collection.)

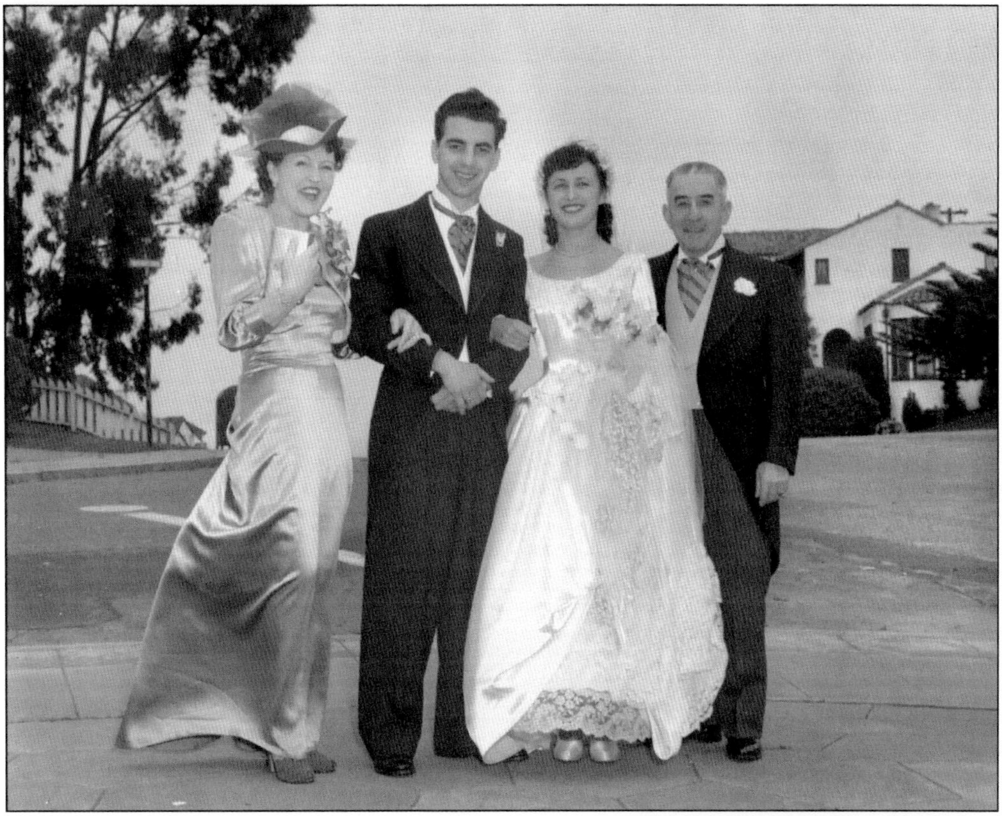

In 1948, Jack and Elvira Dettner Granfield celebrate the marriage of their daughter Elvira "Cis" to Joseph R. Bisho Jr. in front of their Mount Davidson Manor home on Monterey Boulevard on Northgate Drive. Joe Bisho served in the 86th Blackhawk Infantry Division in Germany and in the Battle of the Bulge as a scout for the U.S. Army, receiving two purple hearts and two bronze stars. (Courtesy Dave Bisho.)

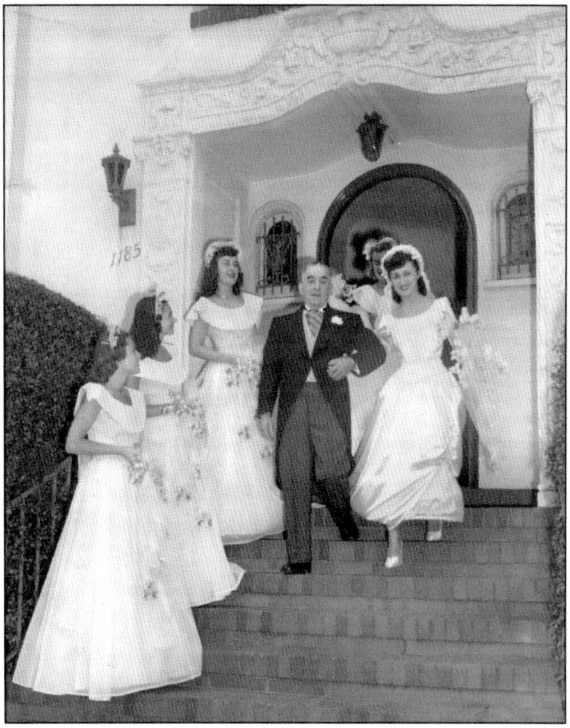

This is Cis with her dad and bridesmaids. Her husband, Joe, got out of the army in 1946 when he was 21, then went back for more service in Korea but was talked out of it by the recruiting officer. From the historic Hobart Building, their son Dave Bisho manages J. R. Bisho Company, Incorporated, the heavy-equipment export business started by his father in 1955. (Courtesy Dave Bisho.)

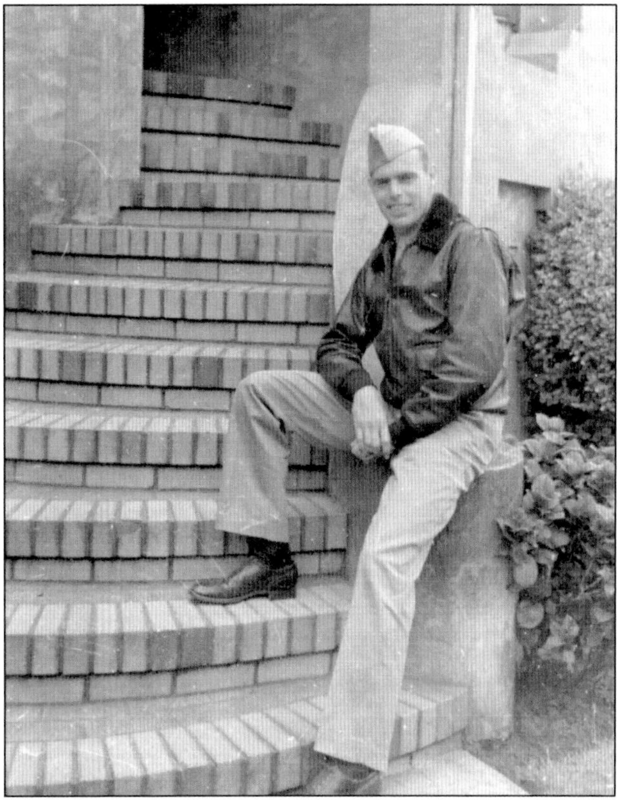

Navy Air Cadet William O'Neill sits on the attractive winding stairway entrance of his family's home in Mount Davidson Manor in September 1942. The pre–World War II development of detached single-family homes by Fernando Nelson for middle-class families was described in a real estate article as "a conservative well manicured neighborhood." (Courtesy Tom O'Neill.)

U.S. Air Corp 2nd Lt. Ray Gallagher and U.S. Navy Lt. J. G. John O'Neill stand next to the O'Neill home at 826 Darien Way in 1942. The Gallaghers lived next door on this curvilinear street of tile-roofed view homes that distinguish this San Francisco neighborhood. (Courtesy Tom O'Neill.)

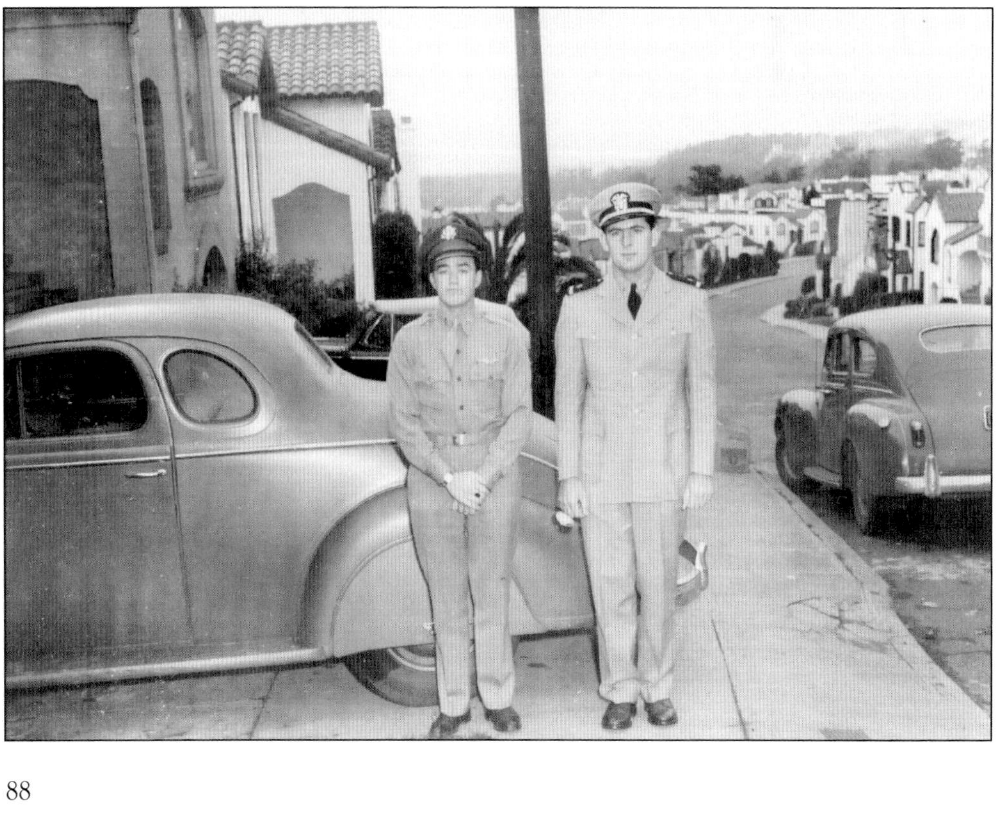

St. Brendan's Church was built in 1929 on Laguna Honda Boulevard at the foot of Mount Davidson. Edward Eames designed the California Mission-style "gem of Miraloma" for a final cost of $40,000. With the postwar boom to the economy and the population west of Twin Peaks growing, the grammar school was added in 1947. Under a foggy shroud, a 1938 Chrysler awaits the wartime newlyweds. (Courtesy Margie Brown Whitnah.)

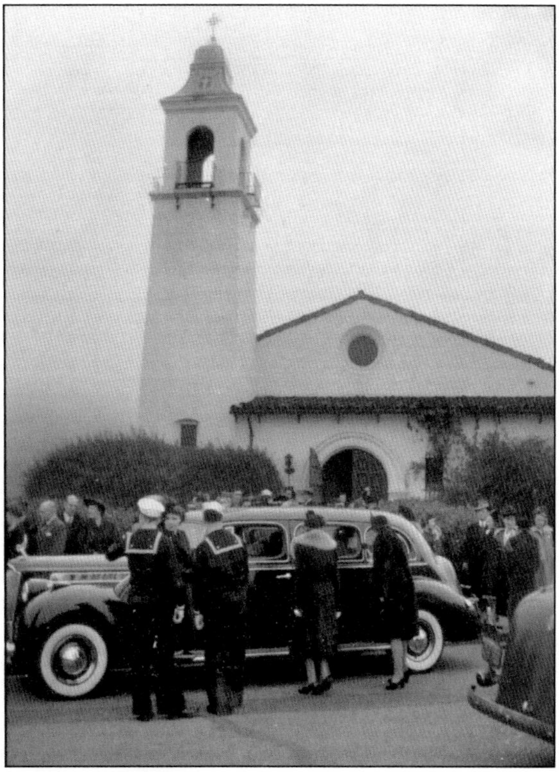

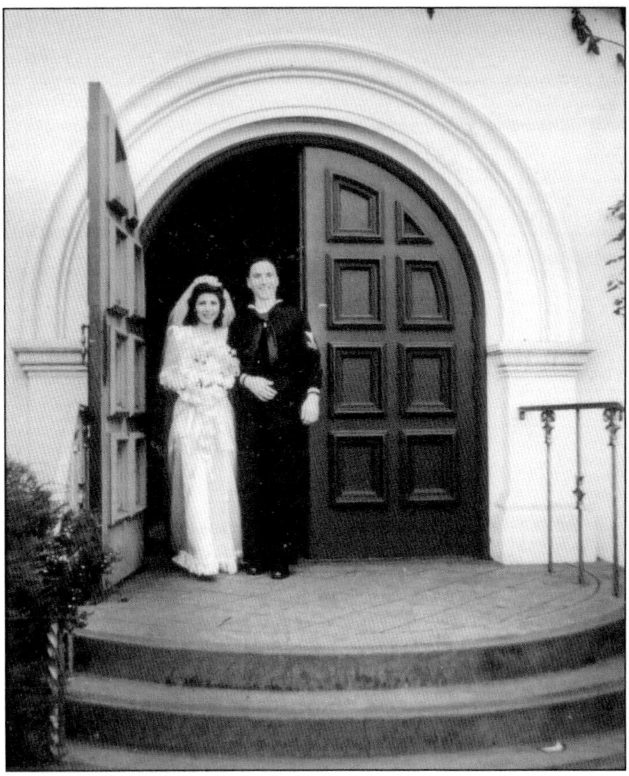

Falling in love at first sight when he moved in across the street from her in Ingleside Terraces, William "Bill" Brown married Esperanza "Espie" Puente at St. Brendan's on December 13, 1942. They settled west of Twin Peaks to provide a home for their two children, Steve and Margie, in Mount Davidson Manor. (Courtesy Margie Brown Whitnah.)

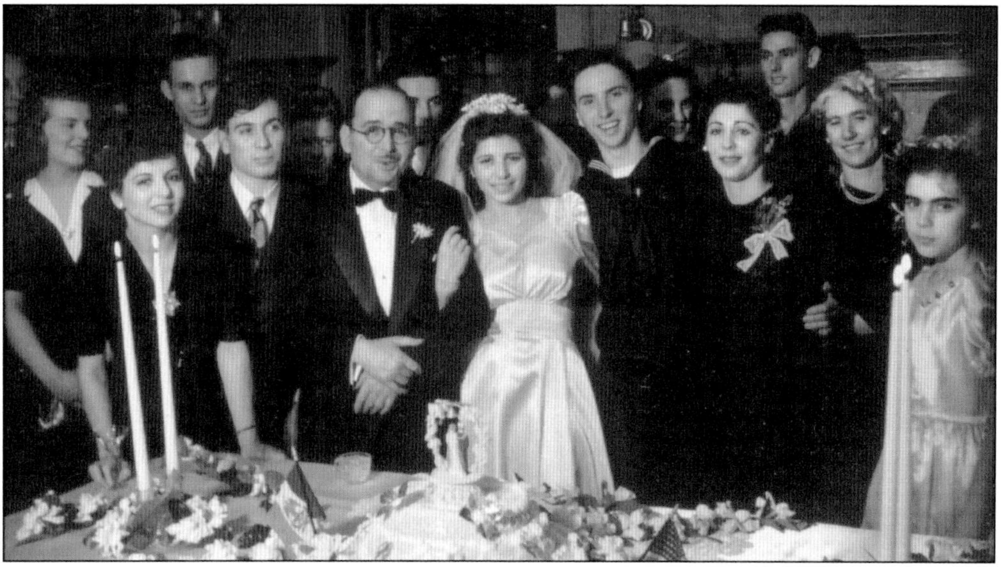

The Puente and Brown-Hancock families held the 1942 wedding reception for Espie and Bill at 262 Moncada Way. Felipe Puente was affectionately called *el puente de San Francisco*, the San Francisco bridge, by the Commonwealth Club for his efforts to promote good relations with the United States as the representative of the president of Mexico. (Courtesy Margie Brown Whitnah.)

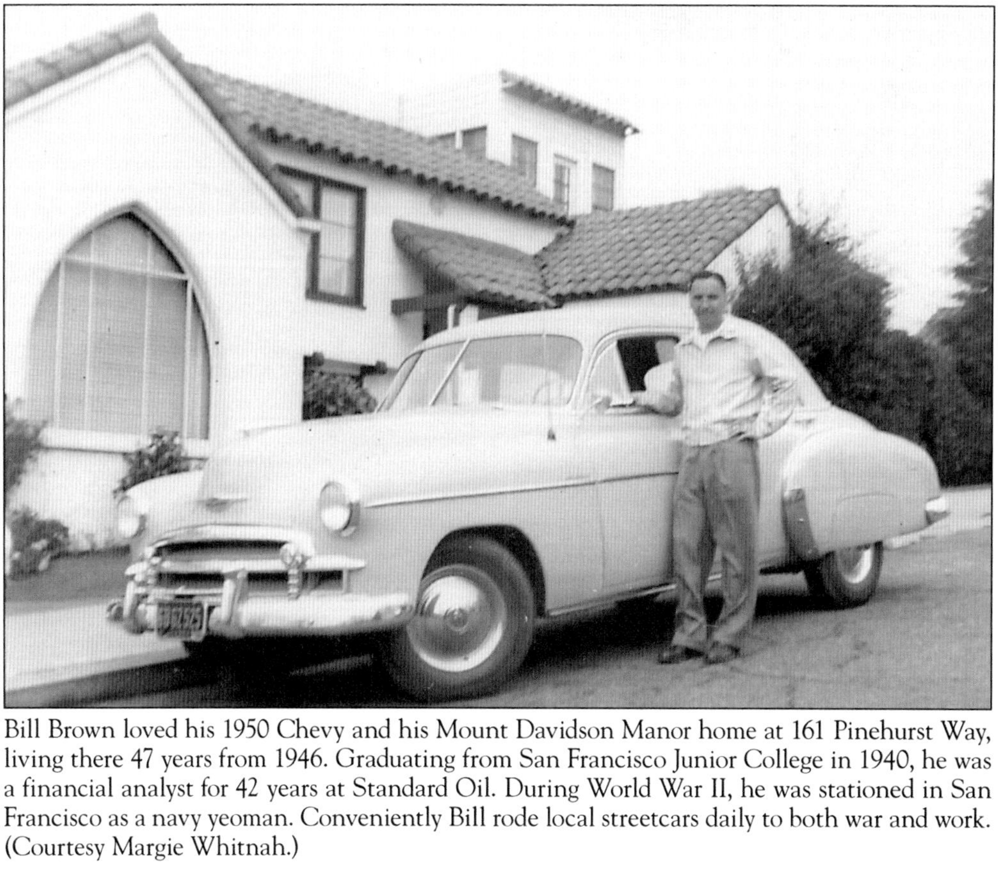

Bill Brown loved his 1950 Chevy and his Mount Davidson Manor home at 161 Pinehurst Way, living there 47 years from 1946. Graduating from San Francisco Junior College in 1940, he was a financial analyst for 42 years at Standard Oil. During World War II, he was stationed in San Francisco as a navy yeoman. Conveniently Bill rode local streetcars daily to both war and work. (Courtesy Margie Whitnah.)

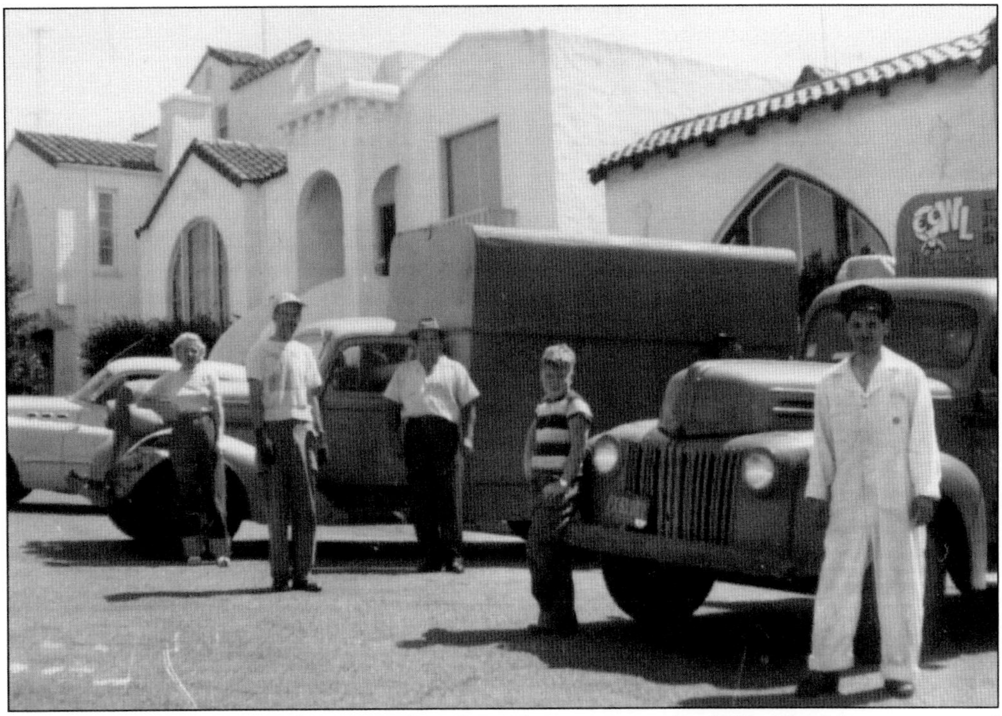

Moving day is underway on this Mount Davidson Manor street in the 1950s. Neighbors appreciated Bill's helpfulness with repairs, advice, and getting things done well. The "Bill Brown method" was responsible for spurring the completion of the Golden Gate Park Pavilion at Stow Lake. (Courtesy Margie Brown Whitnah.)

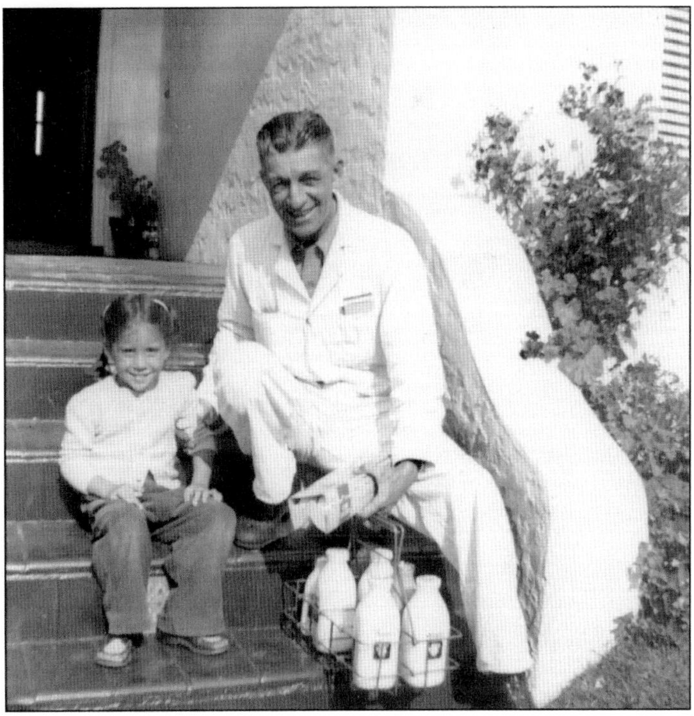

Around 1952, Margie Brown enjoyed visits with Borden's Dairy milkman Leo, who delivered dairy products every weekday to Mount Davidson Manor homes. The mothers (and their little helpers) used Borden's small fan of colored cardboard tags to request items such as chocolate milk, cream, and even cottage cheese in colored tin drinking cups. The fan rested in the neck of one of the glass milk bottles being returned. (Courtesy Margie Brown Whitnah.)

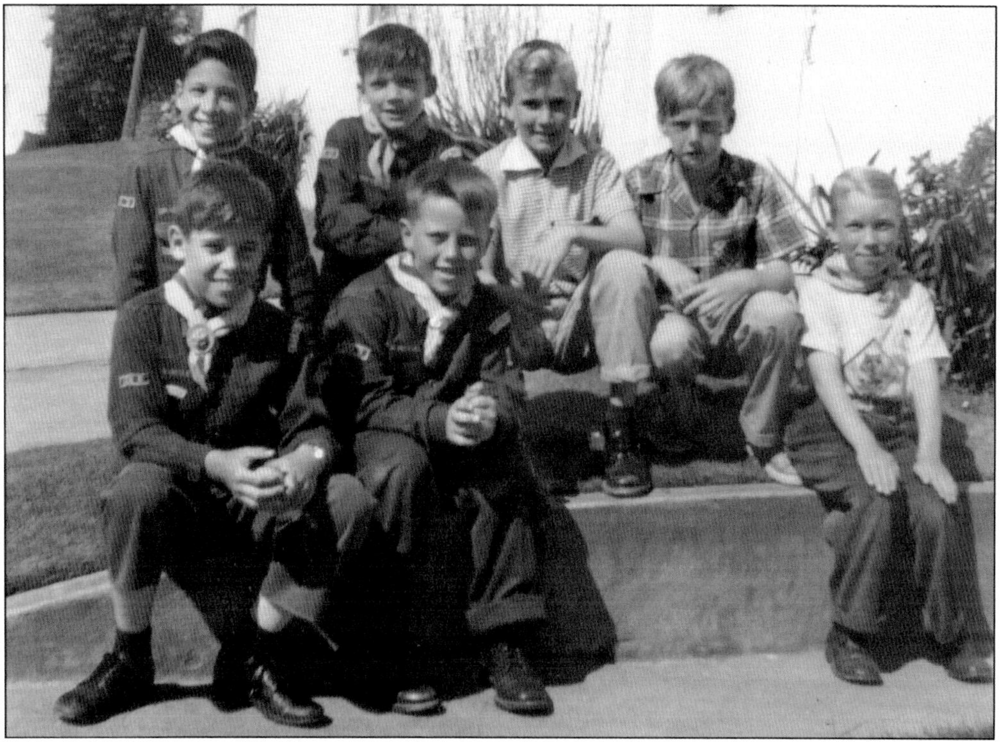

These 1950s Cub Scouts met regularly at the Mount Davidson Manor home of Steve Brown (upper left), whose mother was den mother for the troop. This den was one of many in Cub Pack One, organized in 1930 and the first on the Pacific Coast west of the Rockies. Ben Teshara, a Darien Way resident and owner of Sun Valley Dairy in Pacifica, was Pack One's legendary Cub Scout master from 1937 to 1962. (Courtesy Margie Whitnah.)

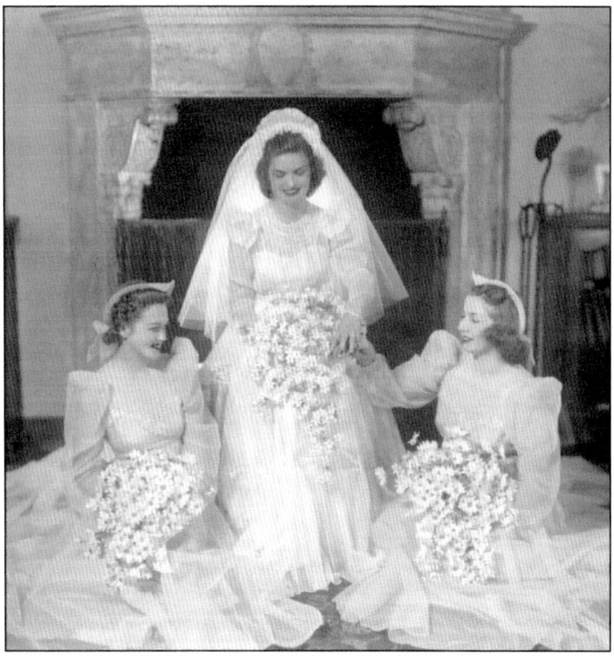

Betty Kern is getting ready for her marriage to Commodore Sloat Elementary School classmate John Bryan at the Monterey Heights home of her aunt and uncle, Morgan and Grace Walsh, at 55 St. Elmo Way on August 16, 1941. (Courtesy Corinne Bryan.)

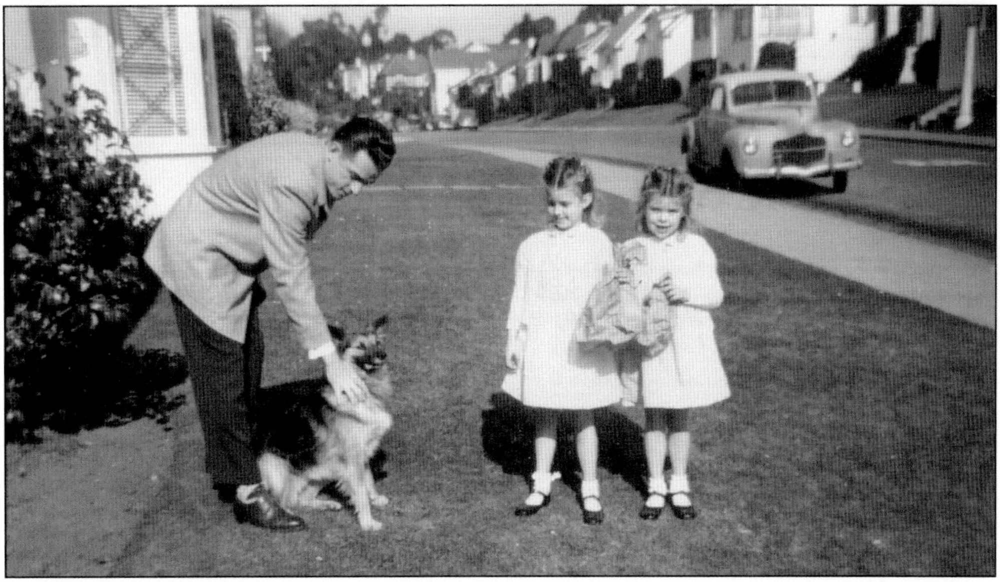

Second-generation San Francisco radiologist Dr. John Bryan is pictured here enjoying the "residence park" atmosphere on the lawn in front of their 316 Santa Ana Avenue home in Balboa Terrace with daughters Corinne and Cathy. Both girls also attended Commodore Sloat School. (Courtesy Corinne Bryan.)

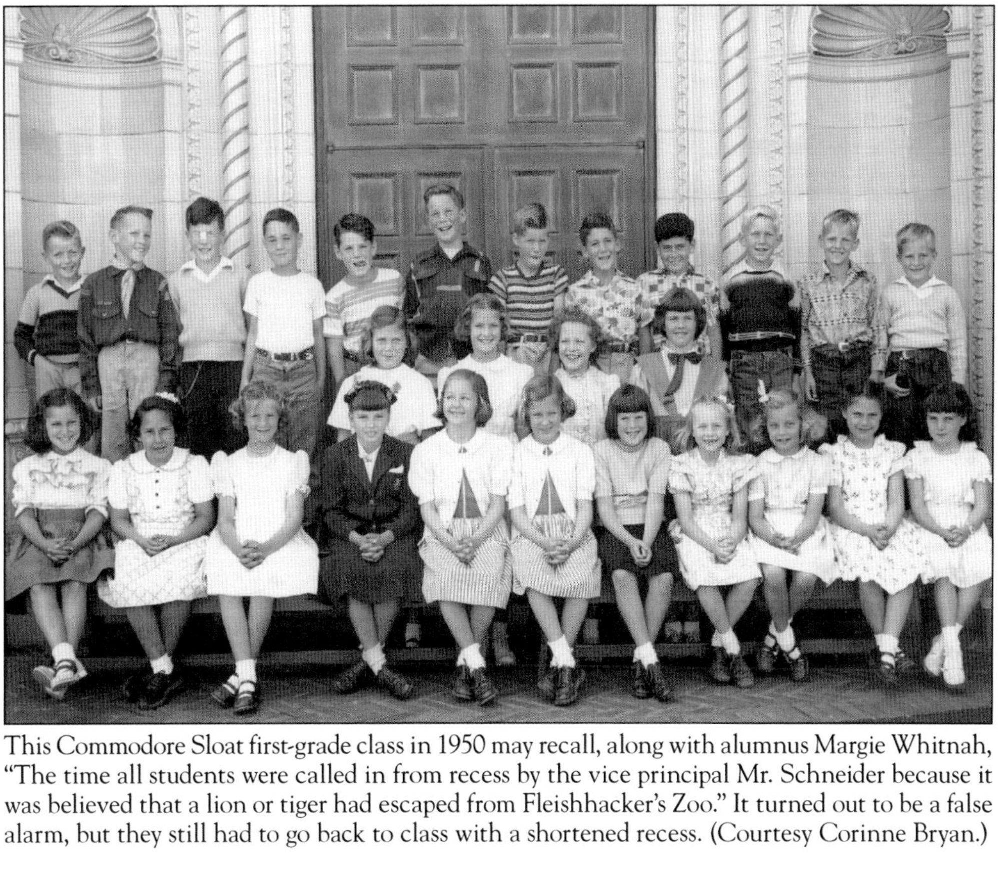

This Commodore Sloat first-grade class in 1950 may recall, along with alumnus Margie Whitnah, "The time all students were called in from recess by the vice principal Mr. Schneider because it was believed that a lion or tiger had escaped from Fleishhacker's Zoo." It turned out to be a false alarm, but they still had to go back to class with a shortened recess. (Courtesy Corinne Bryan.)

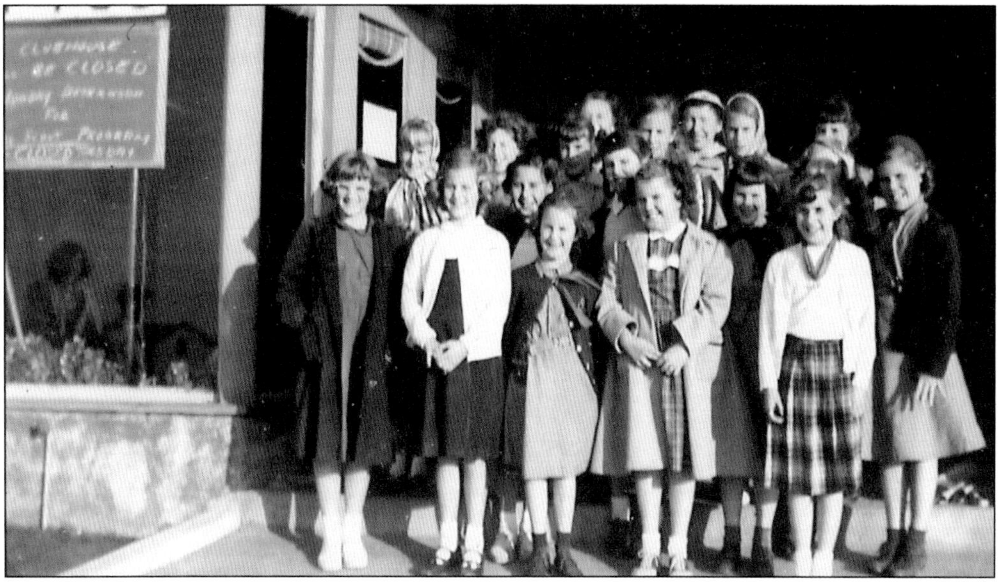

Commodore Sloat Brownie Troop is out on Ocean Avenue in 1952. A nickname for the school, "Commodore slop with the cherries on top," referred not to the food but the red-tile roofs on the school built in 1924. The cafeteria had premier cooks who baked all the breads and cakes and fixed hearty meals. (Courtesy Corinne Bryan.)

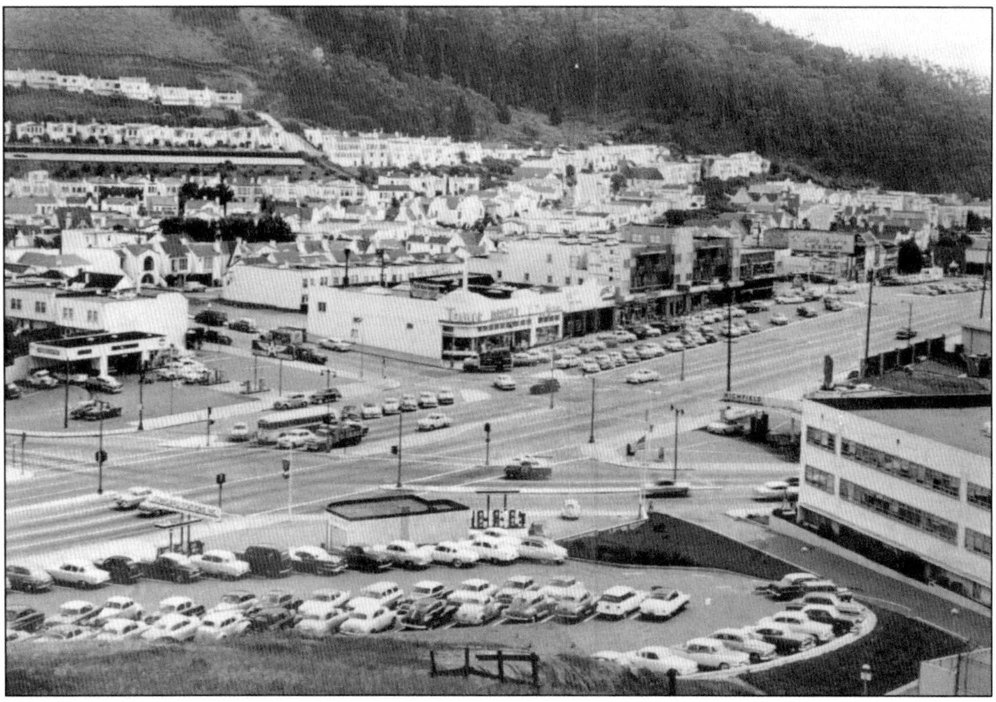

Miraloma Park, pictured here in 1951, was described as being an enclave of stable, straight society in San Francisco of mostly detached homes with well-kept gardens in front and others that back onto the heavily forested slopes of Mount Davidson, the site of the annual Easter morning religious services. Next to Miraloma Park, Tower Market was noted for catering to a gastronomically inclined clientele. (Courtesy John Pommon.)

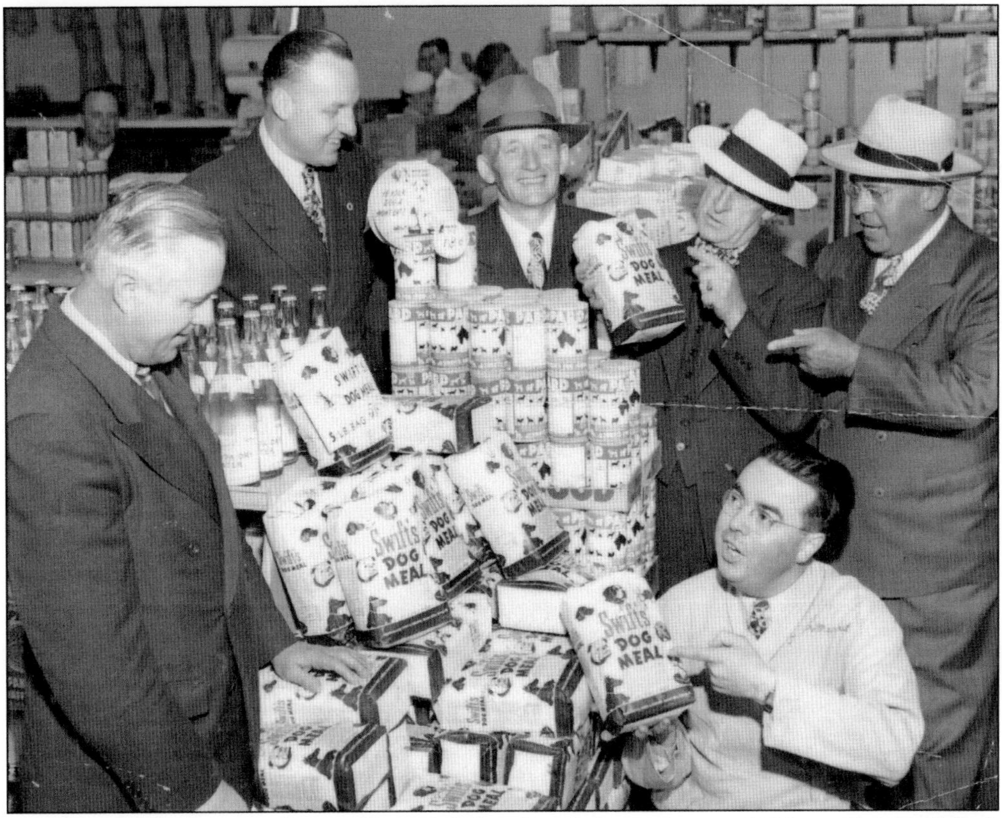


Admiring Swift's Dog Meal inside Tower Market, from left to right, are Al Masar, Bob Neill, Jack Robertson, "Doc" Davis, Mark Pommon, and Danny Pommon. Dan, Mark's son, took over the business when his dad passed away in 1953. John Pommon recalls, "Whenever a customer asked for a new item, Dad [Dan Pommon] would spend the rest of the day if necessary to find a supplier for it." (Courtesy John Pommon.)

A three-foot, eight-inch pumpkin pie, which weighed 165 pounds, ushered in the holiday season at Tower Market in 1954. Dan Pommon is pictured slicing the first piece for his 11-year-old son Marcus and the second for 3-year-old Lindsay Durling of 28 Marietta Drive. According to the newspaper article, "The next step was to cut up the monster and feed it to some 500 other children from the Miraloma Park neighborhood." (Courtesy John Pommon.)

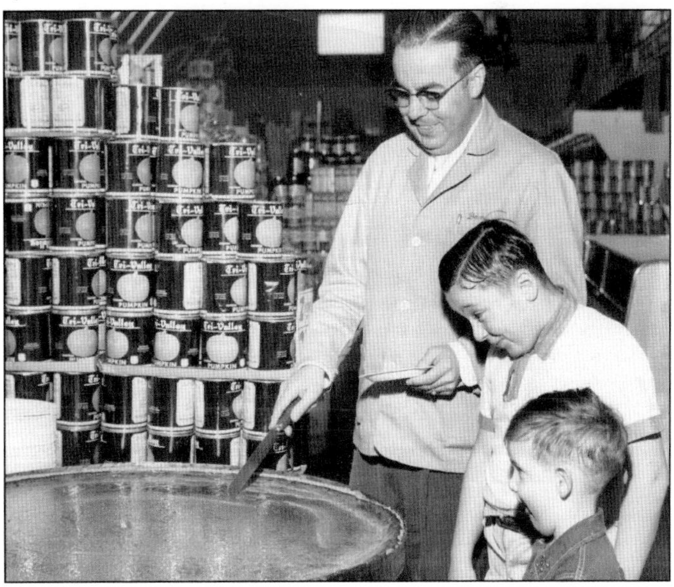

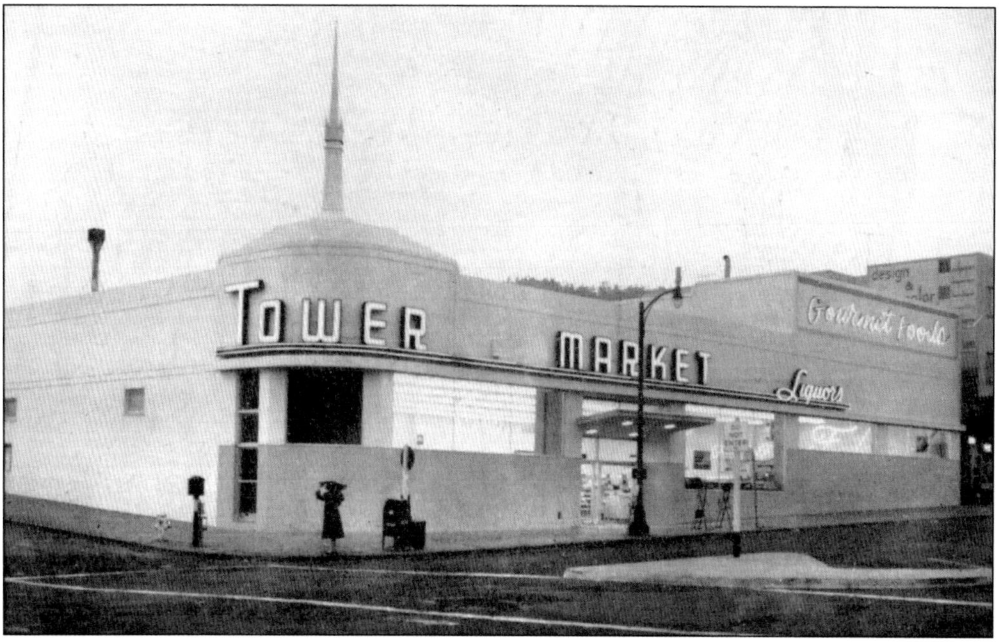


Tower Market is twice its original size here in 1958. Buying out the small businesses next door, Dan Pommon invested everything he had to increase the store to 10,000 square feet. West of Twin Peaks residents their entire lives, the Pommon family expanded their store three times and invested in many other improvements throughout the years in order to continue offering their customers the very best. (Courtesy John Pommon.)

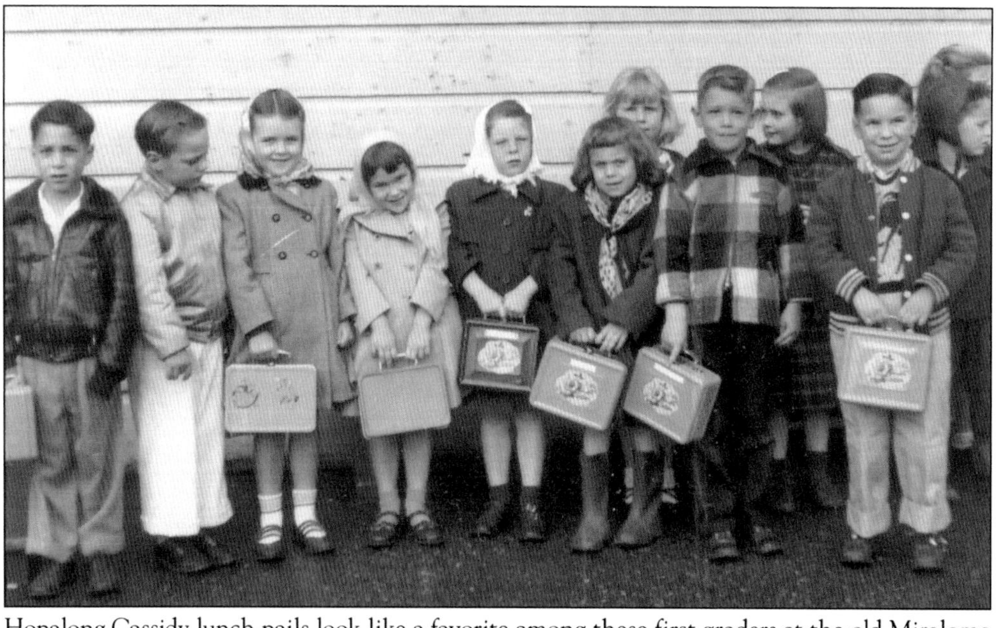

Hopalong Cassidy lunch pails look like a favorite among these first graders at the old Miraloma School in 1951. Parents called the temporary bungalows built in 1936 "shacks." Still heated with wood-burning stoves, children had to go to the bathroom out in the cold. Evening programs had to be held outside as well, and older children were transferred to West Portal School because of lack of space. (Courtesy Bertha Jones.)

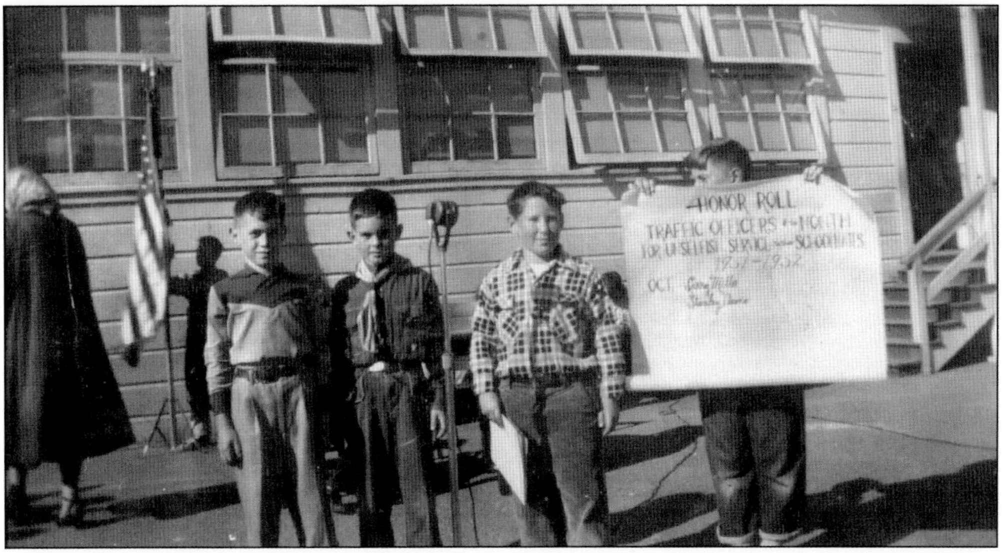


The honor-roll traffic officers of the month, a reward given for unselfish service to their schoolmates, include Larry Miller and Stanley Davis (in the plaid shirt) in October 1951. Many students went on to the best high schools and universities. Stanley earned a scholarship to Stanford University when he graduated from Lowell High School. (Courtesy Jeanne Davis MacKenzie.)

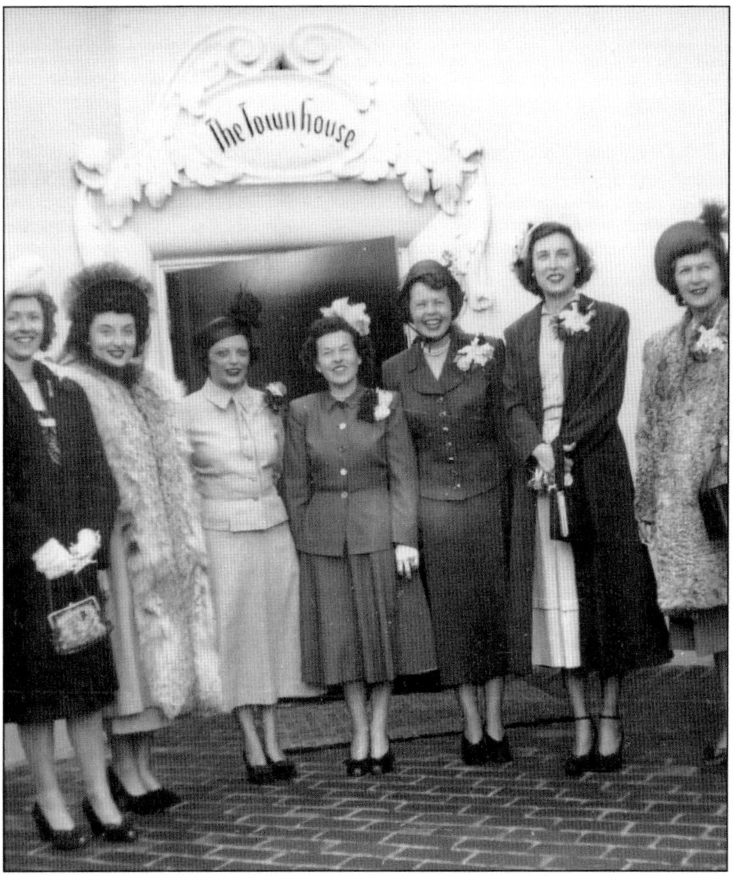


Parents treat Miraloma School teachers to a special lunch in March 1949 at the Townhouse Restaurant (now Villa d' Este). Pictured here are Mrs. Long, Mrs. Inman, Mrs. Patton, and Mrs. Rosenberg, as well as Miss Goldstein, Miss Green, and Miss Learned. Many fund-raising events held by the club have split proceeds with the school. (Courtesy Bertha Jones.)

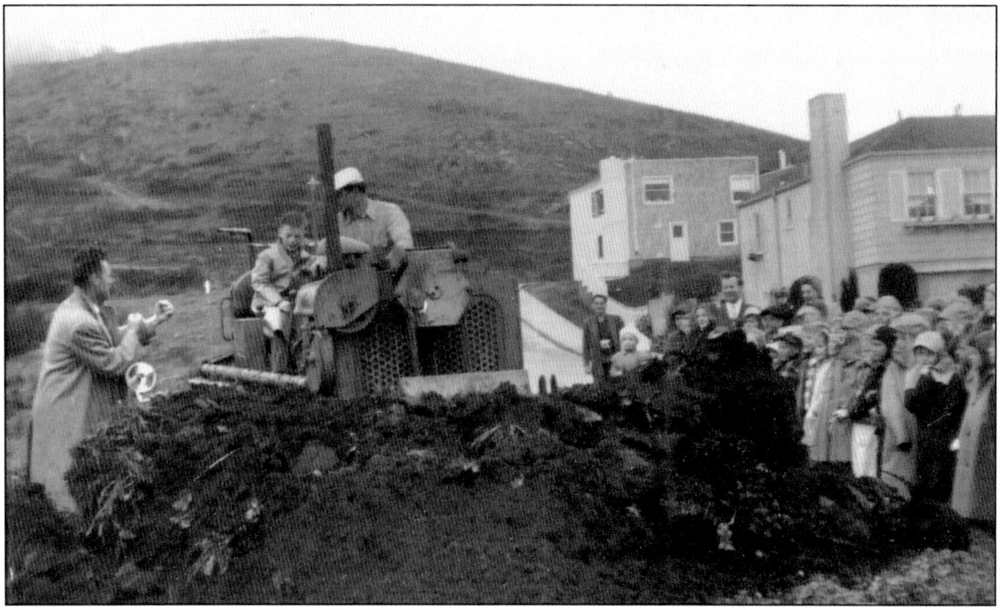

Parents, led by Dale Jones, conducted a census of current and potential neighborhood children and successfully advocated for the building of a new permanent Miraloma School. In this photograph of the groundbreaking ceremony on February 5, 1951, the newspaper photographer puts down his camera to give the students a demonstration on how to move the gears on the bulldozer. (Courtesy Bertha Jones.)

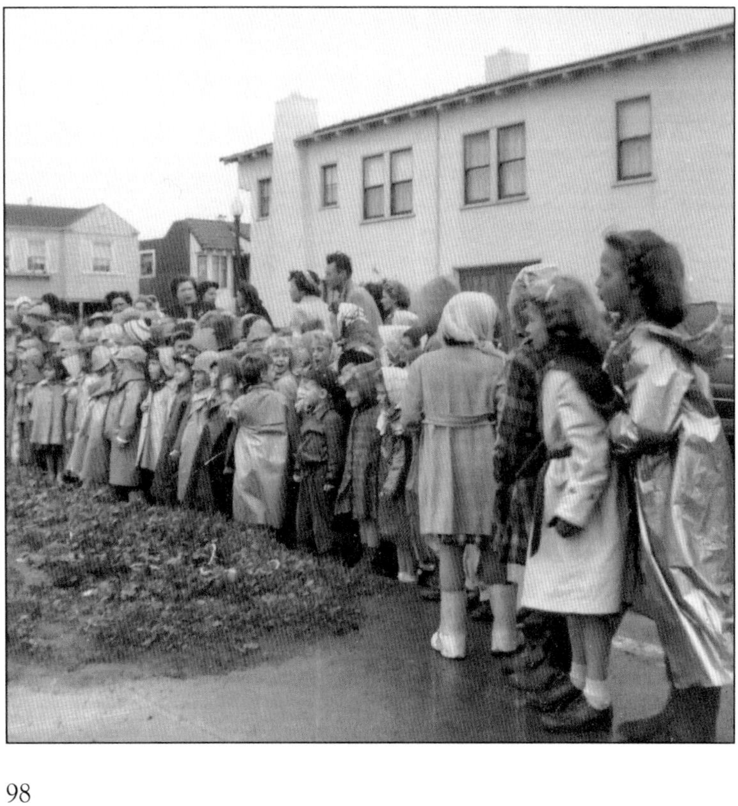

Miraloma students and parents are lined up to watch the groundbreaking ceremony despite the inclement weather. The contractor was the same Munson Brothers who built the Mount Davidson Cross in 1934. In November 1952, the new school at 174 Omar Way was opened with 400 pupils in kindergarten through grade six. (Courtesy Bertha Jones.)

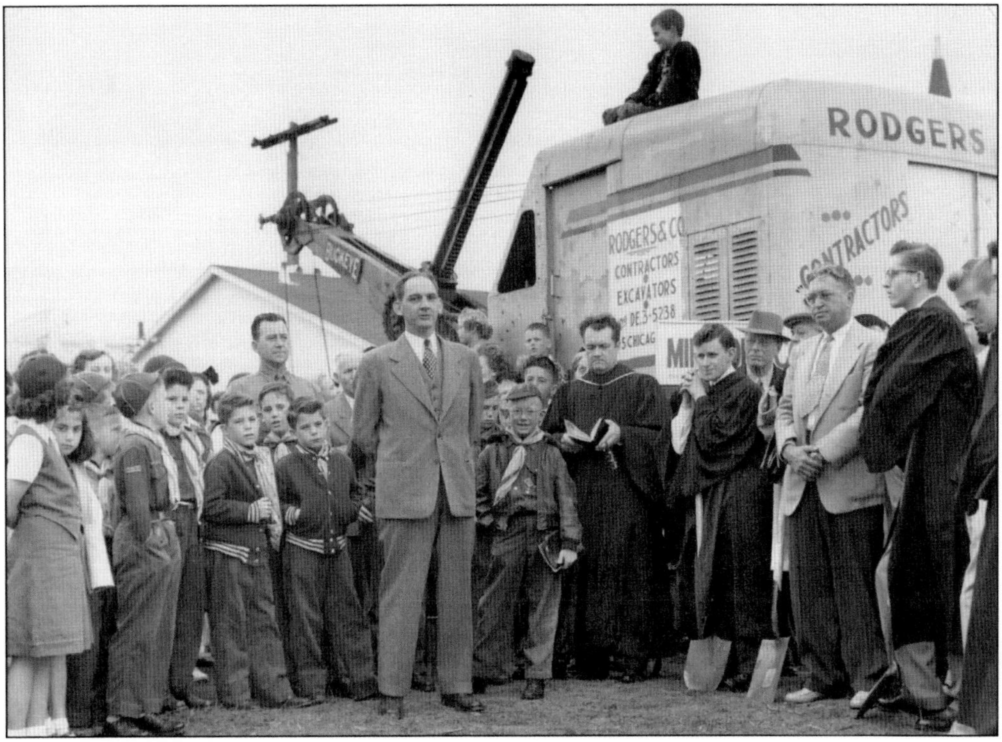


Pictured, from left to right, are Jeanne Davis, Judy White, Dale Jones (behind the Cub Scouts), architect Stanley Fuller Davis (front center), Rev. Leroy Nattress (with book), Stanley Davis Jr. (above Nattress on the backhoe), and grandfather Herman Quast II (watching with the hat) observing the Miraloma Community Church groundbreaking in October 1950. Fifteen Miraloma Park families pledged their personal worth as surety to get the loan to build the church. (Courtesy Jeanne Davis MacKenzie.)

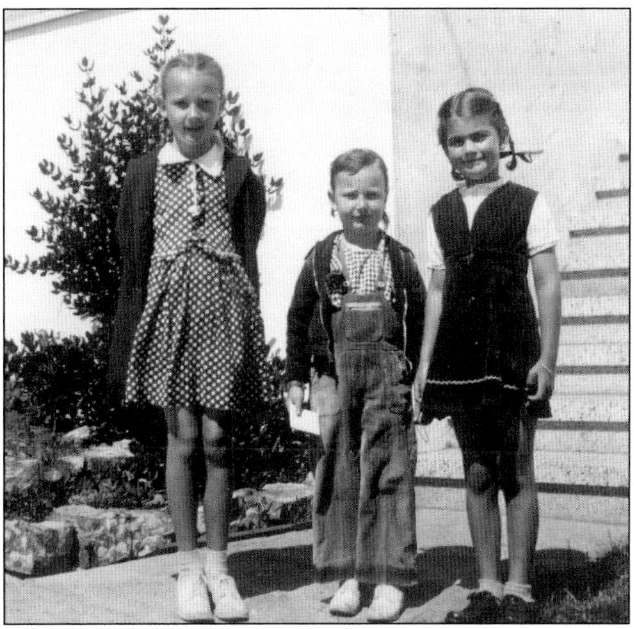

Stanley and Jeanette Quast Davis lived down the block from the church he designed at 2 Arroyo Way. Posing in front of their home built in 1941 is daughter Jeanne (right) with friends Jean (left) and Louise Clay (center). In 1936, the improvement club worked to get the 36 bus line established for Miraloma Park with Mayor Rossi driving the first bus on July 23, 1939. (Courtesy Jeanne Davis MacKenzie.)

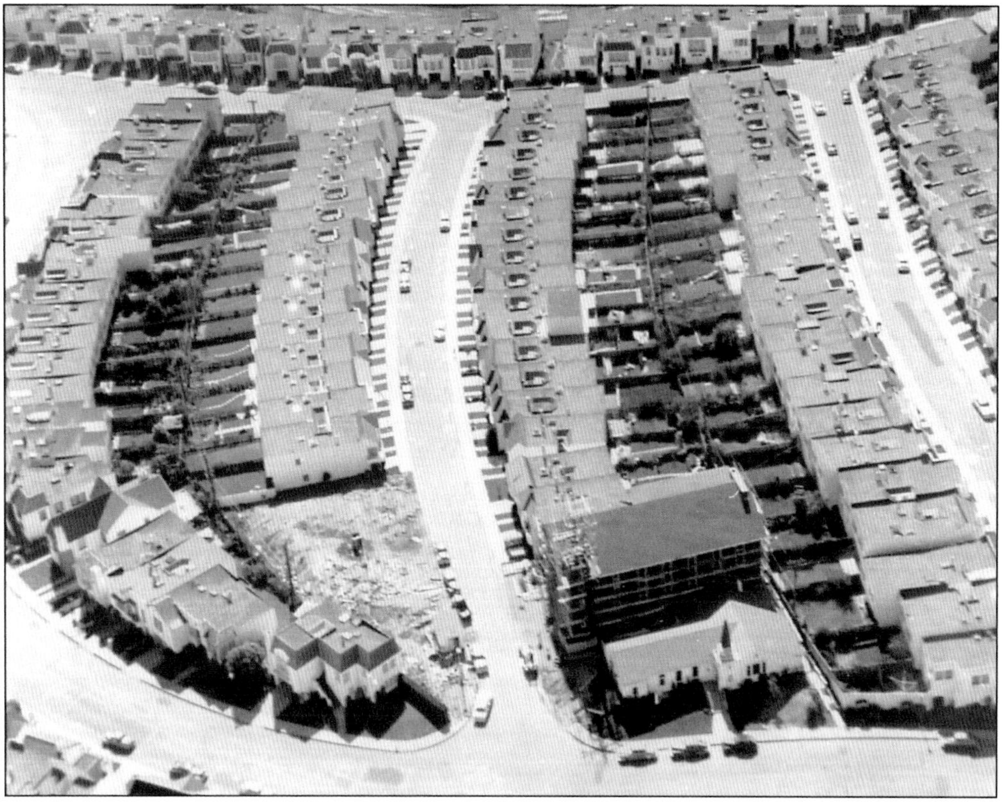

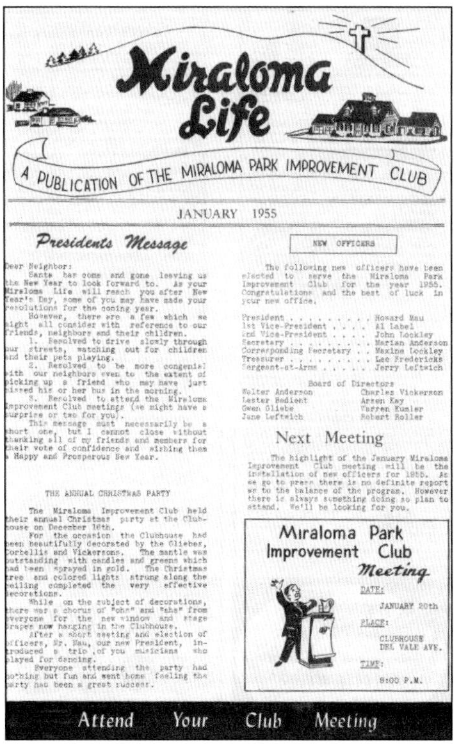

# Miraloma Life

A PUBLICATION OF THE MIRALOMA PARK IMPROVEMENT CLUB

JANUARY 1955

## Presidents Message

Dear Neighbor:

Santa has come and gone leaving us the New Year to look forward to. As your Miraloma Life will reach you after New Year's Day, some of you may have made your resolutions for the coming year.

However, there are a few which we might all consider with reference to our friends, neighbors and their children.

1. Resolved to drive slowly through our streets, watching out for children and their pets playing.

2. Resolved to be more congenial with our neighbors even to the extent of picking up a friend who may have just missed his or her bus in the morning.

3. Resolved to attend the Miraloma Improvement Club meetings (we might have a surprise or two for you).

This message must necessarily be a short one, but I cannot close without thanking all of my friends and members for their vote of confidence and wishing them a Happy and Prosperous New Year.

### THE ANNUAL CHRISTMAS PARTY

The Miraloma Improvement Club held their annual Christmas party at the Clubhouse on December 18th.

For the occasion the Clubhouse had been beautifully decorated by the Gliebes, Corbellis and Vickersons. The mantle was outstanding with candles and greens which had been sprayed in gold. The Christmas tree and colored lights strung along the ceiling completed the very effective decorations.

While on the subject of decorations, there was a chorus of "ohs" and "ahs" from everyone for the new window and stage drapes now hanging in the Clubhouse.

After a short meeting and election of officers, Mr. Mau, our new President, introduced a trio of you musicians who played for dancing.

Everyone attending the party had nothing but fun and went home feeling the party had been a great success.

### NEW OFFICERS

The following new officers have been elected to serve the Miraloma Park Improvement Club for the year 1955. Congratulations and the best of luck in your new office.

President . . . . . . . . . . Howard Mau
1st Vice-President . . . . Al Label
2nd Vice-President . . . . John Lockley
Secretary . . . . . . . . . . Marian Anderson
Corresponding Secretary . . Maxine Lockley
Treasurer . . . . . . . . . . Lee Fredericks
Sergeant-at-Arms . . . . . Jerry Leftwich

Board of Directors

| | |
|---|---|
| Walter Anderson | Charles Vickerson |
| Lester Bedient | Arsen Kay |
| Gwen Gliebe | Warren Kumler |
| June Leftwich | Robert Roller |

### Next Meeting

The highlight of the January Miraloma Improvement Club meeting will be the installation of new officers for 1955. As we go to press there is no definite report as to the balance of the program. However there is always something doing so plan to attend. We'll be looking for you.

Miraloma Park Improvement Club Meeting

DATE: JANUARY 20th

PLACE: CLUBHOUSE DEL VALE AVE.

TIME: 8:00 P.M.

Attend Your Club Meeting

This aerial view in 1951 shows a now-completed section of the "suburb in the city" along Arroyo Way in Miraloma Park. The church under construction was deliberately built tall so it could be seen from all around. Moving to the neighborhood with her husband in 1945, Velma Salcido calls it "the friendly church at the foot of the cross." (Courtesy Jeanne Davis MacKenzie.)

The Miraloma Park Improvement Club has distributed a free monthly newsletter, *Miraloma Life*, to the 2,200-home neighborhood since the 1950s. Funded by advertisements, this 1955 edition includes a message from president Howard Mau, an editorial, the Miraloma Church news, the stork reports, the merchant of the month, the Miraloma Cooperative Nursery School news, Troop 57 news, Campfire Girls news, Whist Club news, folk dance news, shopping in Miraloma, Miraloma PTA news, and "Mountain Chatter." (Courtesy MPIC.)

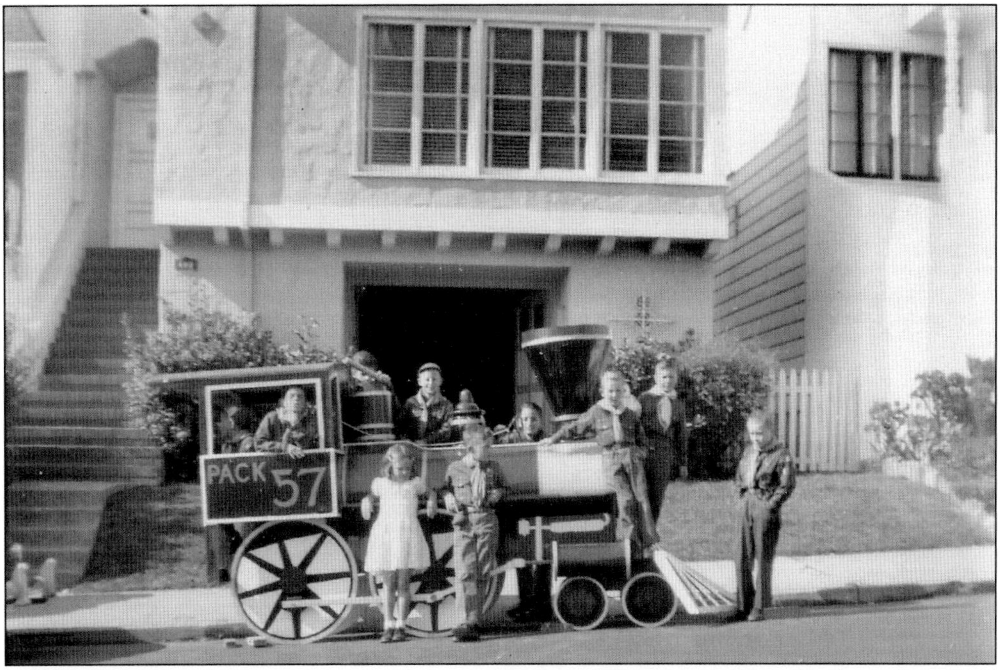


Miraloma Park Cub Scouts pose in front of the Jones home on Teresita Boulevard in 1951, showing the train engine built for their scout jamboree that was later donated to the children at the Infant Shelter on Nineteenth Avenue (now the Conservatory of Music). Pack members included Dennis Anderson, Richard Bach, Lucian Vance, Douglas Dickson, Charles Harris, David Berkowitz, Stephen Strange, Alan Lacy, and Dennis Jones, with his sister Nancy in front. (Courtesy Bertha Jones.)

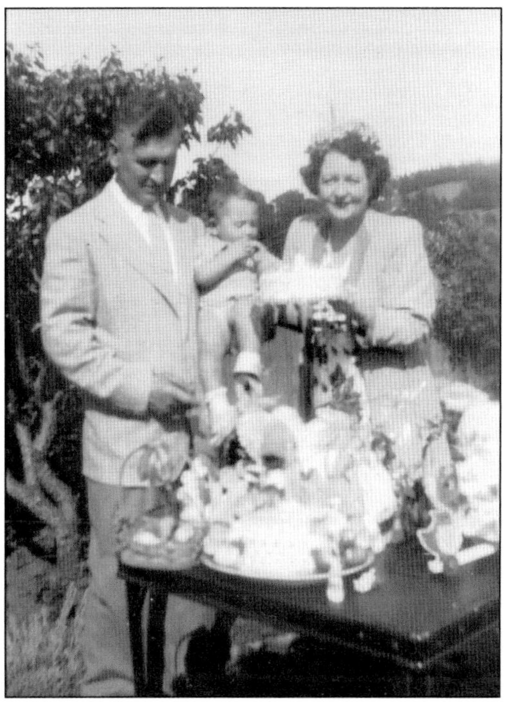

Future director of the Miraloma Park Improvement Club, young Ken Hoegger celebrates his birthday on Prague Street in 1947. Ken could see Mount Davidson from his home and at age seven took the Monterey bus with his young neighbor to see it firsthand. His friend's dad watched over them with his telescope as they enjoyed their adventure hiking up to the city's highest point. (Courtesy Ken Hoegger.)

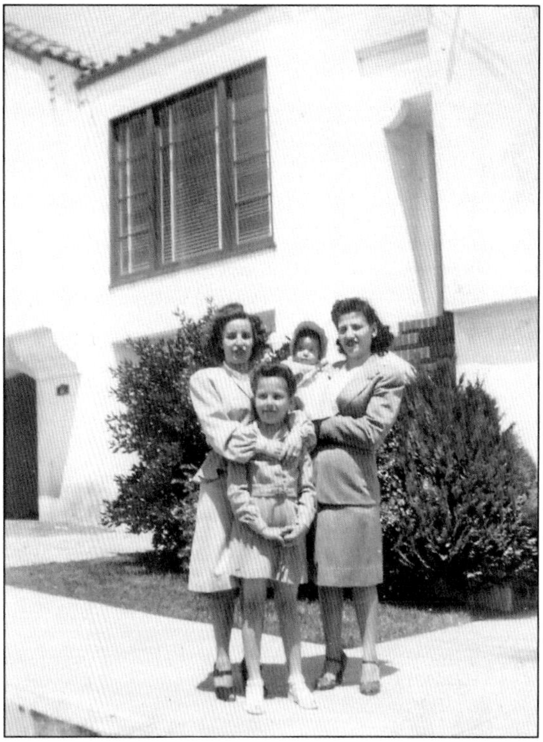

This is the future Mrs. Hoegger as baby Kathy Conte with her mother Josephine, aunt Yolanda Conte, and sister Ann Marie at their Lamartine Street home in 1947. Born in Calabria, Italy, Josephine joined her father in San Francisco at age 13. She married Joe Conte in 1938, whose father came from Calabria in 1905. In 1957, the State of California bought their house to make way for the 280 Freeway. (Courtesy Kathy Hoegger.)

In 1954, architect Milton Pflueger wrote about how the innovative contemporary house he designed for his own family in Sherwood Forest was his favorite because it demonstrated how "those advantages which are sometimes thought to be available only in our suburban communities can be matched right here in the City." The front of the natural lacquered redwood house pictured here has an in-line plan conforming to natural slopes. (Courtesy John Pflueger.)

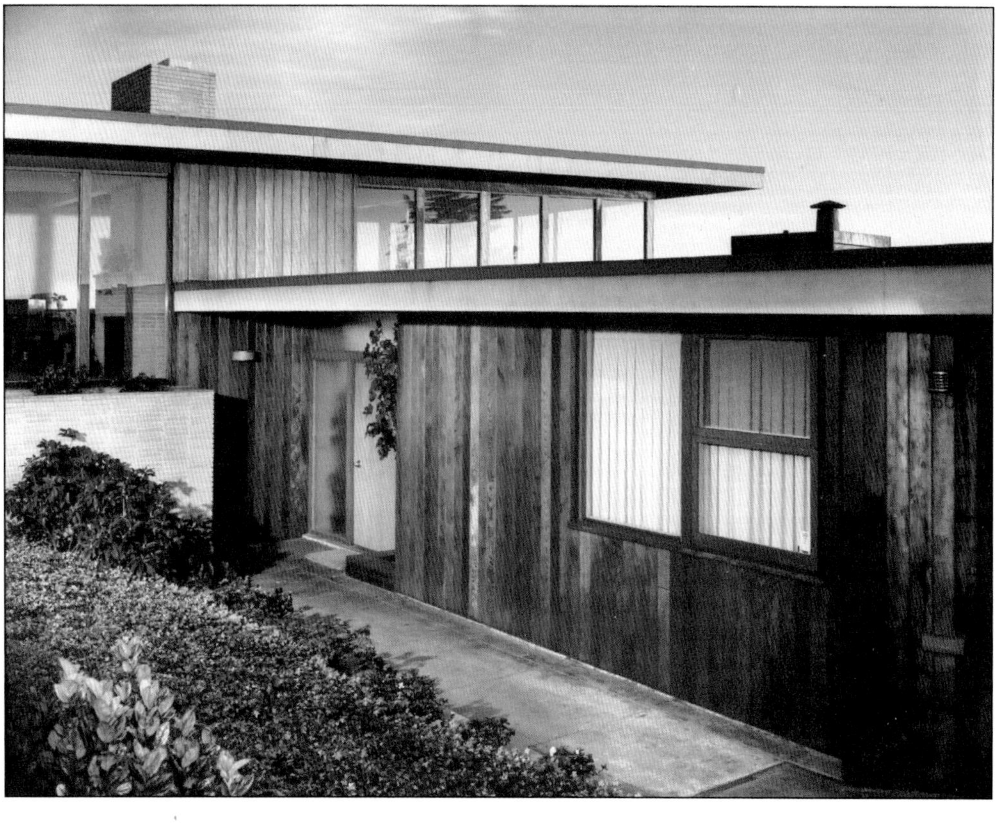

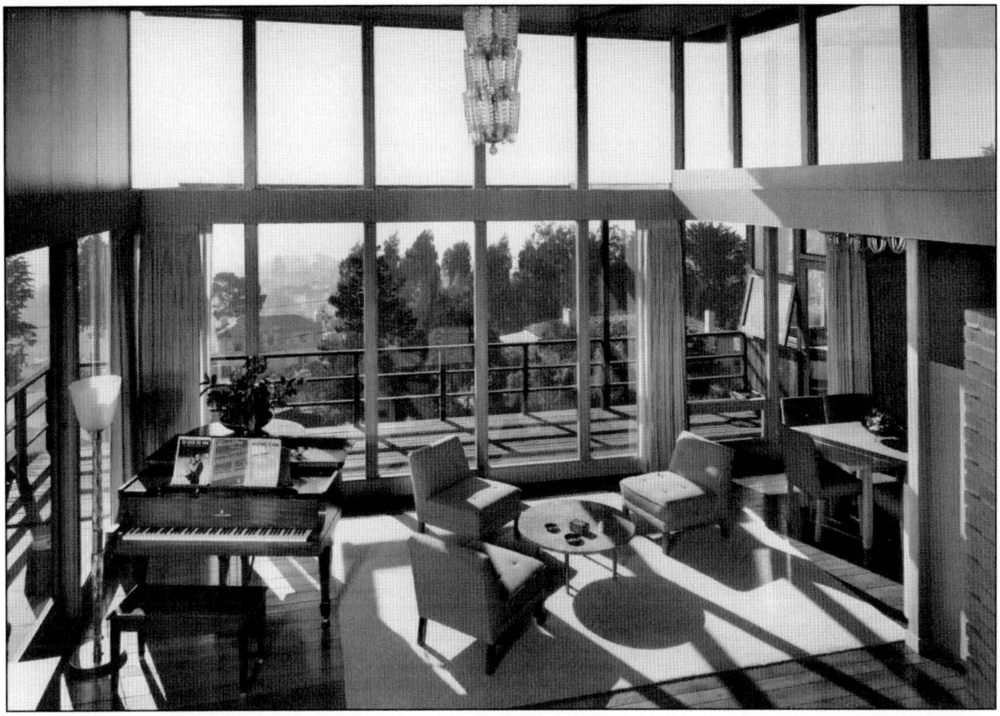

A half-story difference in level, dictated by grades, separates the main living area from the bedrooms. The two-level living room provides for additional entertaining space on the lower level. Plank oak flooring, indirect lighting, golden tan Roman brick in the double fireplace, and exposed wood ceilings were described by Milton Pflueger as creating "a warm neutral background which in combination with the glass walls and clerestory windows to the west, provides spacious uncluttered living space." (Courtesy John Pflueger.)

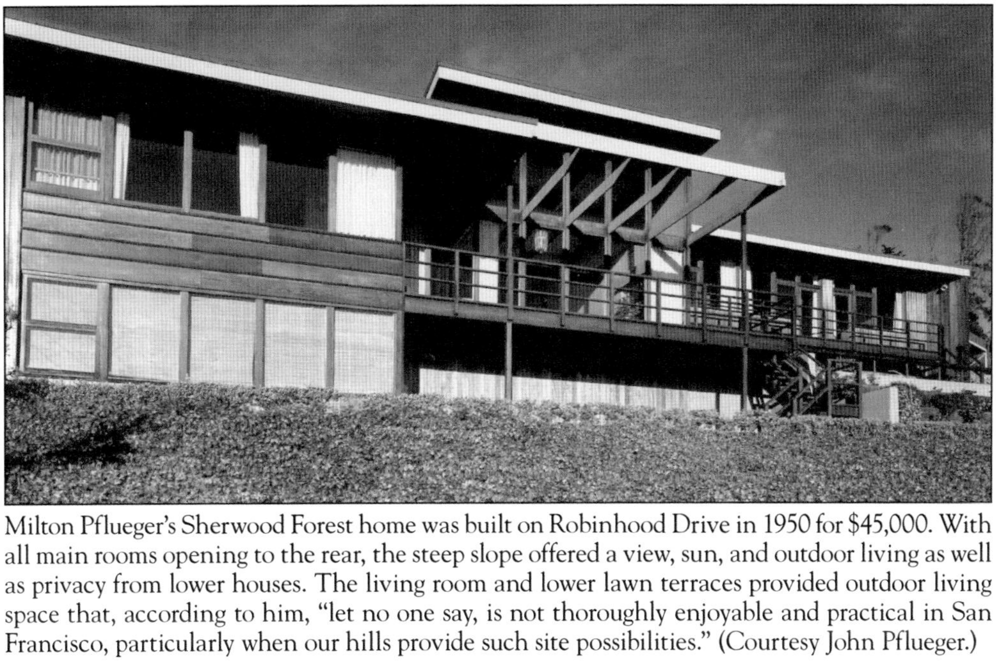

Milton Pflueger's Sherwood Forest home was built on Robinhood Drive in 1950 for $45,000. With all main rooms opening to the rear, the steep slope offered a view, sun, and outdoor living as well as privacy from lower houses. The living room and lower lawn terraces provided outdoor living space that, according to him, "let no one say, is not thoroughly enjoyable and practical in San Francisco, particularly when our hills provide such site possibilities." (Courtesy John Pflueger.)

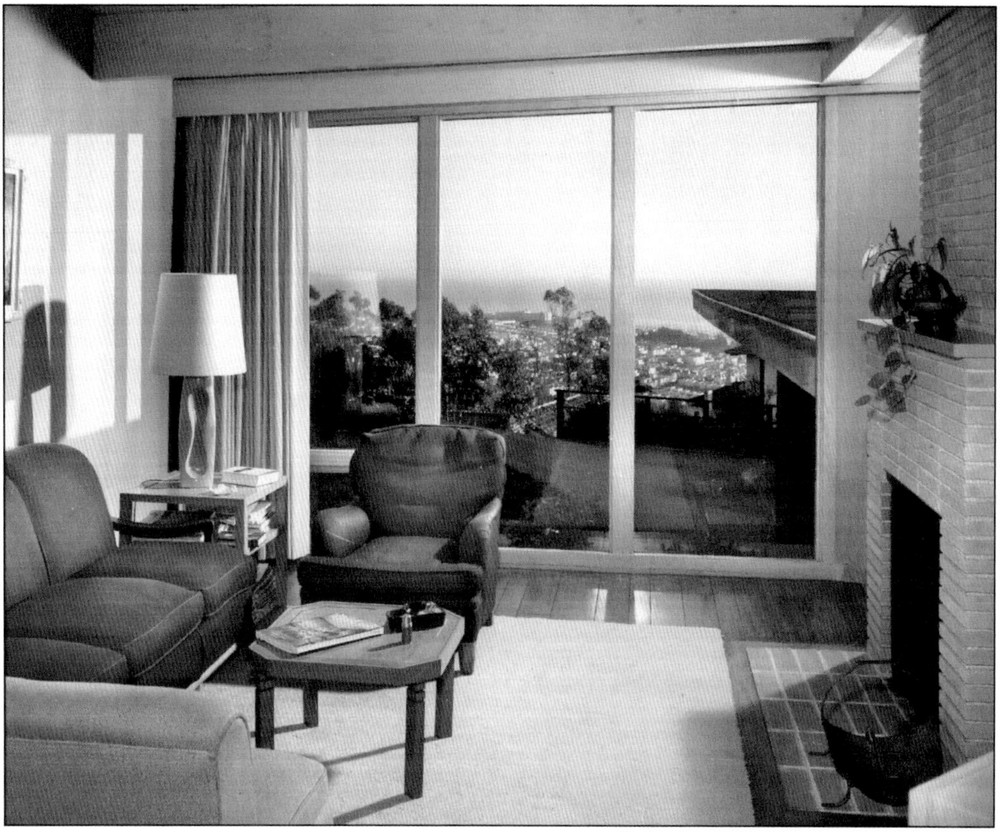

Milton's article concluded that the panoramic indoor and outdoor views of the city, hills, and ocean, combined with the natural, straightforward design, "provide ever-interesting, practical and thoroughly enjoyable living." His son, architect John Pflueger, recalls how he used to get out of bed and get out his telescope to watch the drive-in movie on San Bruno Mountain. "*Singing in the Rain* was my favorite." (Courtesy John Pflueger.)

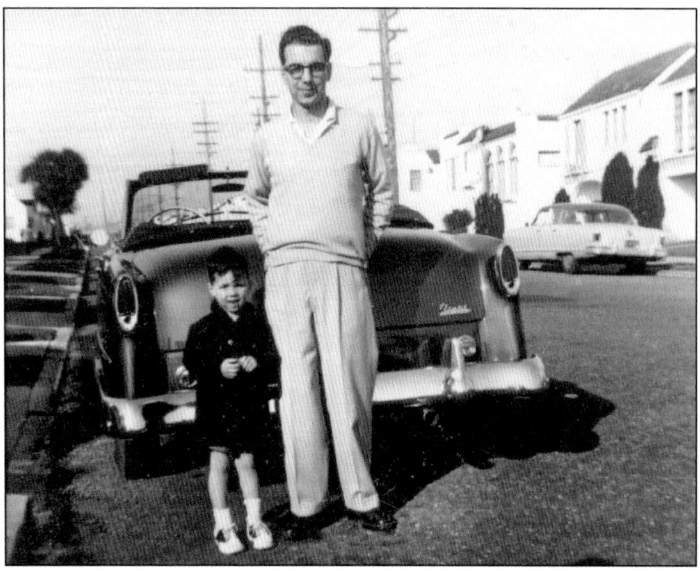

Future West of Twin Peaks council presidents Joseph Bisho Jr. (1981) and his son Dave (1994–1996 and 2004–present) stand next to their Sunset District home before moving to St. Francis Woods in 1952. With delegates from 17 homeowner associations, collectively representing 90,000 San Franciscans, the council continues working to preserve their historic City Beautiful neighborhoods. (Courtesy Dave Bisho.)

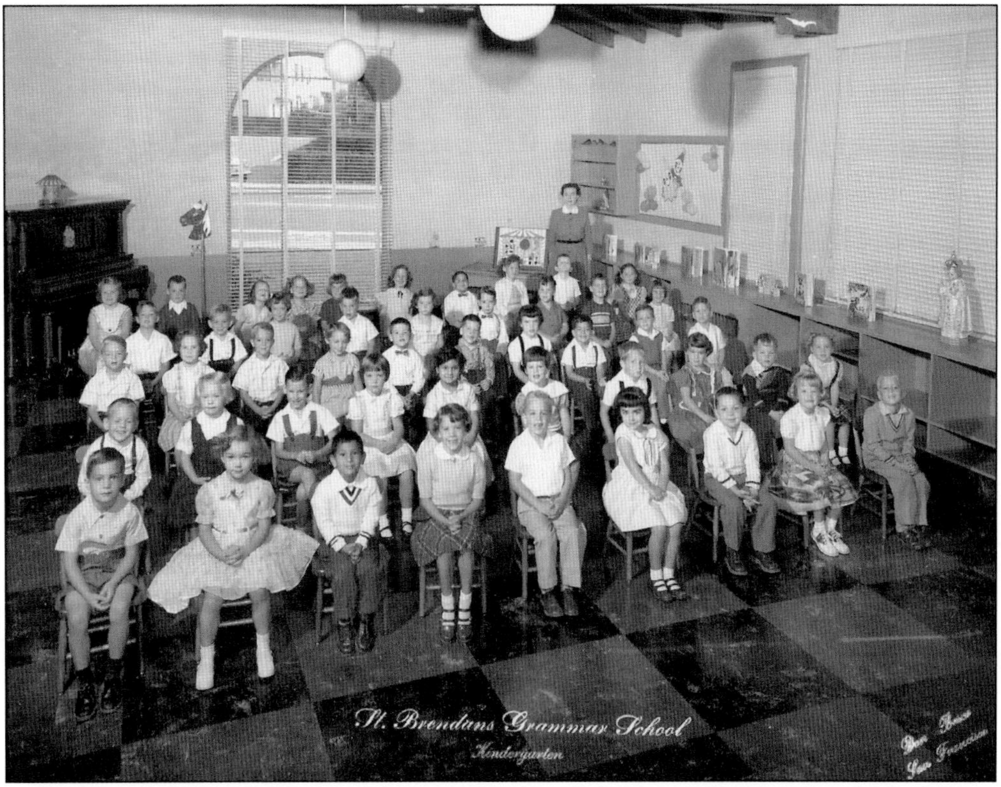


This is Mrs. Burke's kindergarten class at St. Brendan's School in 1956. The identifiable children pictured here are Dave Bisho (first row, third from right), Mike Lunny (third row, second from right), Margaret Schweifler (first row, second from left), future owner of Harrington's Bar on Front Street Mike Harrington (fifth row, far right), and future president of West of Twin Peaks Central Council Paul Conroy (fourth row, far right). (Courtesy Dave Bisho.)

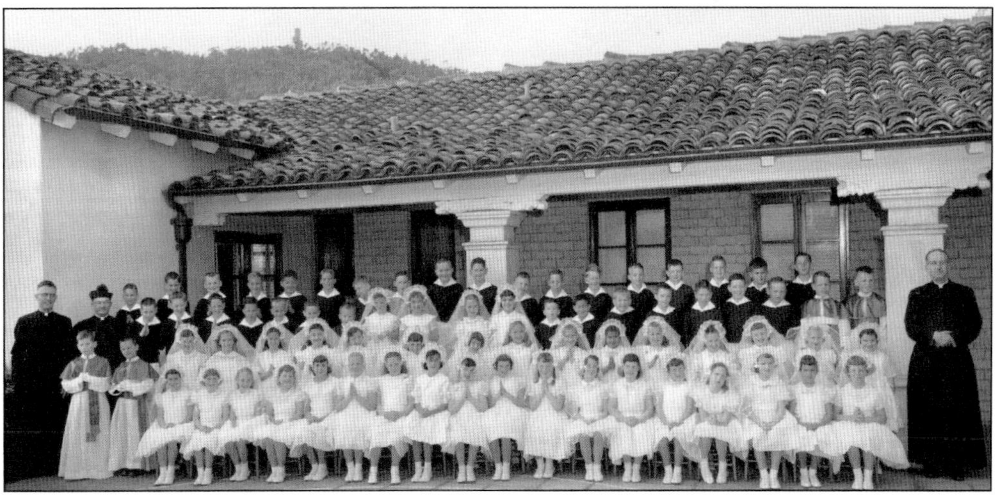

Celebrating first communion at St. Brendan's Church are Paul Conroy (also a future president of the San Francisco Fire Commission), Mike Harrington, Mike Lunny, Dave Bisho, Rod Bisho, David Holdener, and other children west of Twin Peaks in 1958. Mount Davidson Cross is visible in the background. (Courtesy Dave Bisho.)

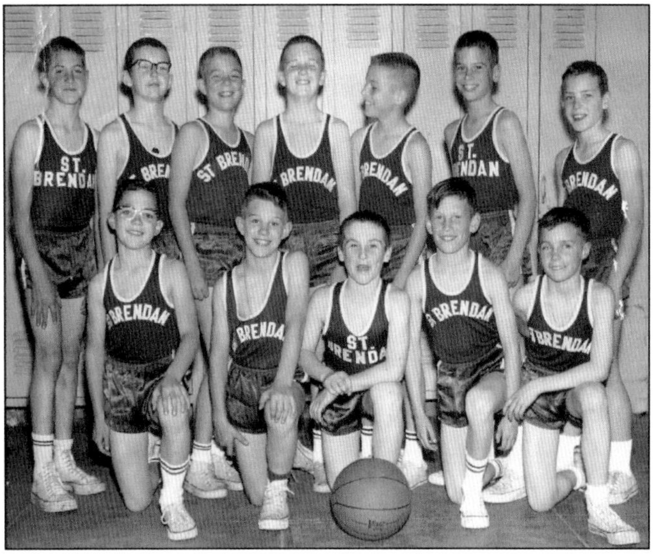

St. Brendan's seventh-grade boys basketball team lines up in 1962. The identifiable boys pictured here are Dave Bisho, future president of Westwood Highlands Homeowner Association and cofounder of the Friends of Mount Davidson Conservancy (first row, left), Mike Harrington (second row, second from left), and Mike Lunny (first row, far right), the future part owner of the Dubliner Bar on West Portal, which used to be TK's and The Road to Mandalay. (Courtesy Dave Bisho.)

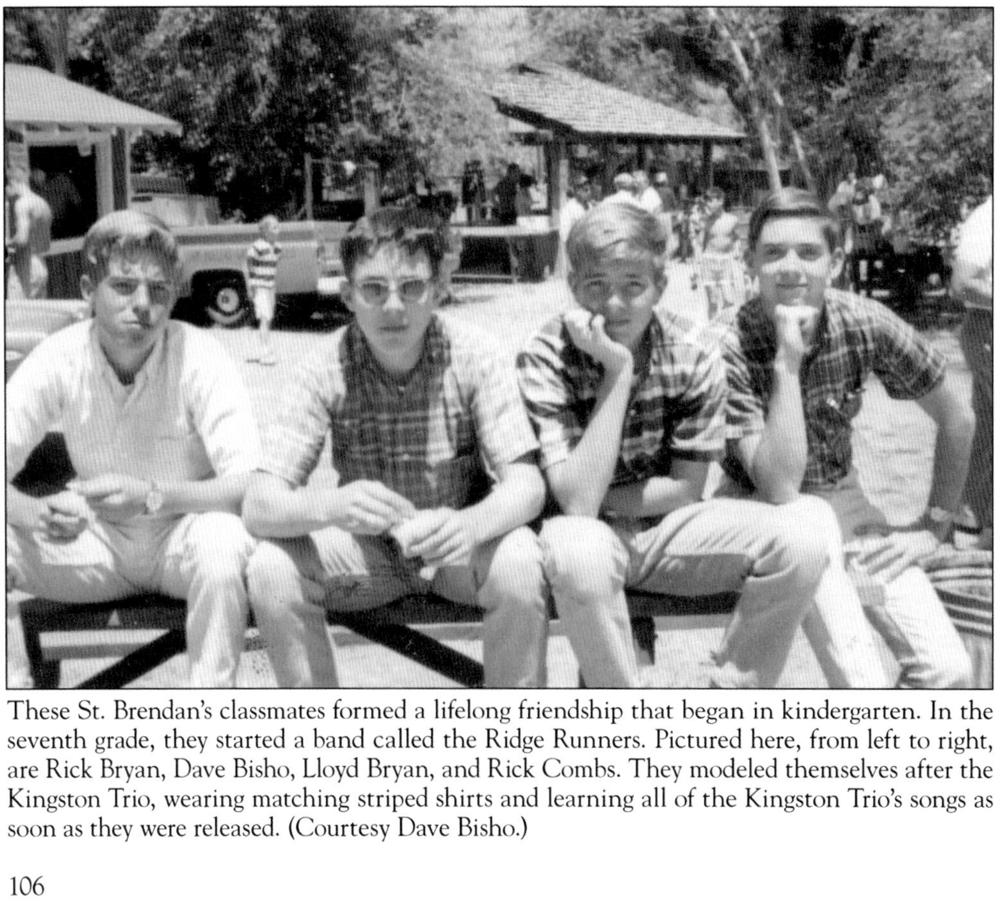

These St. Brendan's classmates formed a lifelong friendship that began in kindergarten. In the seventh grade, they started a band called the Ridge Runners. Pictured here, from left to right, are Rick Bryan, Dave Bisho, Lloyd Bryan, and Rick Combs. They modeled themselves after the Kingston Trio, wearing matching striped shirts and learning all of the Kingston Trio's songs as soon as they were released. (Courtesy Dave Bisho.)

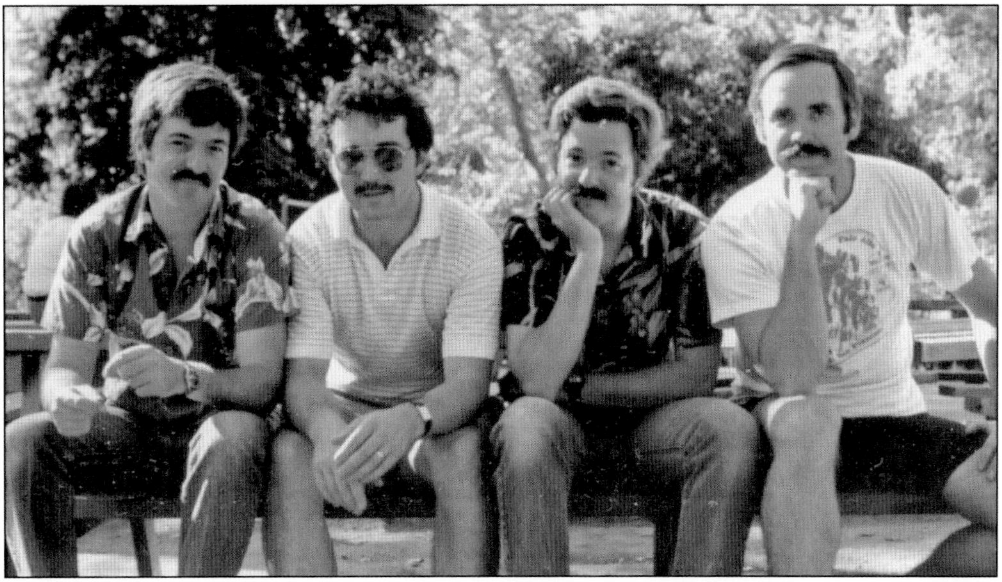

Calling themselves "America's slowest rising pop band," the Ridge Runners were still together and playing 20 years later, as pictured here in 1984. Even their name had an association with the Kingston Trio, as one of their members, John Stewart, had a brother who had been in the since-disbanded Ridge Runners. (Courtesy Dave Bisho.)

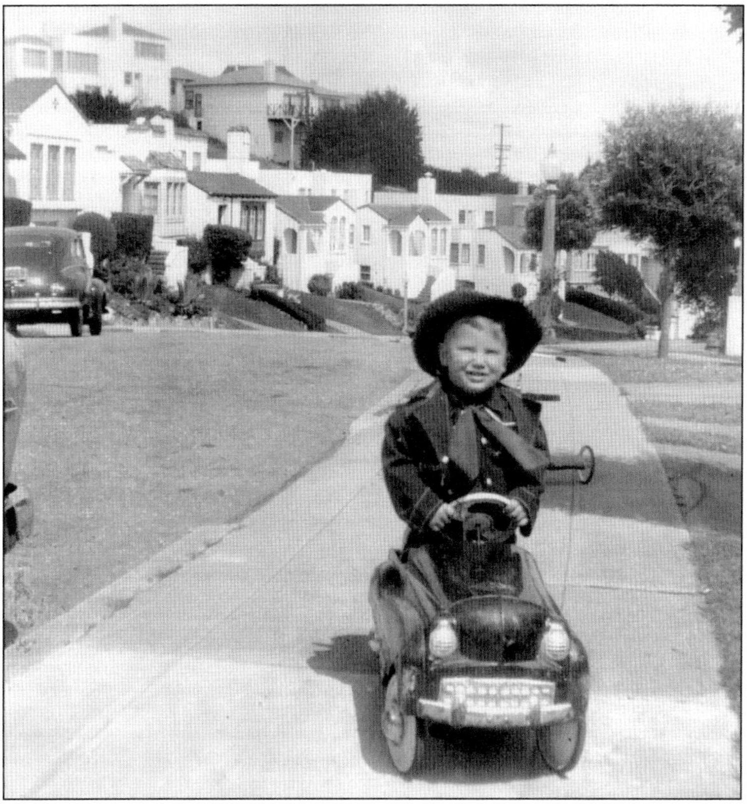

Greg Gaar, in front of his Westwood Highlands home in 1953, fondly recalls building forts with friends on Mount Davidson to reenact movies with air rifles and dirt clods on the mountain. As young as eight years old and, as he states, "running away from home for a few hours," he felt the long climb to the top was worth it. "A peaceful forest, a view of downtown and that overwhelming cross awaited." (Courtesy Greg Gaar.)

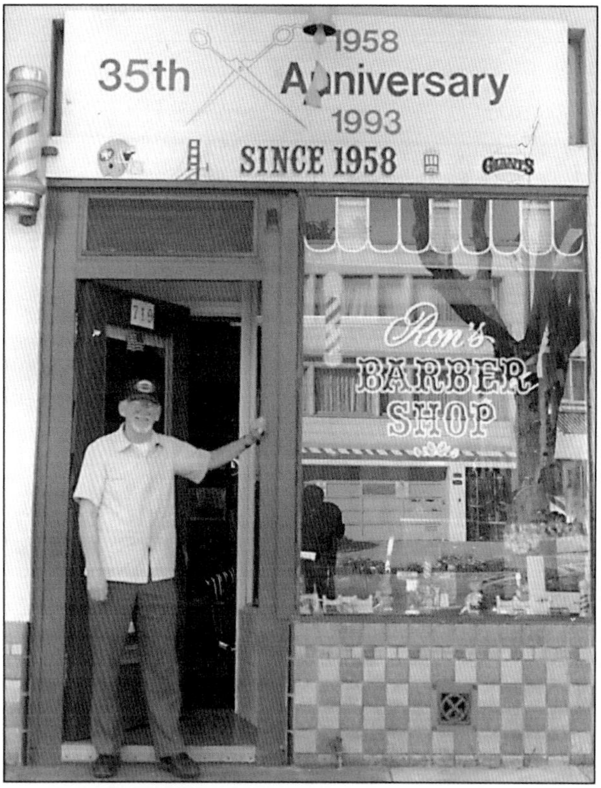


In 1954, four years after marrying San Francisco native Joann Johnson, Ron Davis opens Ron's Barbershop at 719 Monterey Boulevard in Sunnyside. He became the neighborhood historian, accepting photographs in exchange for haircuts. They raised their two children, Debbie and Ronnie, just down the street in their historic house on Gennessee Street built in 1915. They now have three grandchildren named Jacob, Madison, and Christopher. (Courtesy Ron Davis.)

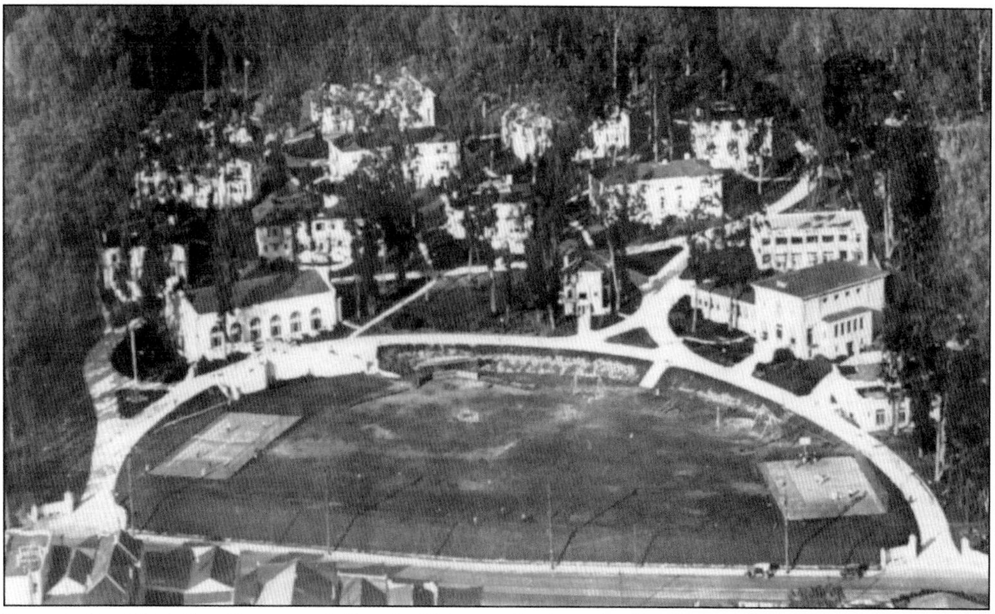

Founded in 1894, San Francisco's Pacific Hebrew Orphan Asylum opened at Homewood Terrace on Ocean Avenue between Faxon and Ashton Avenues in the 1930s. This aerial photograph from the 1950s shows the facility for 125 children, which included a synagogue, library, laundry, commissary, gym, workshop, and dormitories. Each dormitory had room for 10 boys and 10 girls of varying ages. (Courtesy Tasia Melvin.)

# *Six*

# A CITY FOR ALL

## HONORING THE PAST AND MAKING NEW DREAMS COME TRUE

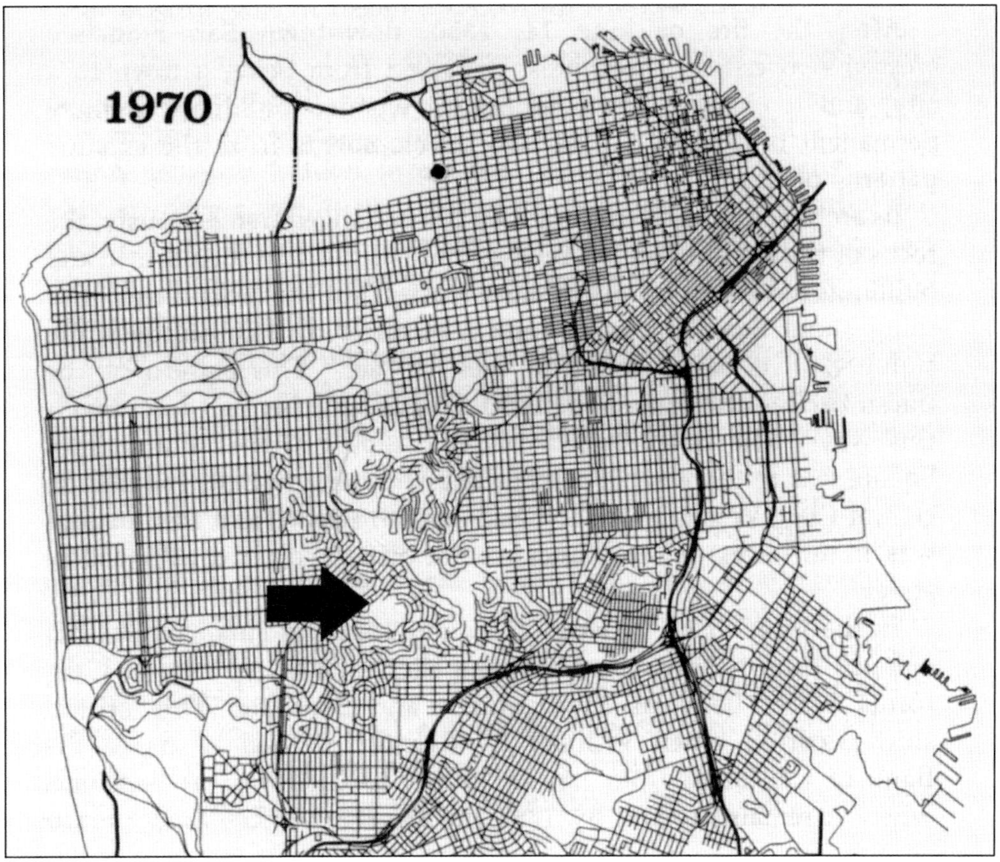


A. S. Baldwin's vision for West of Twin Peaks as the future of San Francisco is complete by 1970, with Mount Davidson's open space preserved as recommended by Daniel Burnham in his 1905 City Beautiful plan. (Courtesy San Francisco Planning Department.)

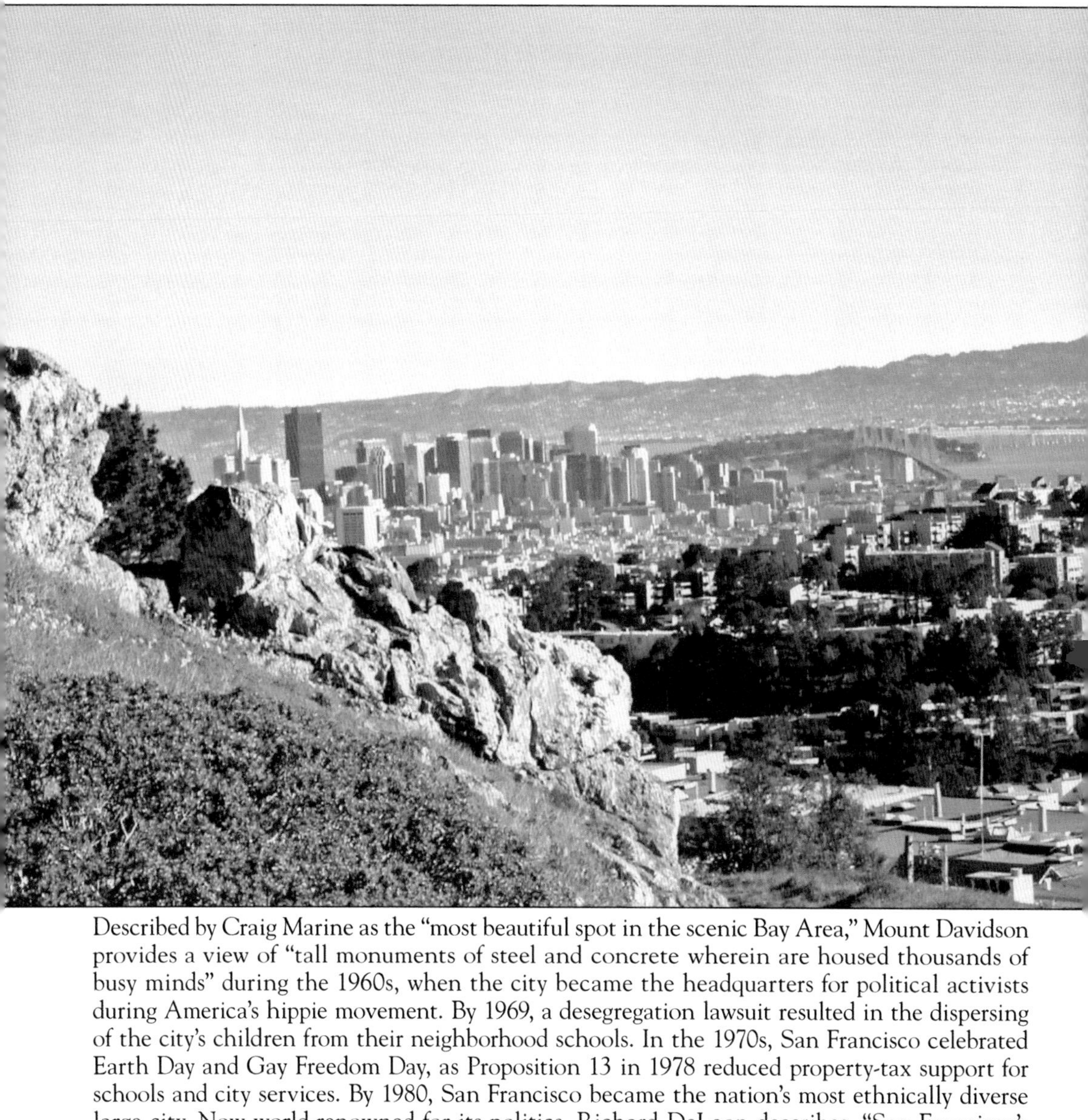

Described by Craig Marine as the "most beautiful spot in the scenic Bay Area," Mount Davidson provides a view of "tall monuments of steel and concrete wherein are housed thousands of busy minds" during the 1960s, when the city became the headquarters for political activists during America's hippie movement. By 1969, a desegregation lawsuit resulted in the dispersing of the city's children from their neighborhood schools. In the 1970s, San Francisco celebrated Earth Day and Gay Freedom Day, as Proposition 13 in 1978 reduced property-tax support for schools and city services. By 1980, San Francisco became the nation's most ethnically diverse large city. Now world-renowned for its politics, Richard DeLeon describes, "San Francisco's progressivism is concerned with . . . protection of the city's environment, architectural heritage, neighborhoods, diversity, and overall quality of life from the radical transformations of turbulent American capitalism." (Courtesy Ron Proctor.)

Tower Market owner Dan Pommon cheers with Mayor Christopher, police chief Frank Ahern, and fire chief Frank Kelly as they enjoy opening day for the San Francisco Giants at Seals Stadium in 1958. One of the finest in the world when built by Henry Brunnier in 1931 for $1 million, the stadium featured a loudspeaker system and state-of-the-art lighting. In 1960, the baseball team moved to a new stadium at Candlestick Point. (Courtesy John Pommon.)

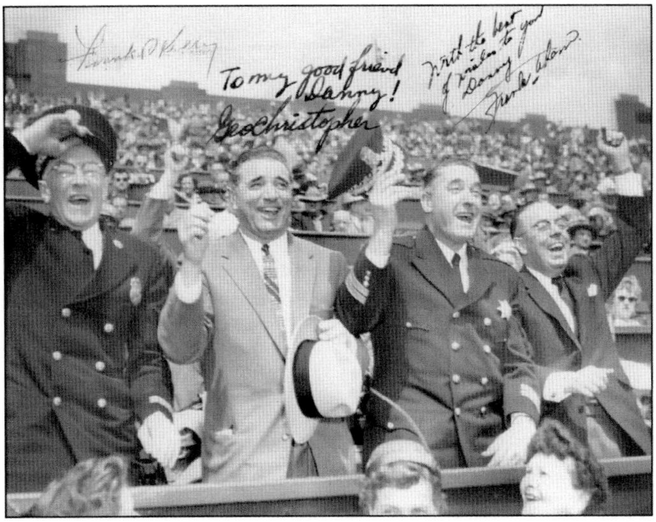


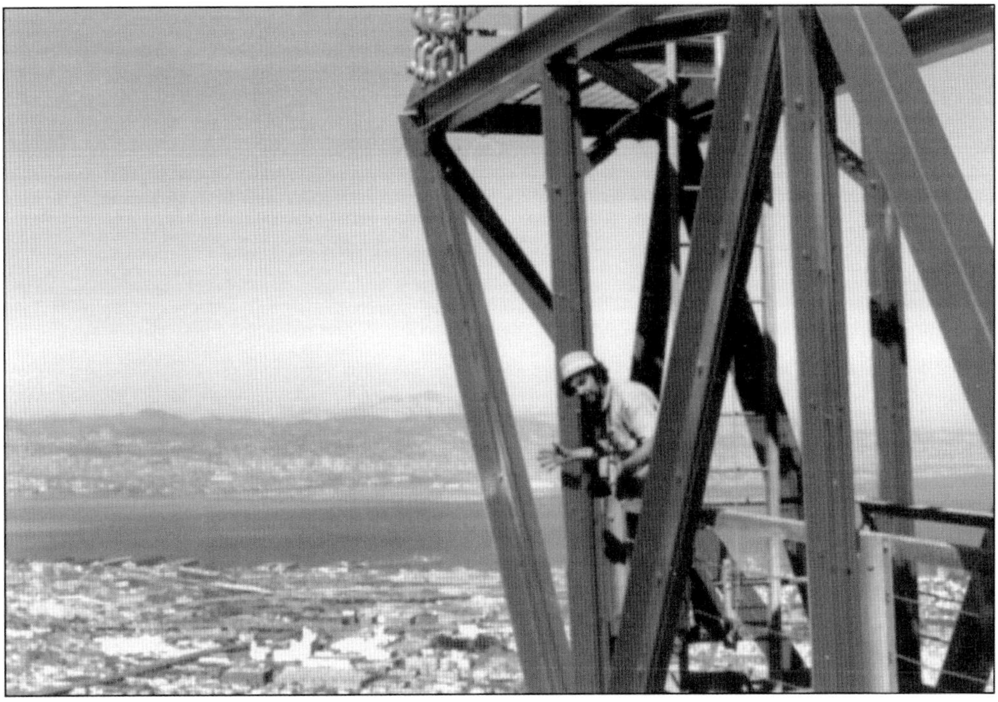

Fred Ulrich waves from atop the new 977-foot-tall Sutro Tower with the East Bay in the background. Constructed in 1972 on the peak Adolph Sutro named Mount Parnassus, it is nine times taller than the Mount Davidson Cross. This new monument of steel and icon for broadcast media on Mount Sutro becomes the most dominant feature of San Francisco's skyline. (Courtesy Ron Davis.)

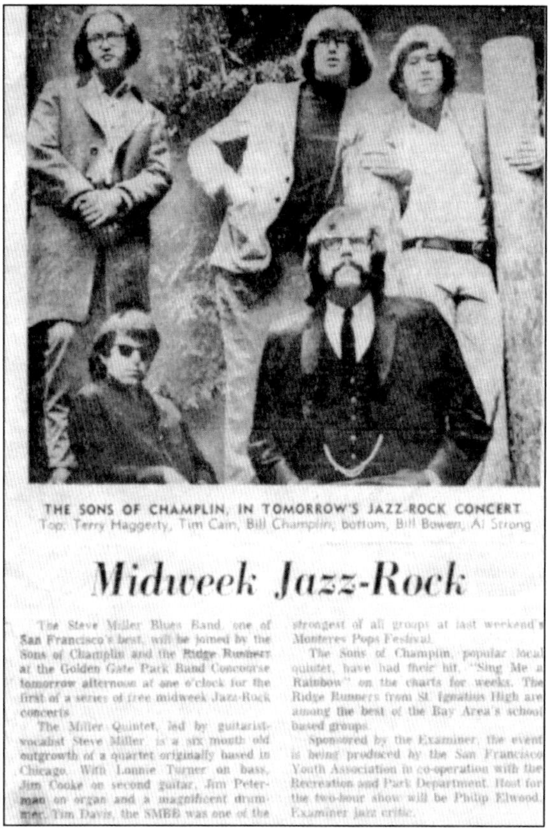

THE SONS OF CHAMPLIN, IN TOMORROW'S JAZZ-ROCK CONCERT
Top: Terry Haggerty, Tim Cain, Bill Champlin; bottom, Bill Bowen, Al Strong

## Midweek Jazz-Rock

The Steve Miller Blues Band, one of San Francisco's best, will be joined by the Sons of Champlin and the Ridge Runners at the Golden Gate Park Band Concourse tomorrow afternoon at one o'clock for the first of a series of free midweek Jazz-Rock concerts.

The Miller Quintet, led by guitarist-vocalist Steve Miller, is a six month old outgrowth of a quartet originally based in Chicago. With Lonnie Turner on bass, Jim Cooke on second guitar, Jim Peterman on organ and a magnificent drummer, Tim Davis, the SMBB was one of the strongest of all groups at last weekend's Monterey Pops Festival.

The Sons of Champlin, popular local quintet, have had their hit, "Sing Me a Rainbow" on the charts for weeks. The Ridge Runners from St. Ignatius High are among the best of the Bay Area's school-based groups.

Sponsored by the Examiner, the event is being produced by the San Francisco Youth Association in co-operation with the Recreation and Park Department. Host for the two-hour show will be Philip Elwood, Examiner jazz critic.

In 1967, the first free Midweek Jazz-Rock Concert, sponsored by the San Francisco Youth Association along with the recreation and parks department, drew an unexpected audience of thousands to see the headlining band, Sons of Champlain. The Ridge Runners, described as one of the best of the Bay Area's school-based groups, played after them before giving the stage to Boz Scaggs and the Steve Miller Blues Band. (Courtesy Dave Bisho.)

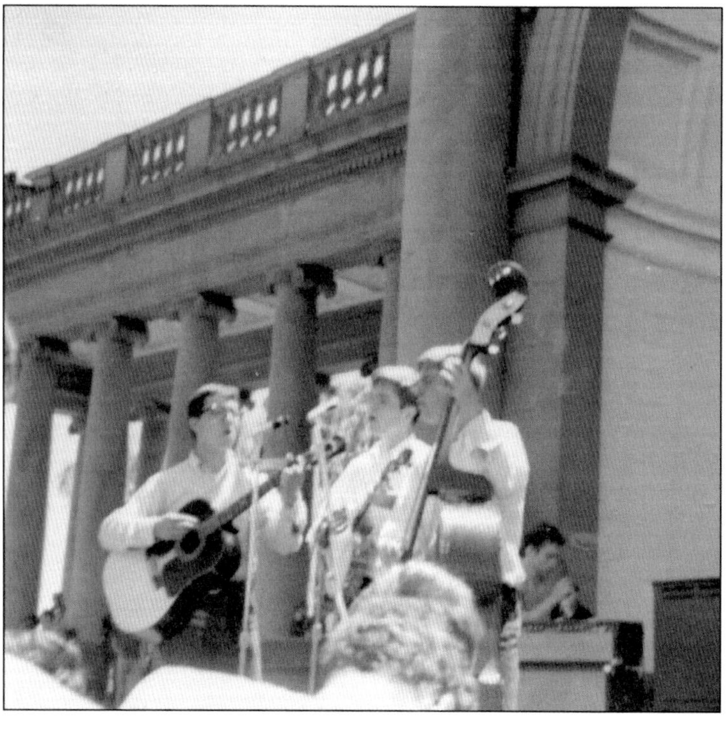

Classmates at St. Brendan's, Ridge Runners Dave Bisho, Lloyd Bryan, and Rick Bryan perform at the Golden Gate Park Bandshell Concert. They were juniors at the old Saint Ignatius High School on Stanyan Street when that "summer of love" marked the beginning of the end of old San Francisco as they knew it. Haight Street changed from a family-oriented neighborhood district to an international pop-culture mecca. (Courtesy Dave Bisho.)

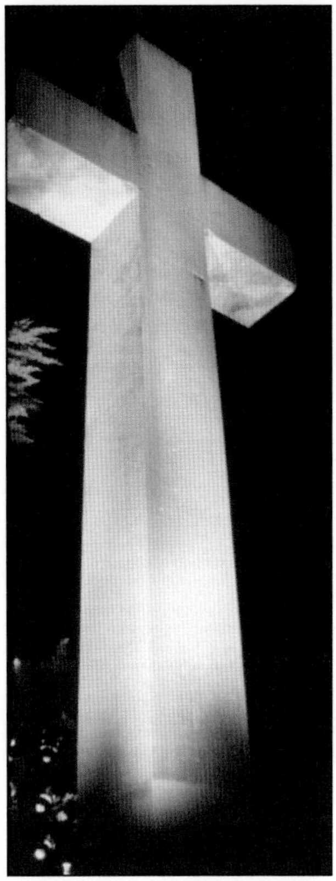

Year-round lighting of the Mount Davidson Cross began in 1955 after a soldier bound for Korea wrote that the lit cross was his last sight of home. The night-lit cross brings Clint Eastwood home in 1971 to fight Psycho Scorpio at its base in his first *Dirty Harry* film. In the film, Psycho says to Harry, "Now turn, face the cross. Come on, put your nose right up against the cement."

The first-grade class at Commodore Sloat is pictured here in 1962 with teacher Mrs. Genevieve Parrott. Jane Werthimer came back to do her student teaching with Mrs. Parrott while attending San Francisco State University. West of Twin Peaks residents have historically made education a priority, maintaining the highest percentage of college graduates of any San Francisco district. (Courtesy Peg Kaplan.)

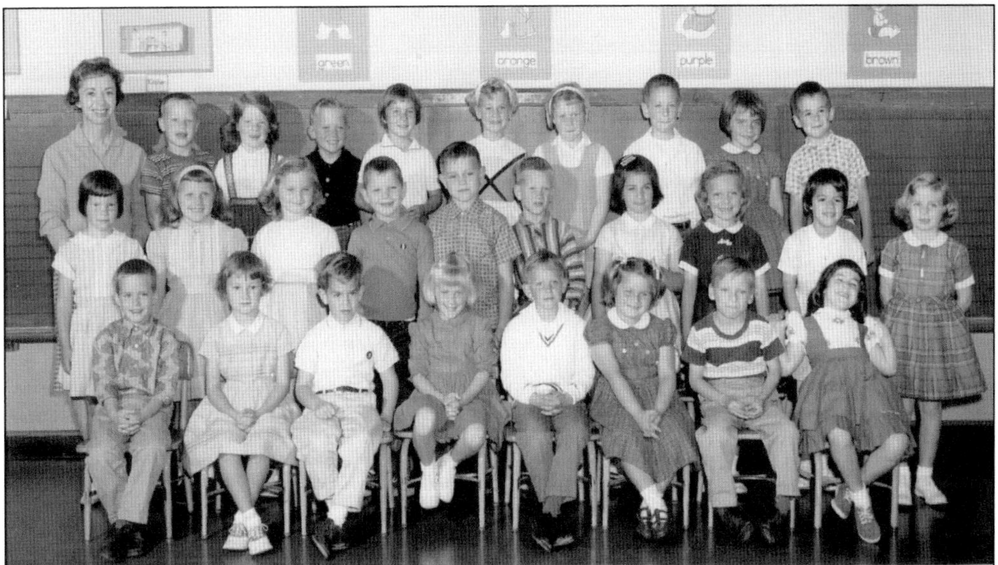

Commodore Sloat School 1962 Mrs. Genevieve Parrott Room 27

Front Row - Paul O'Looney, Cindy Born, Gregory Cronin, Kathleen Mulhearn, Gary Bogdan, Jane Werthimer, William Blue, Valerie Shalin. Center Row - Holly Cronan, Elizabeth Erickson, Peggy Taylor, Dwight Runner, David Dierke, James Aanestad, Michelle Mountanos, Cornelia Aschauer, Nicolette Trasvina, Joan Maggi. Back Row - James Trabucco, Ana Dale, Kevin Collins, Carolyn Webster, Susan Utter, Antoinette Taylor, George McCaffrey, Susan Kaplan, Peter Simpson.

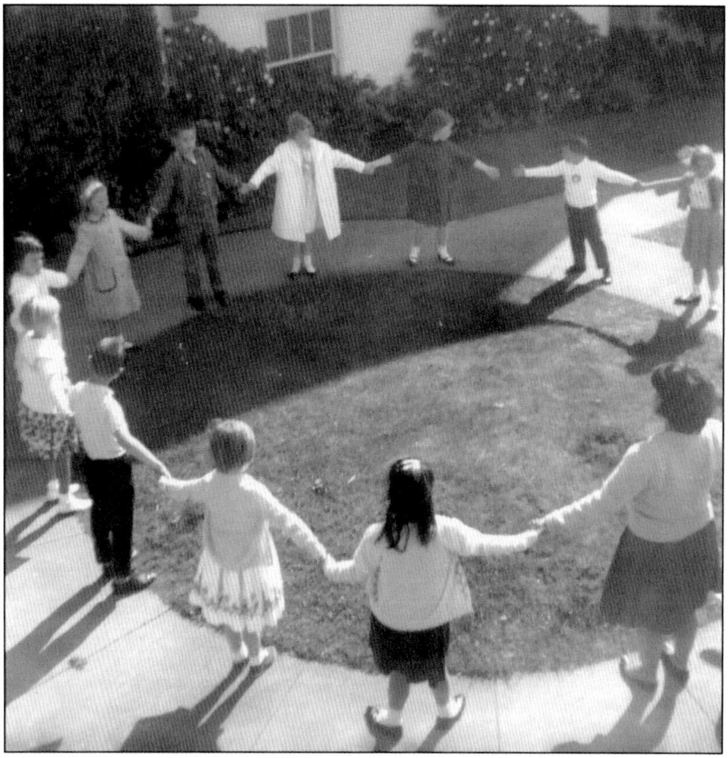

When Peg and Bill Kaplan moved to Balboa Terrace in 1954, along with many other young families, there were 58 children living within just one street block of houses. There is room for Susan Kaplan's 1963 birthday party to be held outdoors in one of the landscaped pedestrian walkways that distinguish the now-historic City Beautiful character of the neighborhood. (Courtesy Peg Kaplan.)

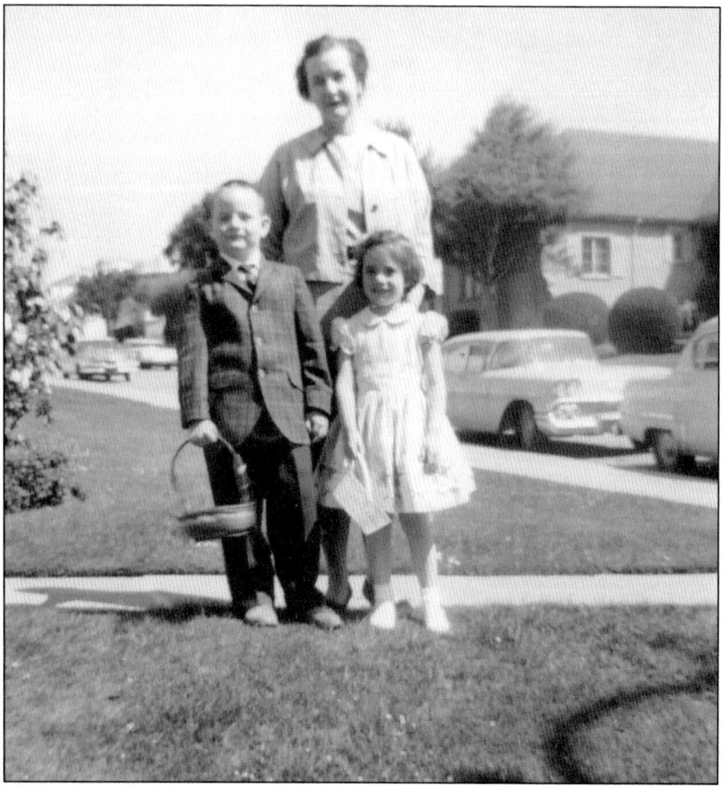

Ready for an Easter egg hunt in 1961, Peg Kaplan poses with son Paul and daughter Susan on the lawn in front of their home. The Kaplans are members of their neighborhood association working to preserve the residential character described by K. Barton in 1926, "It is the lavish planting of fine shrubs and flowers that has so properly earned a residential section of this character the designation of Park." (Courtesy Peg Kaplan.)

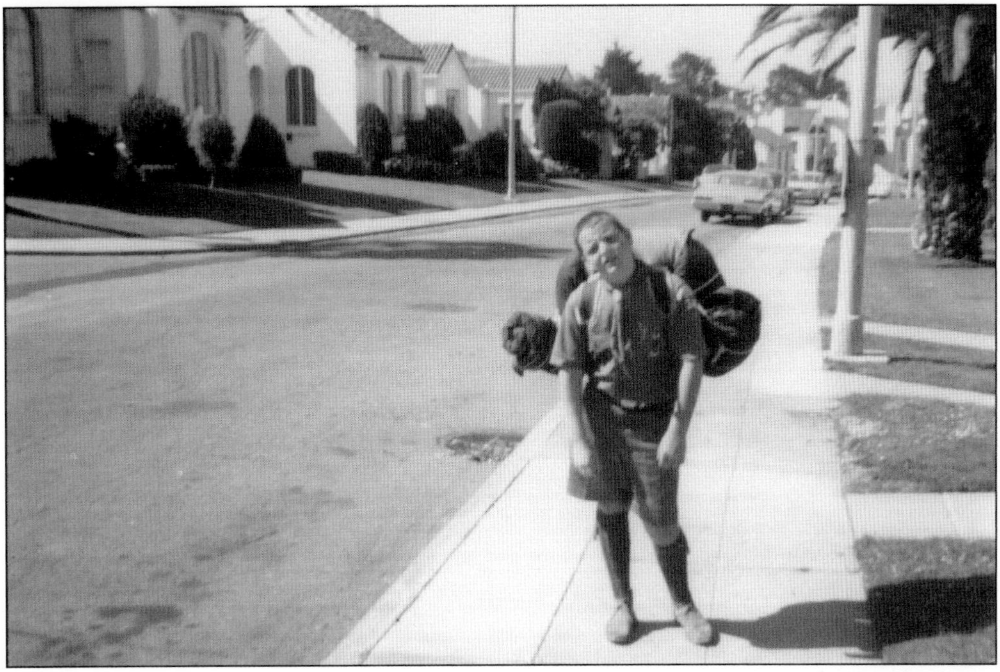

All garages in Balboa Terrace are entered from rear easements or paved alleyways. This eliminates the front-entrance driveway and leaves an unbroken expanse of land for the planting of ornamental shrubs and flowers. This 1966 photograph of Paul Kaplan, with a much too-heavy pack, on the way to Boy Scout camp, shows the still unbroken and landscaped front yard setbacks decorating San Benito Way. (Courtesy Peg Kaplan.)

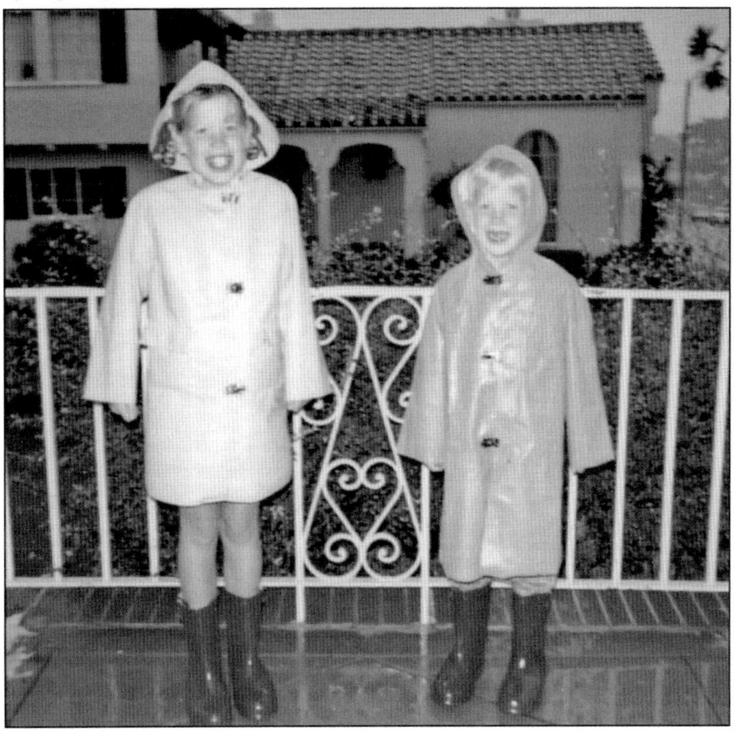

Balboa Terrace residents Shelly (left) and David Wentker are outside their home enjoying one of those very rare snow days in San Francisco in 1972. Like many children who grew up in this and other West of Twin Peaks single-family neighborhoods, David Wentker stayed to raise his family here as well. (Courtesy Joann Wentker.)

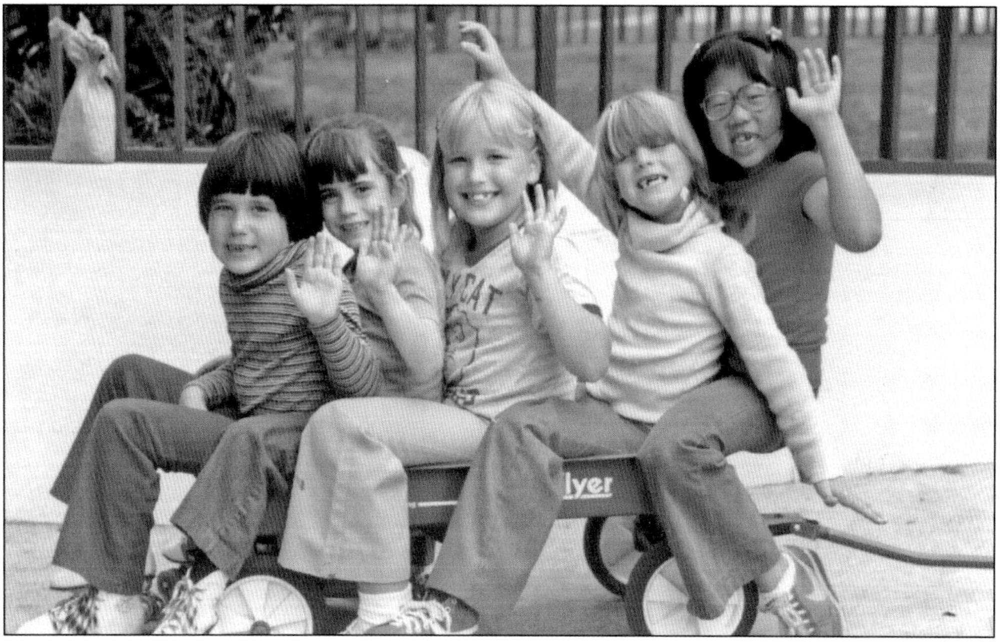

Pictured here in 1975, from left to right, are Rebecca Handler, Alison Dondero, Alison Wentker, Melissa Biele, and Andrea Hom continuing the tradition of neighborhood children using the Balboa Terrace rear alleyways as a playground for everything from kickball to kick the can, hide and seek, and riding bicycles and wagons. Rebecca's brother Daniel grew up in the neighborhood as well and eventually wrote the *Lemony Snicket* books. (Courtesy Joann Wentker.)

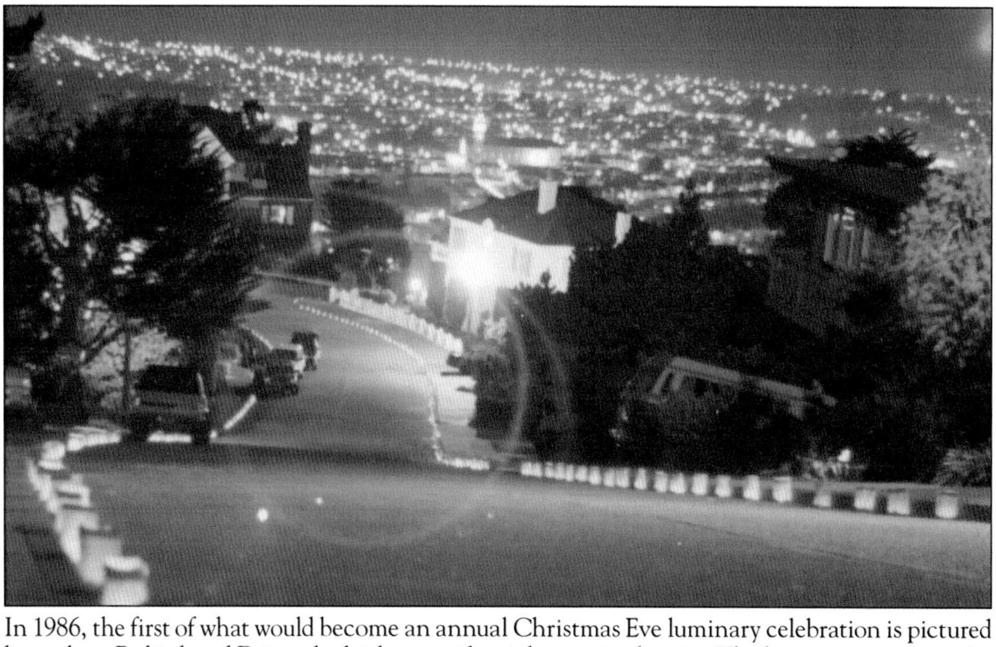

In 1986, the first of what would become an annual Christmas Eve luminary celebration is pictured here along Robinhood Drive, the highest residential street in the city. The homes comprising the original Sherwood Forest subdivision are still linked by their original globe streetlights. With some of the more elaborate ranch-style homes in San Francisco, one was described in a real estate article as having "enough rocks in its retaining walls to dam Islais Creek." (Courtesy Bob DeLiso.)

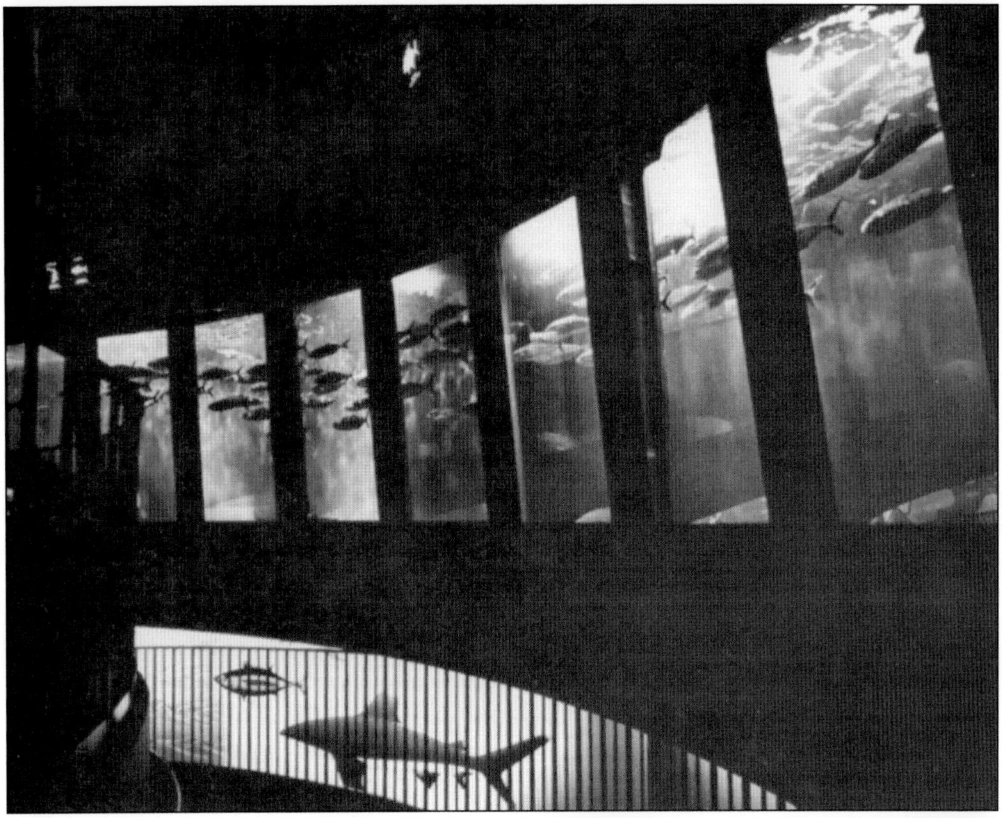

Living on a mountain named for the president of the California Academy of Sciences from 1871 to 1887, Milton and John Pflueger maintained the city's oldest continuously operating architectural firm. They have designed the GHC Meyer Fish roundabout and other academy improvements in addition to Moffitt Hospital and Millberry Union at the University of California. Their work also includes the Shriners Hospital, Ebenezer Lutheran Church, and most of San Francisco City College. (Courtesy John Pflueger.)

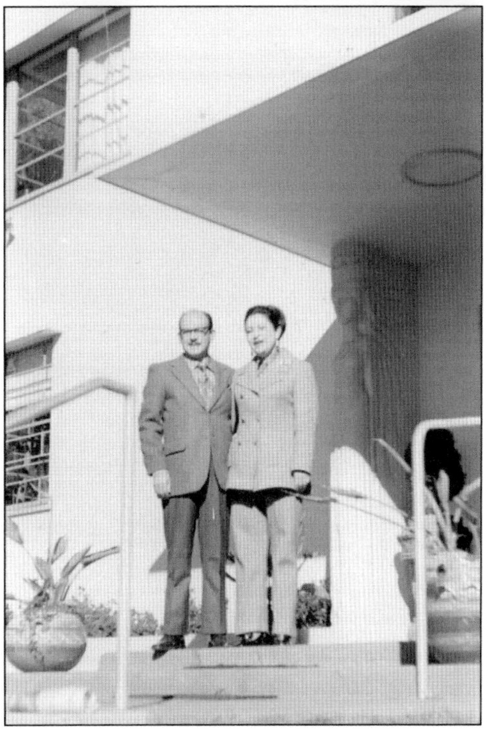

The Pinto family was outgrowing their home on Rosewood Drive in Monterey Heights in 1969 when Dr. Pedro Pinto bought the historic house designed by Timothy Pflueger for Drs. Delprat in Sherwood Forest. Coincidently Dr. Pinto attended a party given there by the Delprats when he was an intern. Alicia Pinto is pictured at the entrance to their Streamline Moderne-style house with her brother Patricio Perez, who was visiting from Quito, Ecuador. (Courtesy Denis Pinto.)

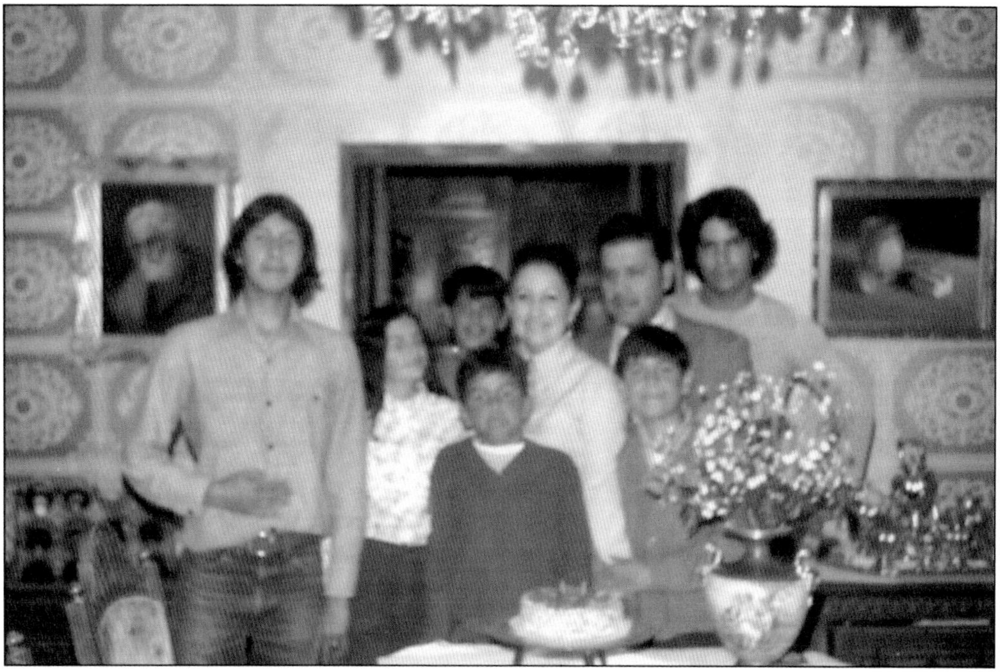

The Pinto home had lots more room for five growing boys, as seen here in 1972 inside their Lansdale Avenue dining room. Pictured, from left to right, are Denis, Denis's young aunt Fina (visiting from Ecuador), Nelson (back), Norman (front), mother Alicia, father Dr. Pedro Pinto (back), Richard (front), and Peter-Stephan Pinto. (Courtesy Denis Pinto.)

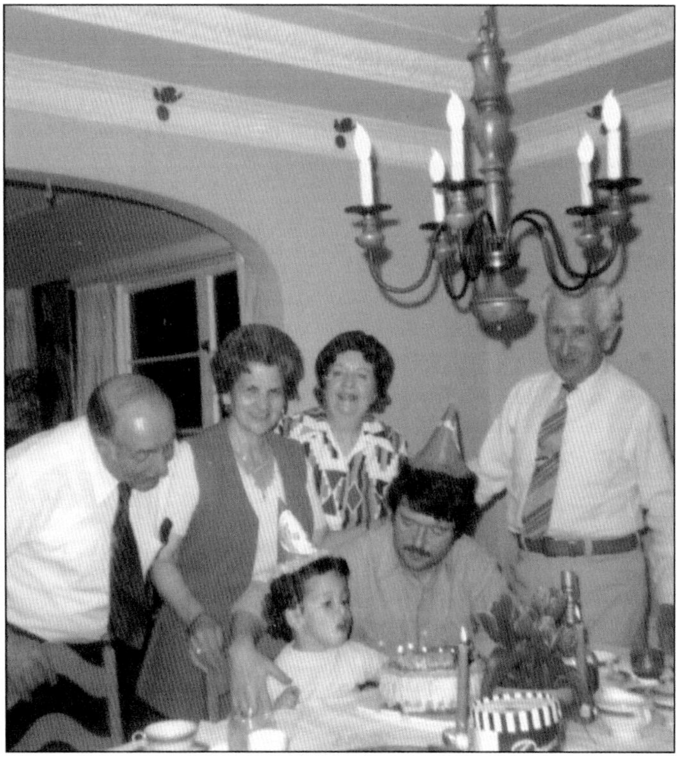

Three generations gathered at the Hoegger home in Westwood Highlands to celebrate Eric Hoegger's third birthday in 1977. Pictured, from left to right, are grandparents Joseph and Josephine Conte, birthday boy Eric, Kathryn Hoegger, proud father Ken, and Joseph Hoegger. A mail carrier, Joe Conte read letters to the Italian families on his route from their sons fighting in World War II. Joseph Hoegger came from Switzerland to San Francisco, where he met his wife Kathryn. (Courtesy Hoegger Collection.)

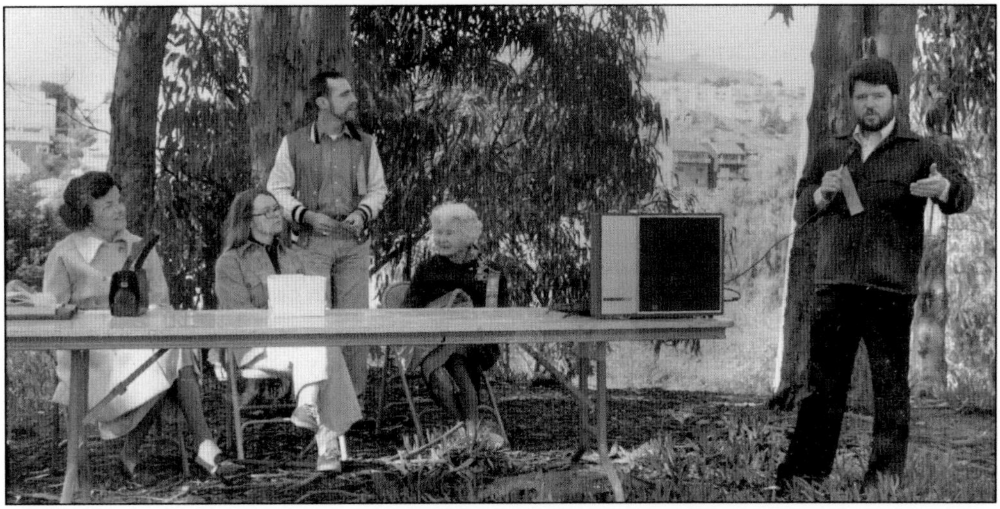

Greg Gaar, Ken Hoegger, and members of the Sunnyside Neighborhood Association saved the open space on Martha's Hill from development. Attendees at the 1979 dedication of Dorothy Erskine Park (named for the founder of the Greenbelt Alliance), from left to right, are Dianne Feinstein, the first female mayor of San Francisco; Mary Burns; Tom Molloy, director of parks and recreation; Dorothy Erskine; and Ken Hoegger. (Courtesy Ken Hoegger.)

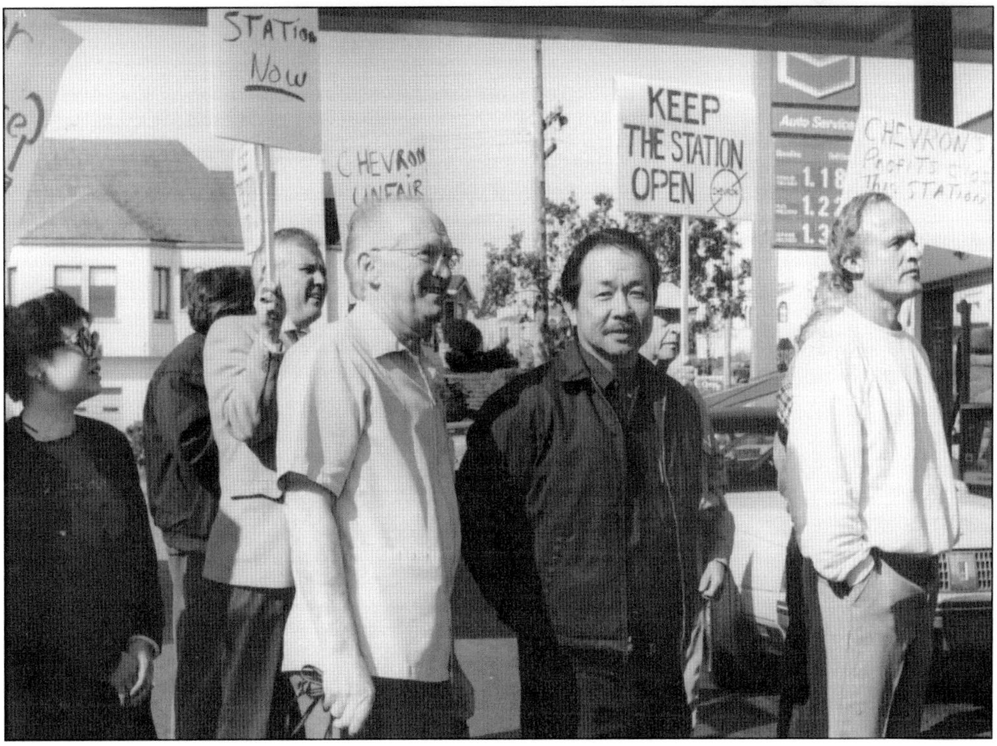


Forty years after the West of Twin Peaks Central Council argued to prevent the building of gas stations, Sunnyside residents, led by "mayor of Monterey Boulevard" Ron Davis, protest the planned closure of a Chevron station, calling it part of a dying species of neighborhood businesses. Supervisor Terence Hallinan sponsors legislation to oppose large chains moving into small neighborhoods and chasing out mom-and-pop businesses. (Courtesy Ron Davis.)

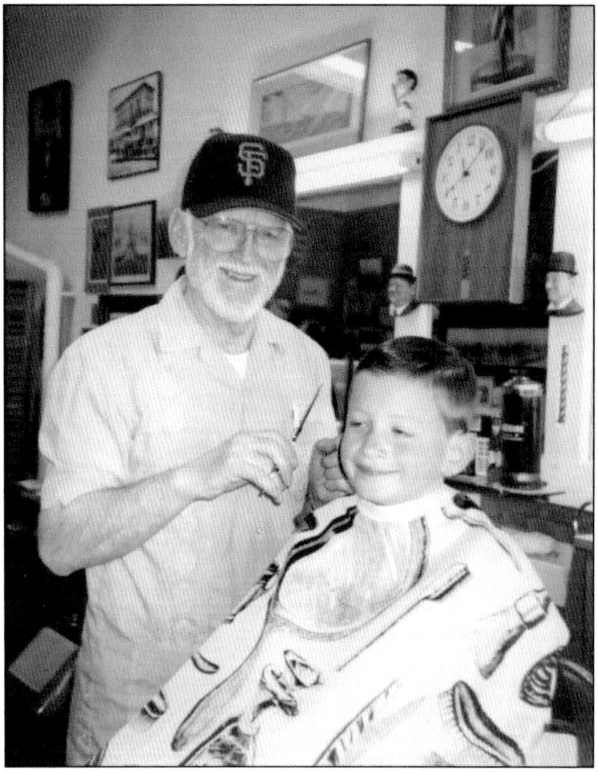

Ron Davis, with grandson Christopher in his Sunnyside barbershop, was mentioned in Herb Caen's popular newspaper column: "Sign in the window of Ron's barber shop on Monterey Boulevard: 'Super Bowl Haircuts. Size 19 Bowl.' . . . It's the Year of the Hare in Chinatown, but the sign outside Ron's barber shop proclaims 'Year of the Hair,' ta-da, and so much for NICE items." (Courtesy Ron Davis.)

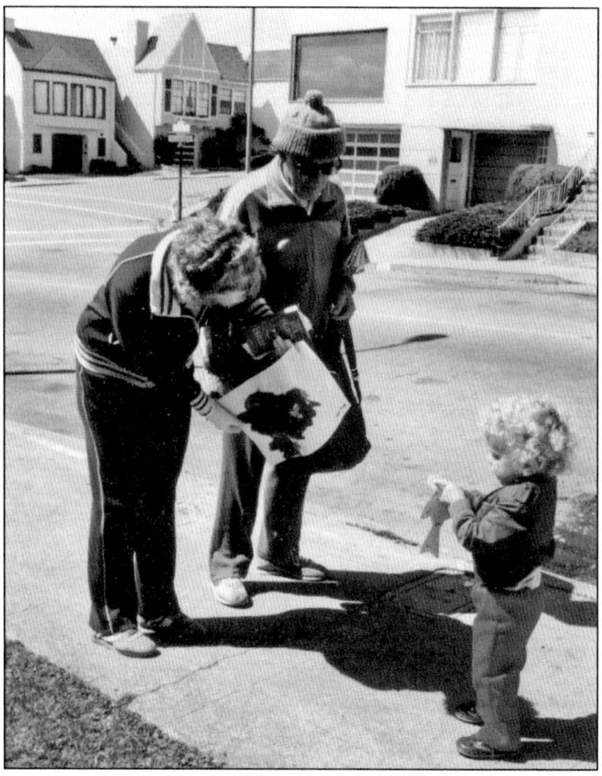

The peaceful pedestrian environment of the innovative curvilinear streetscapes designed by John Punnett for the West of Twin Peaks residential parks encourages walking outdoors and getting to know the neighbors. Longtime residents Bob and Virginia Larribeau, returning from their daily swim, admire next-door neighbor Aaron Proctor's artwork from his first day of preschool. (Author's collection.)

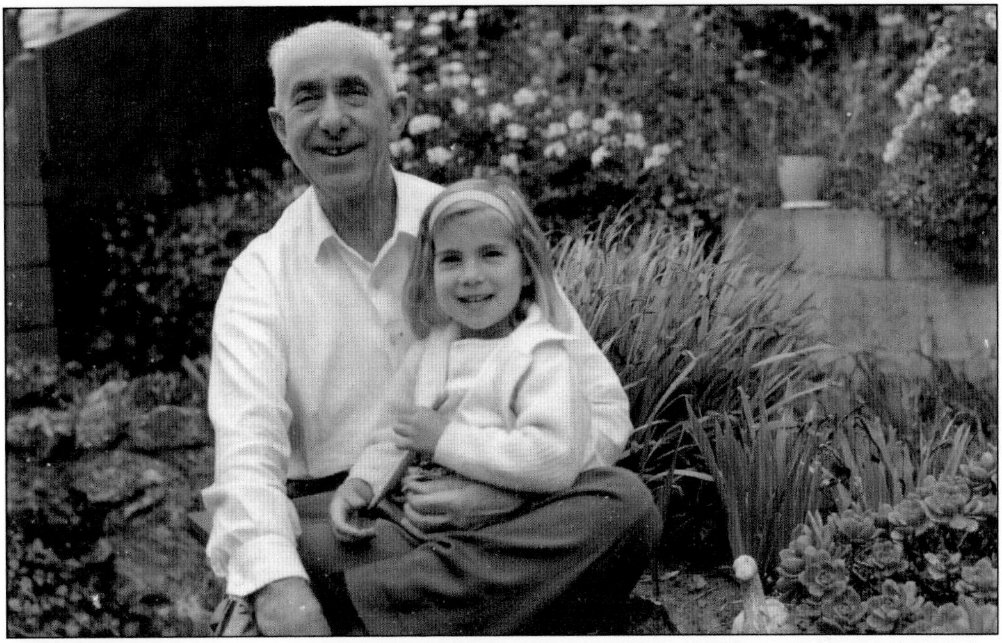

The unique "suburb in the city" quality of life in West of Twin Peaks encourages those who bought their homes in the 1930s and 1940s to remain in their retirement to welcome new families. Fourth-generation San Franciscan and future president of the Miraloma Park Improvement Club Cassandra Mettling enjoys the backyard garden of her great-aunt Sally Grusser's next-door neighbor, Leonard DeHaan, in 1964. (Courtesy Elizabeth Mettling.)

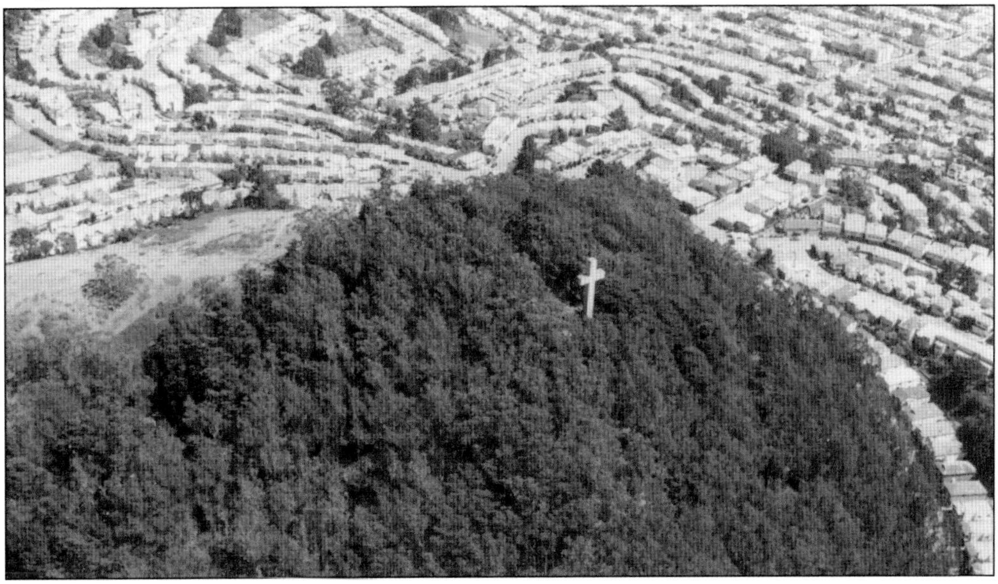

San Francisco's largest regularly scheduled religious observance has continued every year since 1923 without interruption. CBS televised the 1979 event nationally after Harvey Milk and George Moscone were assassinated. Margot Patterson Doss wrote, "Bridges, towers, pyramids, radar fixtures, microwave relay stations, Nike missile sites and other recent soaring monuments notwithstanding, San Francisco's most enduring landmark for the last 200 years has been a cross on a mountaintop." (Courtesy Ron Davis.)

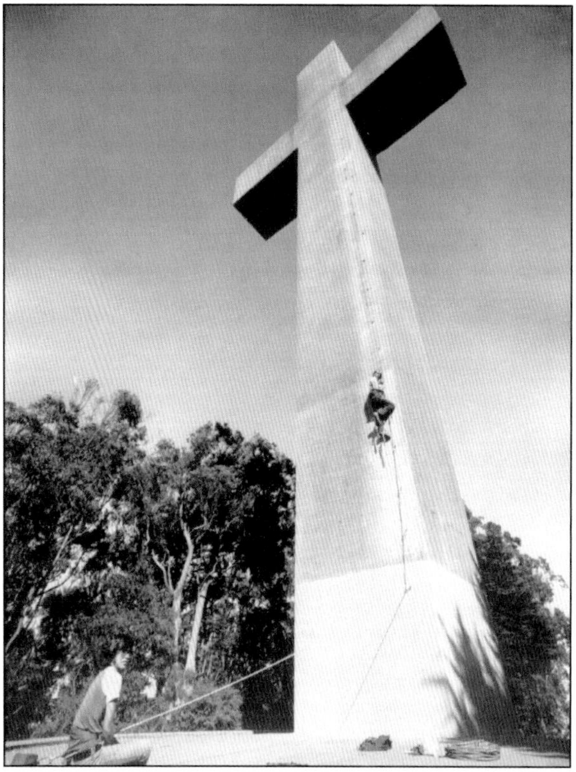

Margot Patterson Doss noted that although it hasn't always been the same mountaintop, the landmark cross has always stood near the sea. Thousands of people have made the climb, despite the predawn chill, heavy fog, or pouring rain, to attend the Easter sunrise sermons on the mountain. She wrote that people were "impelled by the same conviction that has led pilgrims to walk to Rome, to Jerusalem, to Mecca and up Fujiyama." (Courtesy Miraloma Community Church.)

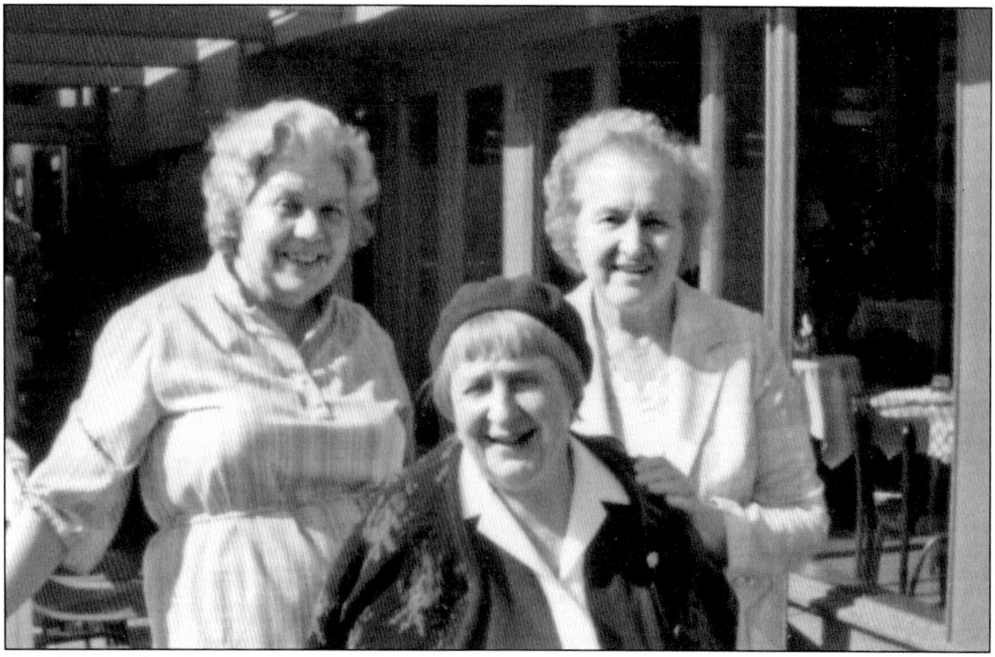

Miraloma Park neighbors since the 1940s have become lifelong friends. After years of community volunteering at the neighborhood school, improvement club, and church, "Miraloma girls" Ruth Snowberg, Judy Krause, and Jeanette Quast Davis enjoy their retirement together with a San Francisco lunch out on the town. (Courtesy Jeannie Davis MacKenzie.)

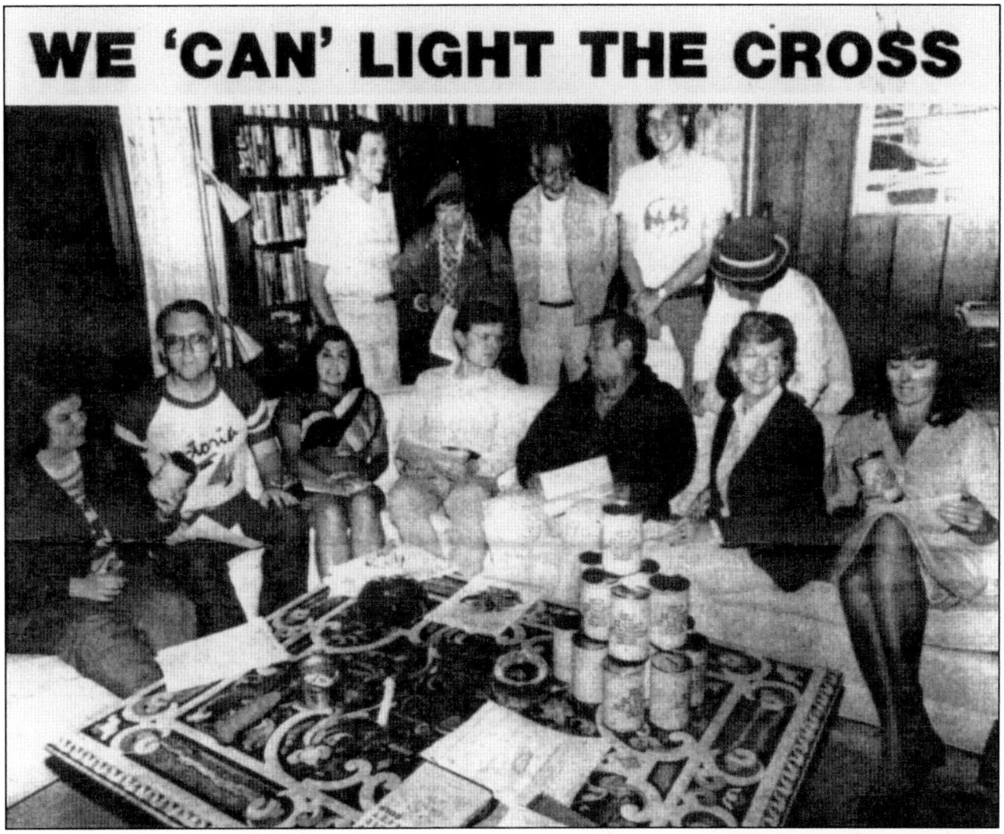


Lighting of the Mount Davidson Cross was restricted to Christmas and Easter weeks in response to the 1976 energy crisis. After the 50th anniversary lighting of the Golden Gate and Bay Bridges, the Re-Light Mount Davidson Committee organized in 1987 to raise funds for the full-time lighting of the monument that neighbors, led by Terence McAteer, described as "inspirational, comforting, and dramatic . . . it's very important as a historical symbol." (Courtesy Jim Ferry.)

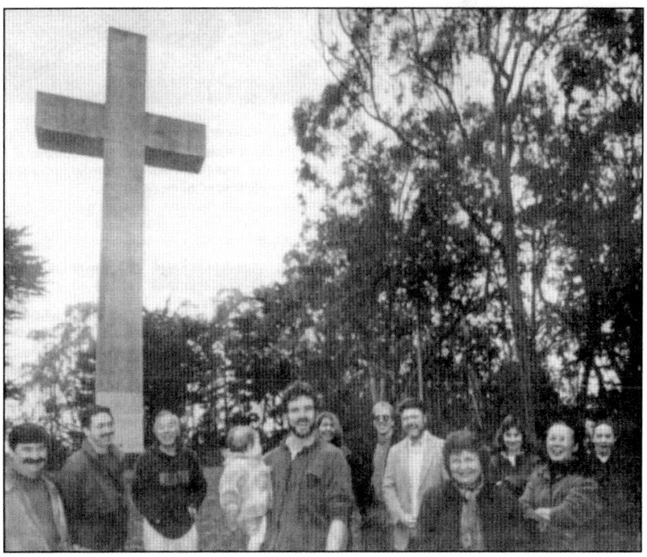

Conflict over ownership of Mount Davidson made its way to the California Supreme Court a second time when it ruled in 1996 that it was illegal for the city to own a religious monument on its highest point. Neighbors organized the Friends of Mount Davidson Conservancy to protect Madie Brown's legacy. The group, pictured here, included Bob DeLiso, Dave Bisho, Denise LaPointe, Glenn Gullmes, Ken Hoegger, Jacquie Proctor, and Michele and Danielle Bisho. (Courtesy Glenn Gullmes.)

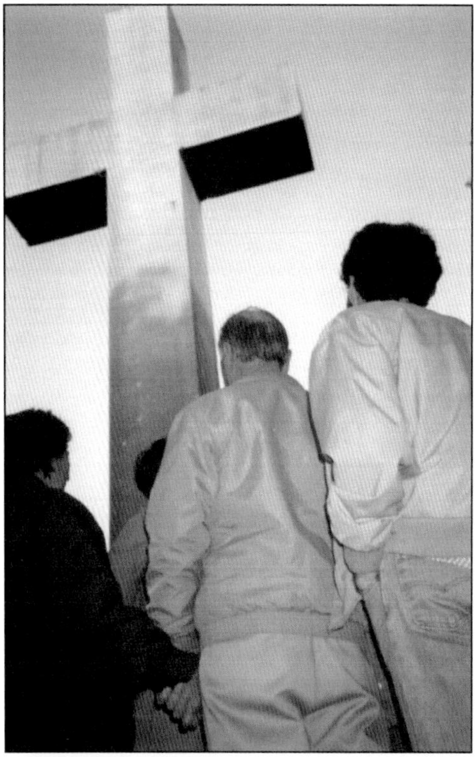

Just after Mount Davidson Manor resident Bill Brown was diagnosed with an inoperable brain tumor at the age of 72, he took his family on a pilgrimage to the cross for his last Easter sunrise in 1993, the 70th anniversary of the event. Photographed here during his last months, he holds hands with his wife of 50 years, Espie, who passed away the following year at the exact same age of 72. (Courtesy Margie Brown Whitnah.)

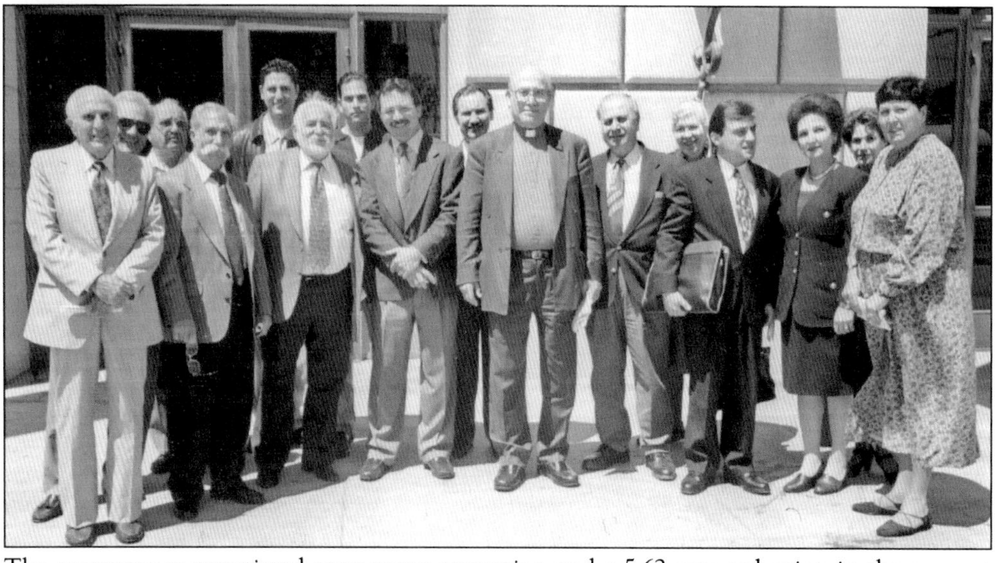

The conservancy negotiated open-space protection and a 5.62-acre reduction in the amount of parkland to be auctioned by the city. Dave Bisho offered the opening bid of $25,000 for the conservancy, who then supported the winning bid of the Council of Armenian American Organizations of Northern California. Among the auction winners pictured here are Gorune Hayrapetian (fourth from left), Edward Aslanian (sixth from left), Dave Bisho (eighth from left), Bishop Aris Shirvanian (center), Elizabeth Mettling (fifth from right), Paul Tour-Sarkissian (fourth from right), Roxanne Makasdjian (second from right), and Ashkhen Mouradian (far right). (Courtesy Dave Bisho.)

In 1997, the $26,000 sale of 0.38 acres of Mount Davidson Park to the Council of Armenian American Organizations of Northern California, including the land upon where the cross is located, was approved by 68 percent of the voters in Proposition F. The terms of the sale required that the land remain open space for public access and prohibit the buyer from making commercial, industrial, or residential use of the land. (Author's collection.)

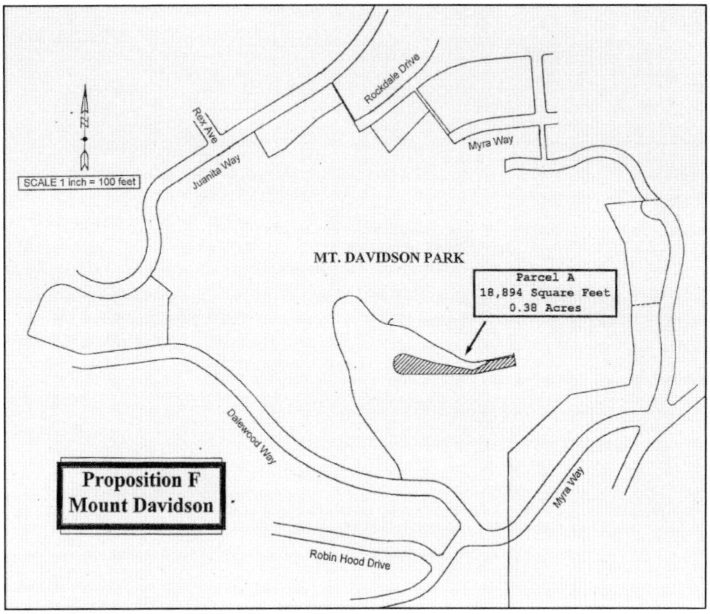


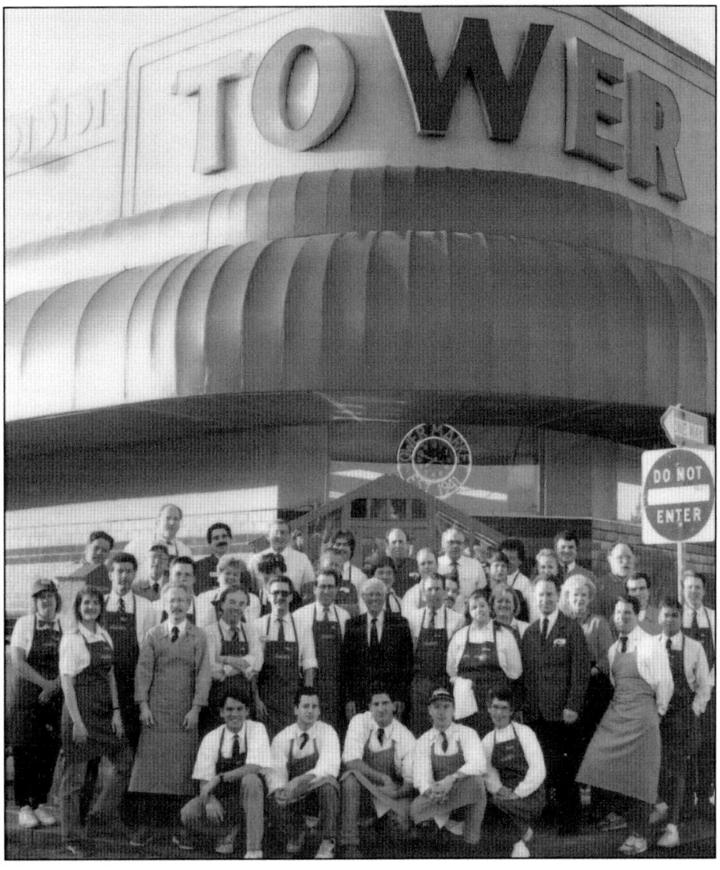


Dan (center, wearing suit) and John Pommon (same row, arms folded) pose in front of Tower Market for this 50th-anniversary photograph with their staff. Mollie Stone's Markets came forward in 2005 to preserve what *San Francisco Chronicle* writer Steve Rubenstein described in 1991 as the "best market in town—fabled Tower Market, on Portola Drive, where a tomato tastes like a tomato and not a soggy tennis ball." (Courtesy John Pommon.)

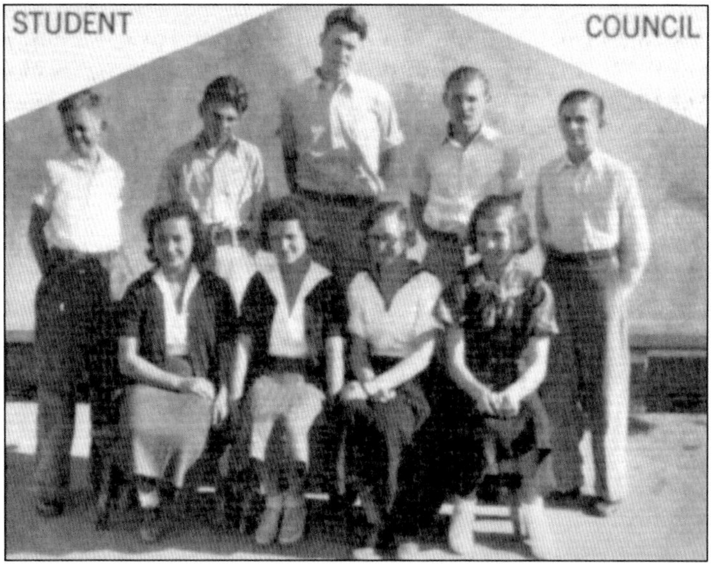


Aptos Middle School was built in 1931 at 105 Aptos Street for the families of West of Twin Peaks. Carol Channing (first row, right) was secretary of the seventh grade in 1932. At 82 years old, Carol married her Aptos classmate Harry Kullijian in May 2003. Mount Davidson Manor resident Bill Brown attended Christian Science Sunday school with Carol. (Courtesy Margie Brown Whitnah.)

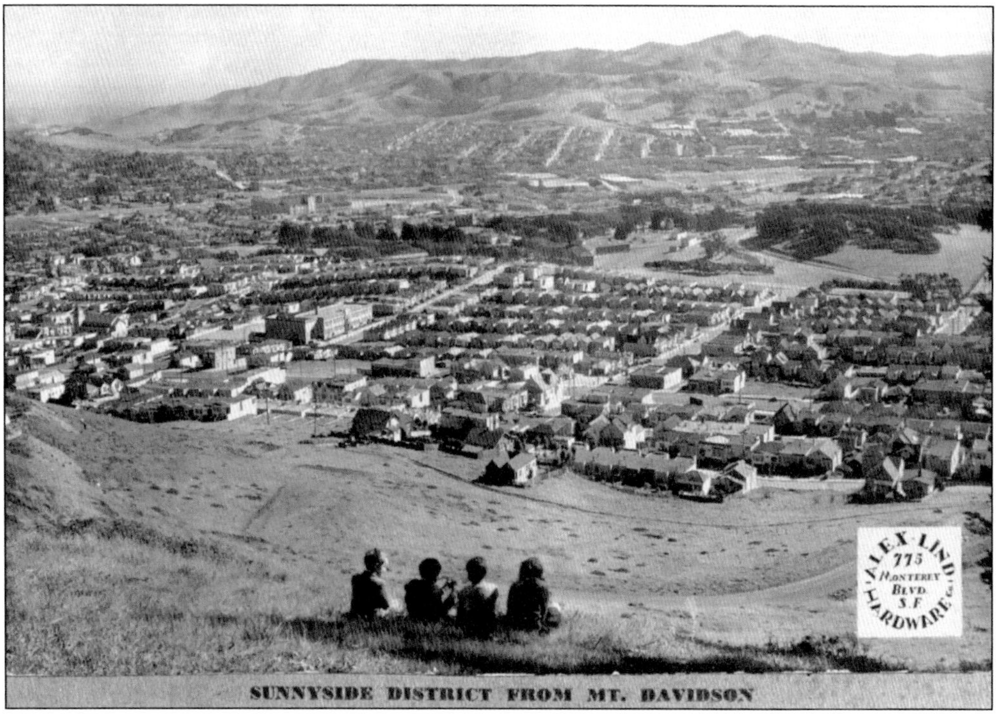


In 1985, Daniel Burnham's City Beautiful innovation is reborn as Livable Cities, which states as one of its planning principles the importance of making cities worthy of a child's affection. Acknowledging how children need to feel at home in cities and be able to find their special places, advocates say it should be possible for children to get to know their city inside out, to be able to hold their city in the palm of their hand, because they are the ones who will inherit the city and become responsible for its future. Pictured here in 1934, this special place for children on Mount Davidson and the areas within the West of Twin Peaks District neighborhoods around it are still beautiful and livable because those living in them not only dared to dream, but worked to make their dreams come true. (Courtesy of Ron Davis.)

# BIBLIOGRAPHY


Binkley, Cameron. *A Cult of Beauty: The Public Life and Civic Work of Laura Lyon White*. San Francisco: California Historical Society, 2005.

Cole, Tom. *A Short History of San Francisco*. Nevada City, California: Lexikos Publishing, 1988.

Delehanty, Randolph. *Walks and Tours in the Golden Gate City*. New York: The Dial Press, 1980. pp. 122–123.

DeLeon, Richard. *Left Coast City: Progressive Politics in San Francisco, 1975–1991*. Lawrence, Kansas: University Press of Kansas, 1991.

Doss, Margot Patterson. *San Francisco at Your Feet*. New York: Grove Weidenfeld, 1991.

Duenwald, Mary and Greg Gaar. "The Changing Face of Mt. Davidson." *Pacific Magazine*. April 1980, pp. 28–33.

Fontes, Marsha. "The Terraces Emerge—After the Quake." *San Francisco Independent*. August 16, 1987.

Fracchia, Charles A. *The Argonaut*. San Francisco: San Francisco Museum and Historical Society, Fall 1998, Summer 2003, Winter 2004.

http://www.outsidelands.org

Kuwatch, Rosalie. *Miraloma Park, A Suburb Within a City*. Unpublished, 1984.

Malim, Thomas W. *The Sunnyside District*. Unpublished, 1976.

McGrew, Patrick. *A Landmark Nomination for the Sunrise Easter Cross*. Unpublished, 1996.

Pflueger, Milton T. *Time and Tim Remembered*. San Francisco: Pflueger Architects, 1985.

Silver, Mae. *Rancho San Miguel*. San Francisco: Ord Street Press, 2001.

Starr, Kevin. *Endangered Dreams: The Great Depression in California*. New York: Oxford University Press, 1996.